# BUILDING WEALTH WITH MUTUAL FUNDS

by

JOHN H. TAYLOR, Ph.D.

*"Wealth is not without its advantages"*

John Kenneth Galbraith

# CONTENTS

The Types Of Risk
How To Measure Risk — Risk-Adjusted Return
How To Avoid Unnecessary Risk

## PART THREE.  PROTECTING YOUR INVESTMENTS

**PART FOUR.  SUMMARY**

# LIST OF TABLES

# LIST OF FIGURES

# CHAPTER 1

# WHAT THIS BOOK CAN DO FOR YOU

This book is not for everyone. If you are an impatient speculator trying to get rich overnight, or a gambler willing to risk your assets on a game of chance, this book is not for you.

On the other hand, if you are a thoughtful, long-term investor who wishes to build real wealth over time - while avoiding unnecessary risk - then this book can do a great deal for you.

It will remove the emotional confusion and complexity that so often surrounds investment decisions. It will show you a logical, step-by-step approach to profitable investing; how to make investment decisions based on simple probabilities, using the investment experience of past decades.

When you have read this book you will no longer be swayed by the day-to-day financial news and the random short-term fluctuations of the stock market. You will be working towards your chosen goal of building wealth, using an all-weather plan which will get you there safely. No longer will you be making a futile attempt to foretell the future, you will simply be following the existing profitable trends of the market place. No predictions, no complicated mathematical formulas and no magic secrets. Just a thorough knowledge of successful investing.

Today's investor has many more choices than ever before. There has been an explosive interest in some of the newer opportunities - international investing in stocks and bonds - the use of index funds to participate inexpensively in entire markets - the practice of socially responsible investing - the tax benefits of mutual funds within variable annuity contracts. Each of these opportunities and many others are explained and critically evaluated.

But there is much more to creating wealth than just selecting a good mutual fund. You need to know the basic rules of the investment game before you can play. You need to know how to set realistic goals and how to develop a balanced portfolio while avoiding the mine fields along the way. Most people never learn the basics of investing and finish up losing money over the long term; even more investors lose purchasing power. This is not why you have worked hard. The first part of this book is devoted entirely to developing a plan that will lead you to a lifetime of successful investing. It will help you lay out a clear road map to get you from where you are to where you need to be.

The book is divided into four parts:
  • **Planning Your Financial Future**
  • **Selecting Your Investments**
  • **Protecting Your Investments**
  • **Summary - The Do's and Don'ts of Successful Investing**

In "Planning Your Financial Future," we first look at what it takes to stay ahead. In Chapter 2 we take a cold hard look at why you need to invest successfully and the unfortunate fate of the majority who do not. It highlights the twin enemies of inflation and taxes and shows what you must achieve to build real wealth. You may find this somewhat daunting, but be assured that later we show you how to overcome the fate of the majority and build real wealth. Right here we outline the ten basic rules of investing which will be further elaborated on throughout the book. These alone will put you on the right path and well ahead of the majority of investors.

Chapter 3 reminds you of the common sense things to do before you start investing; then shows you how to set realistic and achievable though ambitious objectives. You can achieve them using the awesome power of compounding combined with tax deferral. If there is a "secret" to investing, this is it.

The essential concept of putting together a well-balanced portfolio of stocks, bonds and real estate is discussed in Chapter 4. We summarize the entire process of wealth building and give examples representing different levels of risk. This is the most important of all the decisions that you will make. We show you how to get it right.

In "Part 2 - Selecting Your Investments," we first cover in Chapter 5 what you need to know about mutual funds; what they are, how they work and how to make them the investment bargain of our times. We particularly discuss what it costs the investor to use mutual funds and how to minimize that cost - and so increase investment returns without increasing risk.

The question of risk is so important and so little understood that Chapter 6 is devoted to this important subject. We show you the types of risk to which your investments will be exposed. There is no truly risk-free investment. We explain how to measure risk, how to look at all investments on a risk-adjusted basis and, most important, how to avoid unnecessary, unrewarded risk. If you read nothing else, read this chapter.

The choice of mutual funds is almost overwhelming, but in Chapter 7 we classify them into a few basic types and explain what each type offers the investor. This prepares us for an exciting look at how to pick the best funds. This is not as easy as generally assumed, but in Chapter 8 we challenge much of the popular conventional wisdom and explain the progressively selective steps to arrive at the cream of the crop. We explain some little-used and simple ways of picking the winners.

International investing has become so important in a global marketplace that Chapter 9 is devoted to explaining the new world of opportunities and showing you how to take on the world and win. There are a few things that you should definitely not do and we explain why. Another very popular innovation is the use of index funds to buy a whole market; whether it be large company stocks, small company stocks, bonds or international investments. Chapter 10 takes you on a guided tour of what is available and how to pick the best. The use of index funds is the choice of many professional investors.

Your investments need careful protection to avoid losing part of your hard-earned wealth. This is where people become most irrational and undo years of profitable investing. Part 3 of the book is devoted entirely to how to look after what you have. We stand back and look at market cycles in Chapter 11, putting them in some historical perspective and characterizing the various stages of the cycle. We discuss what you may choose to do about market cycles. We take a position on the vexed question of whether to attempt to time the market. This sets the stage for Chapter 12 which is a practical description of managing market cycles using just three criteria, each based on many years of successful use. We mention the hundreds of arcane indicators which frequently contradict each other and we rely instead on a simple analysis of where we are now in the cycle. The discussion concludes with a slightly fanciful but well-founded scenario describing the early stages of a bull and bear market.

The practical question of how to actually manage your investments month-by-month and what choices you have are explained in Chapter 13. This brings together much of what we have learned and lets you select a management style that you feel comfortable with.

Whatever your choice, you will need reliable sources of up-to-date investment information. Finding the best can take a long time and a lot of expense. This has all been done for you and the best sources are described in Chapter 14. This can save you months of searching and give you a competitive edge. We report the best of every medium, from magazines and newsletters to fund reporting services and software.

The last chapter summarizes the key do's and don'ts of successful investing.

This book and the resources it guides you to are all that you need to have both the basic understanding and the practical know-how to achieve investment success. It can lead you to financial independence and a richer life-style.

Whether your assets are large or small you have to play the money game throughout your life - and the stakes are high, particularly if you have children to educate or want a comfortable retirement. This book will show you how to safely play the money game to win!

# PART ONE

# PLANNING YOUR FINANCIAL FUTURE

CHAPTER 2

# WHAT IT TAKES TO STAY AHEAD

There is an age-old saying that there are three good ways of losing money; women, horses and the stock market. Women are the most pleasant, horses are the fastest and the stock market is the most assured.

Experience supports at least the last contention and shows that around 90% of investors fail to make real money over time. The result is a lifetime of hard work followed by a progressively impoverished old age.

In this chapter we will take a look at the shocking decline in living standards of the aging American population and show how you can avoid joining them. We will review the ten basic rules for successful investing. These are the guidelines that can lead you to a lifetime of building and enjoying real wealth. We will also take a hard look at taxation and inflation, the twin enemies of wealth, to determine what level of return you personally need to stay ahead. We will measure the risks involved in some of the traditionally conservative approaches to investing such as Treasury Bills and Bonds.

# POVERTY IN OLD AGE
# IS THE FATE OF THE MAJORITY

It has been estimated that after a lifetime of hard work, as few as 2% of Americans reach financial independence in their retirement years. Government statistics clearly show that very many people outlive their money and become progressively poorer with advancing years. For example, among unmarried people over 85 years of age, more than one-third live below the poverty level and the majority live below 125% of the poverty

TABLE 1

**EMERGING POVERTY WITH AGE**

Median Income of the U.S. Population by Age Group

| Age Group | Median Income (thousands) |
|-----------|--------------------------|
| 55 to 61 | $26.0 |
| 62 to 64 | $19.6 |
| 65 to 69 | $15.7 |
| 70 to 74 | $13.7 |
| 75 to 79 | $10.8 |
| 80 to 84 | $8.9 |
| 85+ | $7.8 |

TABLE 2

**POVERTY IN OLD AGE**

Proportion of Population in Different Income Groups
at Different Ages

| Income Level (thousands of dollars) | Proportion of Population at Age: | |
| --- | --- | --- |
| | 55 to 61 | 85+ |
| up to 6 | 13% | 33% |
| 6 to 12 | 12% | 39% |
| 12 to 30 | 31% | 22% |
| 30 to 60 | 31% | 4% |
| 60+ | 13% | 2% |
| | 100% | 100% |

level. The process of economic decline is progressive with age as can be seen in Table 1. The greater the age, the lower the income. This effect is seen at nearly all levels of income. Table 2 shows that during the working years of 55 to 61, only 13% of people lived on less than $6,000 a year, but in the group 85 years and older this figure had increased to one-third of the entire population. The highest income group, earning $60,000 a year or more, accounted for 13% of the working population, but only 2% of the aged population.

The prospect of increasing poverty with age is not limited to the previously poor or indigent; it applies also to those who have worked hard and had successful careers. When they most need money for a comfortable old age, they just don't have it. The chances of you being in that 85 or older group are substantial and are increasing annually. If you were to retire at 65 today, you have a better than 50% chance of living into your 80's.

What is the cause of this alarming financial decline with advancing years?  Part of it is due to a generally very low rate of saving in this country; half the American work force has no money whatever put aside for retirement. A large part of the problem, however, is due to the inability of most people to invest wisely throughout their working years. Less than one quarter of older people's income comes from their investments, and they finish up primarily dependent upon Social Security. Now is the time to learn how to avoid this, to keep ahead of the crowd, and to ensure your future financial quality of life. You must learn how to invest your hard earned money wisely and knowledgeably as no one else will do this for you. Others can give you advice, for which you pay dearly, but most often it is far from unbiased advice and may not even be well informed advice.

The majority of investors receive advice from a stockbroker or insurance agent. In a survey of over 800 investors reported by the Wall Street Journal, investors although receiving such advice, rated it among the lowest quality advice of any sought. People selling you investments are doing just that. Their jobs depend upon the commissions they earn. Their objectives are not necessarily the same as yours, so you must take charge of your own financial destiny. You must play the money game and you must play it to win. It is not hard, provided you know the basic rules. Let's take a look at them.

## THE TEN BASIC RULES
## FOR SUCCESSFUL INVESTING

Experience has shown that what separates the winners from the losers is knowing the rules of the game. These are the most important rules:

1. HAVE CLEAR-CUT INVESTMENT OBJECTIVES AND A REALISTIC PLAN TO GET THERE
   Whether you have short-term needs to buy a car or take a vacation, medium-term needs to fund college education or long term needs to develop a retirement income, your objectives must be clearly stated with a time horizon and dollar requirements. Competing objectives must be prioritized. Your objective, for example, should be to have so many dollars in so many years, assuming a stated level of risk. You must then have a realistic plan to make it happen. You cannot assume unreasonably high investment returns without assuming unreasonable risk. The level of savings and the time horizon must be sufficient to allow steady and relatively safe compounding of your assets. We will explore this in the next chapter.

2. ACHIEVE A CORRECTLY BALANCED PORTFOLIO
   You should not have all of your assets in any one type of investment, however good it may look today. You must diversify broadly. You should not be all in stocks, all in bonds, all in real estate, or all in cash. Even with a small portfolio it should be spread among several

investment types to protect your assets and minimize your risk. The correct split between different types of investment varies depending upon your unique situation. We shall examine your requirements in the next chapter.

3. ENSURE ADEQUATE DIVERSIFICATION OF STOCKS

The market does not reward the investor for unnecessary risk, only for unavoidable risk. Being inadequately diversified is both unnecessary and dangerous. Two-thirds of investors who own individual stocks hold ten or fewer stocks. Recent studies have shown that many times that number is necessary for adequate diversification. This problem can largely be overcome by owning a diversified mutual fund. However, even then, some diversification between funds is necessary, and it is wise to own several diversified funds having different objectives and management styles.

4. MATCH YOUR INVESTMENTS TO YOUR RISK TOLERANCE

It is obvious that a retired couple living on a fixed income, with limited capital assets, should not purchase the same investments as a young, single, highly-paid person with secure employment and significant assets. The appropriate levels of risk are quite different. Most cases, however, fall between these extremes and require careful analysis. On average, over sufficient time, increasing risk will produce increasing rewards although there are limits to this generalization. In the investment world the race between the hare and the tortoise is often won by the tortoise. There is an optimal level of risk for you, and this is where your investments should be placed. To assume more risk is dangerous for you and to assume less is wasteful. We shall determine just what is right for you.

5. LET YOUR TIME HORIZON DICTATE YOUR IN-VESTMENT VEHICLES

If you are investing for less than a five-year period you should probably not invest in the stock market at all, as you may have to sell when the stock market is depressed. You would be better to invest in money market funds or short-term bond funds. History shows that stocks have the best performance over time, but over a one-year period they have showed a loss in 20 years out of 64 years or about 31% of the time. Even over five-year periods, losses have been recorded but with less frequency. By comparison, over twenty-year periods no losses have been recorded and substantial gains have been achieved.

6. EXPLOIT THE INCREDIBLE POWER OF COM-POUNDING WITH TAX DEFERRAL

The island of Manhattan was bought from the Dutch in 1626 for a mere $24. Today it is worth three trillion dollars ($3,000,000,000,000). The original $24 has compounded at a rate of just 8% per year! This is the awesome power of compounding.

If you are young and can invest fairly small sums of money on a regular basis, you can win the money game quite easily. The power of compounding is on your side. Conversely, if you are in debt and the debt is accumulating, you have the power of compounding working against you.

For example, suppose you can put $2,000 a year or $167 a month into a tax deferred vehicle such as an

I.R.A. or an annuity, starting at age 30. By the time you must start taking some out at age 70 1/2, you will have contributed $80,000, and, assuming a return of 10% per year, it will be worth $975,000. If this is left to compound further, apart from the withdrawal of an annual income for the remainder of your life expectancy, you will enjoy a taxable income starting at almost $60,000 a year and steadily increasing over the next 18 years to over $300,000 per year. All this for an original investment of $80,000 accumulated over 40 years at just $167 per month. Such is the incredible power of compounding. If there is a secret to financial success, then this is it.

7.  CAREFULLY SELECT THE BEST INVESTMENTS
Use top performing no-load mutual funds and measure performance on a risk-adjusted basis. Fund selection must reflect your stated overall investment objectives and appropriate level of risk tolerance. If in doubt, err towards the more conservative. Don't buy funds because they are fashionable or exciting or because they did well last month or last year. Don't buy anything which is complicated or which you don't fully understand. Do your own research, consult a good fund reporting service and read the prospectus. Study. That is what leads to success. We will show you later how to pick the best funds. It is not as simple as most authorities would suggest, but we will give you guidelines. Most of all, be objective; carefully study the choices, and don't buy anything just because someone is trying to sell it to you. Remember, it's your pocket they are putting their hand into. We will show you where to go for the best current information.

8. OBJECTIVELY MANAGE YOUR INVESTMENT PORTFOLIO

Any business needs good management and your investments are your business. Allocate regular time at least monthly to manage your business. Good portfolio management requires discipline and patience. Don't be swayed by the emotions of the moment. Stick to your chosen strategy. You are investing for the long term. Use an objective "automatic" system of decision making that lets you buy, sell, or switch according to a set of rules that you have adopted. We will show you how to do this. Otherwise your decisions will be influenced by short-term random movements of the market. Learn to step back and observe from a distance. Control your normal emotions of fear and greed. They are your worst enemies. Ignore the daily financial news and observe only the longer term trends. Do not try to time the market by short-term trading, as over time you are likely to lose. Your objective system will alert you to important longer term changes of trend in the market or in your funds; it will tell you when to take action. Don't try to be a prophet, you are not. You will not always be right in your decisions but learn from your mistakes. You may still out-perform the professionals. They, too, make mistakes. Study Part 3 of this book, it will greatly help you to protect your investments.

9. EXPLOIT INVESTOR PSYCHOLOGY

Investor behavior is quite consistent and usually wrong. Like a flock of sheep, where one goes and succeeds there they all want to go. When the market is rising, more and more investors will enter the market until, as a group, they have no more money left to invest. At this stage they will be euphoric, convinced that the market can only go up. This is the time to sell. If no one is buying any more, then it only needs one person to sell and the market will rapidly decline. When they finally all get desperate and sell, then is the time to buy because there are no more buyers left.

To follow this advice needs guts and clear objectivity. But to buy when everyone else is selling and to sell when everyone else is buying is the simple way that fortunes have been made through the ages. To do this you must side-step the madness of the moment and keep cool and calm in an excited market. You need to discount the latest market scare on the TV news, you must ignore the magazine cover announcing that the market can now only go up (or down). You must return to your basic strategy, remembering that your time horizon is perhaps ten or twenty years and not just a few days. Pause to check the several trends that indicate market direction. Do not be a sheep. You will only get fleeced.

10. UNDERSTAND THE LONG TERM IMPACT OF TAXES AND INFLATION

The combined effect of taxation and inflation is the most insidious and certain enemy of the investor. Many people tend to ignore it until too late, because it is not as dramatic as a sudden drop in the market, but it is far more serious. Over time, the market will bounce back but losses due to taxes and inflation are gone forever and will be repeated again year-after-year. Unless your investment returns are sufficient to offset this effect, your portfolio will suffer constant and cumulative erosion of purchasing power. Ill-informed investors who are very risk averse tend to place their assets in passbook savings accounts, certificates of deposit or

Treasury Bills in a futile attempt to avoid all risk. What they actually achieve is to exchange a possible market risk for a virtually certain and more insidious purchasing power risk. This subject is so important to understand when developing your investment strategy that we will examine it in detail later in this chapter.

So let us recap the Ten Basic Rules of Successful Investing:
1. Have clear cut investment objectives and a realistic plan to get there.
2. Achieve a correctly balanced portfolio.
3. Ensure adequate diversification of stocks.
4. Match your investments to your risk tolerance.
5. Let your time horizon dictate your investment vehicles.
6. Exploit the incredible power of compounding with tax deferral.
7. Carefully select the best investments.
8. Objectively manage your investment portfolio.
9. Exploit investor psychology.
10. Understand the long-term impact of taxes and inflation.

Follow these ten basic rules, and you will be well on your way to investment success. None of them is particularly difficult, but used together they will put you ahead of the great majority of investors. We shall be discussing them all in more detail throughout this book.

## HOW TO LIVE WITH INFLATION AND TAXES

INFLATION is caused by an excessive increase in the supply of money and credit relative to the volume of goods and services produced. It results in a progressive debasement of the currency and erosion of real purchasing power.

Physical debasement of currency has occurred progressively since coins were first minted in Lydia, a part of Asia Minor, around 600 B.C. After a while, unscrupulous governments reduced the precious metal content of coins, while traders clipped them to reduce their size. This continued intermittently throughout the Greek and Roman civilizations. The basic silver coin of Rome was the denarius. For 300 years it remained of good quality silver. As time passed, Rome found itself with an Empire to rule and defend, the Punic Wars to fight, a large indigent population to feed and an ambitious public building program to finance. During the reign of the Emperor Nero, debasement of the coinage began. During the next 150 years the silver content of the coinage was gradually reduced until by the year 215 A.D. it was only about 50% silver. The ultimate physical debasement of currency occurred as recently as 1946 in the United States when the government removed virtually all the silver from its coins. Price inflation has occurred almost continuously since then.

Periods of price inflation are well documented throughout history. In France during the 16th Century prices increased about six fold. In the United States during the 19th and early 20th Centuries, periods of inflation were followed by long periods of deflation in which the volume of money and credit declined, together with general prices. However, for the past 50 years, inflation has been almost continuous, without the normal compensating periods of deflation. This may be associated with ever increasing government spending and borrowing to meet the escalating expectations of the voting public. It is possible that this 50-year trend may reverse, in which case an extended period of deflation could occur. However, it currently seems more probable that the existing trend will continue and that inflation will continue to eat away at your standard of living and your net worth. Table 3 shows what it takes to turn $1 into 10¢ - just fifty years of inflation! During this time the Consumer Price Index has increased from 14 to over 133. However, this is an average figure which may not be relevant to the types of expenses that are important to you. Table 4 shows the rate of inflation of the various elements of the Consumer Price Index. You will see, for example, that for the past two decades the rate of increase in the cost of medical care and education far exceeded the general rate of price inflation.

TABLE 3

**THE EFFECT OF FIFTY YEARS OF INFLATION ON THE REAL VALUE OF ONE DOLLAR**

| Year | Purchasing Power of $1.0 |
|------|--------------------------|
| 1940 | 100¢ |
| 1950 | 58¢ |
| 1960 | 47¢ |
| 1970 | 36¢ |
| 1980 | 17¢ |
| 1990 | 10¢ |

To some extent, the investment markets adjust to inflation by raising the rate of return to investors. Interest rates rise and bond prices fall. In general, stocks suffer more from the effects of inflation than tangible assets such as houses or gold, and less than debt securities such as long-term bonds. Table 5 measures this effect for the period 1973 through 1989. If there were a perfect correlation with inflation the various values

TABLE 4

**INFLATION RATES FOR SELECTED ITEMS – 1970 to 1990**

| Item | Average Annual Inflation Rate |
|------|------|
| Clothing | 3.8% |
| Entertainment | 5.3% |
| Transportation | 6.0% |
| Food | 6.2% |
| Housing | 6.5% |
| Medical Care | 8.1% |
| Education | 8.2% |
| Total Consumer Price Index | 6.3% |

would be 1.0. If there were absolutely no correlation, the values would be 0, and if they moved perfectly in opposite directions the values would be -1.0. Both stock and bond prices are negatively correlated with inflation and will suffer, particularly in the face of high levels of inflation.

Continuing inflation has a profound effect on both the balance sheet and income statement of operating companies. Selling prices tend to rise but so do costs and expenses. The value of existing inventory increases but so does the cost of replacing it. Most of all, the replacement cost of plant, machinery and equipment rises and this future liability is rarely reflected in the financial statements. A sudden burst of high inflation may boost company profits in the short term, but it has an adverse impact in the long term.

TABLE 5

CORRELATION BETWEEN INFLATION AND INVESTMENT CATEGORIES

**(1973 - 1989)**

| | |
|---|---|
| Inflation | 1.0 |
| Single Family Homes | 0.82 |
| Gold | 0.59 |
| Domestic Stocks | (0.33) |
| International Stocks | (0.52) |
| Long Term Government Bonds | (0.61) |
| Long Term Corporate Bonds | (0.72) |

A value of 1.0 represents complete positive correlation and a value of minus 1.0 (1.0) represents complete negative correlation.

The overriding fact that the investor has to realize about inflation is that you pay taxes on it. This is the main reason why it is a threat to your financial health. The average annual compound total return on government bonds over a recent 64-year period was about 4.5%. The average inflation rate was

3.1%. The real return after inflation was, therefore, 1.4%. Suppose that your total marginal Federal and State tax rate is 33%. If you just paid tax on the real return of 1.5%, you would have an after tax return of 0.9%. This is very modest, but even this is not the case. You are taxed on the entire nominal return of 4.5% although most of this is not a real return. After tax at 33% you would have 3.0% remaining. Now deduct the 3.1% inflation and you have a negative real return. The exact numbers will vary with the time period examined but invariably they will result in very small positive or even negative real returns. This is the true cost to you of inflation. Stocks have historically produced a much higher nominal annual return of 10.1% which, under the same scenario, would have produced a positive but modest real return of 3.7% per annum.

TAXATION will be considered here only as it affects overall investment returns and how it combines with inflation to form a significant challenge to the serious investor. Later, in Chapter 13, we will explore methods to reduce and to defer taxes on investment income. During the past decade we have experienced at least four major new tax bills and several lesser ones. There is no reason to suppose that future changes will by any less frequent. Completely up-to-date and expert tax advice should be sought on specific tax matters.

Not only are taxes here to stay, but the total tax burden on the American public has steadily increased over the past 40 years in spite of many political claims to the contrary. The Tax Foundation calculates each year "tax freedom day." This is the day on which the average person has earned enough to pay their Federal, State and local taxes for the year. In 1950, this day fell on April 3. It has since steadily increased by more than one month and now falls around May 8. In absolute terms the highest 10% of incomes contribute more than half of all Federal taxes and the highest 25% contribute more than three quarters. For most investors taxes are a very real burden on investment income.

To understand their impact we first need to calculate a total marginal tax rate that will apply to investment income. This consists of the sum of:

a) Your marginal federal tax rate. This is not your average rate or effective rate but is the rate which you would pay on the last dollar of total taxable income. This includes allowance for the deductibility of state and local taxes where applicable.

b) Your marginal state tax rate. This is your marginal rate of state income tax plus any additional state taxes on investment income or intangible assets. State taxes vary widely in nature, and you will need to calculate your own current total rates. Seven states currently have no individual state income tax while five states have top rates of 10% or more.

Now calculate the total of these taxes. The answer will vary widely depending upon both income level and state of residence. It may, for example, be as low as 20% or over 40%. Arrive at an approximate figure that applies to your situation and write it down. You will shortly need to use it. We will refer to this as your "total marginal tax rate." Remember that interest on the obligations of the federal government and its agencies is generally not subject to state income tax. The interest on most of the obligations of state and local governments, such as municipal bonds, is generally not subject to federal income tax and most states do not tax the interest on municipal bonds issued within their own state. Capital gains are generally not exempt from federal or state tax and not all municipal bonds are tax advantaged. State tax laws vary widely and should be individually checked.

## THE RISK OF DOING SOMETHING
## AND THE GREATER RISK OF DOING NOTHING

Many investors having a fairly high total marginal tax rate and who are risk-averse want to make money over time in "riskless" investments such as government guaranteed bank deposits or Treasury Bills. They also want a high degree of liquidity. This is quite understandable, but based on historical evidence it is also quite impossible. They will suffer a certain and inexorable decline in purchasing power if the trends of the past 50 years continue. Let us assume an inflation rate of 5% per year, a return on their "riskless" investment of 6% and a total marginal tax rate of 30%. After five years the purchasing power of $1 will have declined to 96¢, after 20 years to 83¢ and after 30 years to 73¢. The power of compounding has turned against them and time simply worsens the problem. If our investor were fortunate enough to achieve a "riskless" return of 7% throughout the entire period in the presence of 5% inflation, he would be getting a return far above the historical norm, but he would still lose purchasing power under this scenario. We can see this effect in more detail in Table 6 which shows what a dollar invested today may be worth in real terms after taxes and inflation, if placed for 20 years in a "riskless" government guaranteed bank account or Treasury Bill. During the period 1960 to 1990 inflation averaged almost 5.0%. In the first column of the table we have selected this level and also show a level of 7.0% which represents periods of higher inflation during the 1970's and 1980's. In the second column we have assumed investment yields of 1% and 2% above inflation. This is generous by historical standards. The long-term historical yield on Treasury Bills from 1926 to 1990 averaged 0.6% above inflation. During the period from 1968 to 1987 it averaged 1.1%. One percent seems the most probable of the two values chosen; that is a 6%

TABLE 6

**THE IMPACT OF TAXES AND INFLATION**

What a Dollar Placed Today in a "Riskless" Investment May be Worth in Twenty Years After Taxes and Inflation

| Inflation Rate (CPI) | Investment Yield (Annual) | Total Marginal Tax Rate (Federal and State) | | | |
|---|---|---|---|---|---|
| | | 25% | 30% | 35% | 40% |
| 5% | 6% | $0.90 | $0.83 | $0.76 | $0.68 |
| 5% | 7% | $1.05 | $0.98 | $0.91 | $0.83 |
| 7% | 8% | $0.78 | $0.68 | $0.57 | $0.45 |
| 7% | 9% | $0.95 | $0.85 | $0.74 | $0.63 |

yield in the presence of 5% inflation and an 8% yield in the presence of 7% inflation. The table shows that, with one exception, at all inflation rates, investment yields, and tax rates the real value of a dollar invested declined. The only exception was a 7% yield with 5% inflation at a 25% total marginal tax rate. In this case real value has grown by a negligible amount over an extended period. Although not shown in the table, at the two higher rates of tax, real values decline even at a 10% yield in the presence of 7% inflation. The only way that you can stay whole is at a very low inflation rate or a very low tax rate or better still, a combination of the two. The successful investor is unlikely to remain in a low tax bracket and although inflation may be low for short periods, it has not been so throughout any recent decade.

Quite clearly, this is not the best way to build wealth. We must achieve investment yields which produce real growth over time. The so-called "riskless" investment produces not only the risk of real loss of principal but actual, almost certain loss on a continuing basis, when evaluated on an after tax and after inflation basis. Leaving your money in the bank or in Treasury Bills is not the way even to preserve its real value. So we now need to know what are the levels of nominal return which produce real growth and what types of investment have historically produced them.

## WHERE IS YOUR BREAK-EVEN POINT?

You should now form your own opinion about likely future rates of inflation. We have discussed the historical values. You also now need to know your current and future probable total marginal tax rate. Perhaps you expect to be in a higher tax bracket within the time horizon of your investment program. Now take both these values and refer to Table 7 from which you can simply read off the nominal returns necessary to break-even, that is to experience neither real gain or loss after taxes and inflation. If, for example, you assume 5% inflation and a 30% total marginal tax bracket, your break-even point is 7.1% average annual compound return. Above that, you are making

TABLE 7

**BREAK-EVEN ANALYSIS**

The Nominal Annual Compound Return Required to Maintain Purchasing Power
of Investments Under Various Inflation and Tax Rates

| Total Marginal Tax Rate (%) | Annual Inflation Rate (%) | | | | | | | | |
|---|---|---|---|---|---|---|---|---|---|
| | 0 | 3 | 4 | 5 | 6 | 7 | 8 | 9 | 10 |
| 0 | 0 | 3.0 | 4.0 | 5.0 | 6.0 | 7.0 | 8.0 | 9.0 | 10.0 |
| 10 | 1.1 | 3.3 | 4.4 | 5.6 | 6.7 | 7.8 | 8.9 | 10.0 | 11.1 |
| 15 | 1.2 | 3.5 | 4.7 | 5.9 | 7.1 | 8.2 | 9.4 | 10.6 | 11.8 |
| 20 | 1.3 | 3.8 | 5.0 | 6.3 | 7.5 | 8.8 | 10.0 | 11.3 | 12.5 |
| 25 | 1.3 | 4.0 | 5.3 | 6.7 | 8.0 | 9.3 | 10.7 | 12.0 | 13.3 |
| 30 | 1.4 | 4.3 | 5.7 | 7.1 | 8.6 | 10.0 | 11.4 | 12.9 | 14.3 |
| 35 | 1.5 | 4.6 | 6.2 | 7.7 | 9.2 | 10.8 | 12.3 | 13.8 | 15.4 |
| 40 | 1.7 | 5.0 | 6.7 | 8.3 | 10.0 | 11.7 | 13.3 | 15.0 | 16.7 |

progress; below it you are slipping backwards. Circle the appropriate number for you and fix it in your mind.

## WHAT IT TAKES TO STAY AHEAD

Now we can see what it takes to achieve real growth using your own tax rate and expected inflation rate. Please refer to

Table 8 which shows the return required to double your money over different time periods, at different levels of inflation and with different tax levels. If, for example, you have chosen a 5% inflation rate and a 25% total marginal tax rate, you will need a nominal return of 9.8% to double your money over 30 years, 11.4% over 20 years, and 16.3% over 10 years. The table also shows the break-even points for the same scenarios. This table summarizes the real challenge facing investors. It faces up to the inescapable fact that rather high nominal returns are needed to gain modest real growth. Can this be achieved?

Historically, the return on stocks has varied, depending upon market conditions and the underlying inflation rate. During the extended period from 1926 to 1990, the compound annual total return on stocks averaged 10.1% while that of Treasury Bills was 3.7% and inflation was 3.1%. During this period small company stocks averaged approximately 12% per year. These averages include all the poor performing stocks as well as the good ones and assumes that the investor remained fully invested through all the recessions, including the Great Depression of 1929. In more recent times stocks have performed much better, producing a total compound return of over 17% per year throughout the 1980's. If we examine the performance of the better performing mutual funds, we see an even more encouraging picture. For example, 20th Century Investors, Inc., have managed two of their oldest funds under a consistent investment philosophy for about 20 years. During the past 15 years, their 20th Century Select fund and their 20th Century Growth fund have each produced a compound total return of more than 20% per year. During the decade of the 1980's, which was generally favorable for the stock market, a number of good funds produced total returns averaging 15% to 20% per year. This very rapidly produces real wealth. Successful market timing by investors during this period would, of course, have increased these returns further.

However, when you invest in stocks you must be emotionally and financially prepared for the virtual certainty of incurring losses in some years. In return for accepting this risk of loss, you can expect to receive a higher return over time than normally

FIGURE 1

**REAL RETURNS AFTER TAXES & INFLATION**

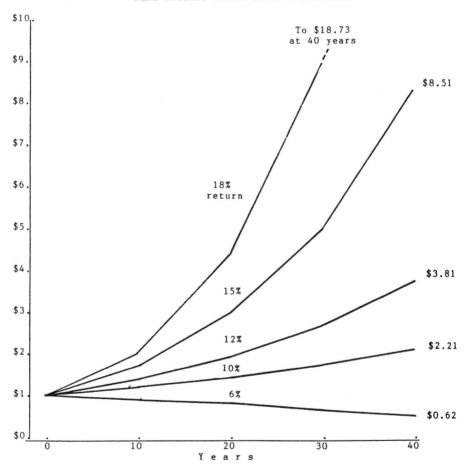

The Real Purchasing Power of One Dollar Invested at Different Nominal Rates of Compound Return After 30% Taxation and 5% Inflation

achieved by less volatile investments.

It is impossible to predict just how the stock market, the better mutual funds, or you as an investor will perform in the future. However, based on the historical record, let's see what would be achieved in real terms with nominal total returns of 6%, 10%, 12%, 15% and 18% per annum in the presence of 5% inflation and a 30% tax rate. The results are shown in Figure 1. The 6% return, more typical of historical Treasury Bill performance, would have produced a decline in real value so that $1 invested would be worth only 62¢ after 40 years. The 10% to 15% returns, more typical of very long-term stock market performance, would all have produced significant real growth, and the 18% return as seen in the very best stock mutual funds turned $1 into $18.73 in real terms. The figure also dramatically shows the importance of just a few extra percentage points of return when measured over long periods. Performance in a tax-deferred account would, of course, increase these returns considerably.

These, then are the types of significant returns that are needed to stay ahead and to build wealth. To achieve them, some market risk must be borne. The alternative is too dangerous over the long term. The traditional "riskless" investment is too risky; your wealth will depreciate. Market risk can be minimized by investing over a long time period and fully diversifying the investments. The ten basic rules of investing will guide you. With this strategy you can build wealth, and over time, achieve financial independence. This is what it takes to stay ahead.

CHAPTER 3

# FIRST YOU NEED A PLAN

If you don't know what you are looking for you probably won't find it. Similarly, with your investments if you don't have clearly thought out measurable objectives and a practical plan to get there, you probably won't succeed. Long-term investment requires patience, discipline and clear objectivity. If you have generalized, fuzzy half-formed objectives and an ill-conceived plan, you will probably wander off the straight line between where you are now and where you need to be. You cannot just copy other people's plans. Your situation is unique.

This chapter will address the important financial matters which must be attended to before you even think of long-term investing. We shall then discuss the setting of clear financial objectives based upon your future likely needs. We will show how to develop a realistic plan to reach those objectives, making the best use of both time and money. Finally, we will review some of the broad classes of investments available to you and how you should combine them into an efficient portfolio having adequate diversification and reduced risk.

## THINGS TO DO BEFORE YOU INVEST

It is important to distinguish clearly between short-term savings to meet a financial obligation, perhaps this year or next year, and long-term investments in which money may be tied up for years to come, or perhaps only available by selling assets at a loss if the market declines. Savings typically would be placed in a money market mutual fund, whereas investments although sometimes held in a money market, would more typically be in stocks, bonds or real estate.

The most important things that you should attend to before even thinking of long-term investing are as follows:

1. ESTABLISH AN EMERGENCY FUND — Most financial planning experts recommend that this should be equivalent to three to six months of after-tax income; more if your job is insecure or you have heavy liabilities, less only if you have other sources of available cash. Such a fund may be essential, if for example, you become unemployed or you have a large deductible amount to pay under your medical or other insurances.

2. HAVE ADEQUATE INSURANCE COVERAGE TO MEET CATASTROPHIC EVENTS — Adequate medical insurance is essential. If it is supplied by your employer, check the terms carefully and ensure that it is truly comprehensive and non-cancellable. If you are an older person, you may want to have insurance coverage for long-term care to cover the expense of a nursing home. Remember that 30% of men and 54% of women over 65 will enter a nursing home. The average stay is over a year and it is not paid by Medicare. Simple term life insurance is necessary if you have dependents, and it should be sufficient to produce an

income of at least 75% of your current after-tax income. You should similarly have disability insurance in case of long-term incapacitation, again reflecting the needs of yourself and your dependents. Adequate automobile and homeowners insurance is, of course, necessary, and you may also need liability insurance in respect of your occupation or profession. When planning your insurance, become very familiar with what coverage your employer already provides. Beyond that, get quotations from several insurers, compare policies carefully and elect to take the largest deductible that you can afford. Evaluate no-load insurance companies. Insurance is important but expensive so get the best value for your money and don't over-insure. You need your money to invest.

3. PROVIDE FOR YOUR HOUSING NEEDS — If you rent, then the rent money is sacrosanct. If you choose to buy a house on a mortgage the same applies to your mortgage payments. Don't buy more house than you need as you cannot be sure that it will be a good investment.

4. PAY DOWN DEBT — One of the best investments you can make is to pay off your consumer debt. Check the rate of interest that you are paying on your credit cards and ask yourself where you can get a safe, liquid after-tax return as great as that. You most probably can't. Pay it off and keep it off, and if necessary, tear up your credit cards. You need that money to invest, not to pay as interest to a credit card company. The same applies to auto loans and unsecured bank loans. Whether you should pay off your mortgage is a more complex question which depends on the mortgage interest rate,

your tax rate and the alternative opportunities. You need to calculate whether the after-tax cost to you is greater than the after tax return that you can get on a secure investment of similar duration.

5. PUT YOUR FINANCIAL AFFAIRS IN ORDER
   a) Seek good tax advice to ensure that you are not paying unnecessary taxes.
   b) Have a realistic personal operating budget which minimizes unnecessary expenditure and lets you know just where your money goes. Is this where you really want it to go?
   c) Update your Will to ensure that if you should not survive to enjoy the fruits of all your hard work, at least your loved ones will benefit, with as little as possible being diverted to legal expenses and taxes.
   d) Update your statement of net worth. List your assets and deduct your liabilities. This is where you are now. Next write down the discretionary income that you can allocate to investment during the coming year. Perhaps you need to express it as so much per month. Now estimate what this amount may be for each of the next several years. This is what you have to work with. No matter if the amount seems small, sufficient time will cure that problem.

## SETTING YOUR INVESTMENT OBJECTIVES

Most people never have enough money to meet what they perceive as their longer term financial needs, and it therefore becomes necessary to prioritize them. The most frequent reason why people invest is to achieve financial independence in retirement, although usually with limited success. Other common reasons are to finance college education for their children, to start a business or to purchase a house. These are all likely to have different time horizons and may therefore require varying investment approaches. Those people with very limited assets and a relatively short time frame cannot afford to achieve the higher returns normally achieved over extended periods with higher risk investments. In contrast, those who have already achieved financial independence, and who perhaps wish to build a large estate for their heirs, have the advantage of a normally long time horizon and the ability ultimately to achieve higher returns from investments having above average risk.

At this stage you should be concerned only with a statement of your long-term financial objective, do not concern yourself at present with how this will be achieved. That will come later. But you should be aware that accumulation of significant wealth with reasonable safety takes many years. This is why you should now define your broad objectives and priorities far into the future. It is never too early, but it may be too late.

Your stated objective should not simply be "to make as much money as possible" or "to become rich" because these are quite subjective. There is no way to devise a plan to achieve these objectives, and there is no way of checking whether you are on track or when the objectives have been achieved. Better defined objectives might be for example: *"To be able to finance college costs of $20,000 a year for each of four years starting in 15 years time."* or perhaps: *"To retire in 30 years at age 65 with a million dollars of investments."*

If you expect to retire with a fixed pension but recognize that it will be steadily eroded by inflation after retirement, then you might want a supplementary income when you have to start withdrawing your I.R.A. and other tax-deferred accounts at age 70 1/2. In this case you could possibly have as an objective: *"To provide an income starting at $100,000 a year, beginning in 30 years and lasting for a 20-year period. Maintain its purchasing power throughout the 20-year period assuming 5% annual inflation."* This is a more sophisticated objective but perfectly feasible if carefully planned. We will take a look at each of these three examples to see how they could be achieved. Meanwhile, you should now finalize your own personal long-term objective and write it down. Be ambitious!

## HAVE A PLAN TO GET THERE — THE AWESOME POWER OF COMPOUNDING

Your plan should basically be a realistic and achievable program to build a stated sum of money within a given period of time. The value of an investment at the end of a given period is determined by only three factors:
- The cash flow into the investment
- The time period during which the assets may grow, and
- The average rate of return achieved during the investment period.

The final value will be determined both by the magnitude and the interaction of each of these three factors. We will look at each factor separately but focus particularly on the best use of the investment time period.

THE CASH FLOW into the investment may be either as an initial lump sum, as periodic investments, or frequently as a combination of the two. In the case of investment vehicles having fluctuating market values, which is the case for most long-term investments, any lump sum should be invested either when the market is clearly below its historical average price, or alternatively, the lump sum should be divided into ten equal parts and one part invested quarterly. This will avoid having the

TABLE 8

**REQUIRED RETURN ON INVESTMENTS**

Nominal Return Required to Meet Investment Objectives at Varying Rates of Taxation and Inflation

| Investment Objective | Total Marginal Tax Rate | | | | | | | | |
|---|---|---|---|---|---|---|---|---|---|
| | 0% Inflation | | | 25% Inflation | | | 35% Inflation | | |
| | 3% | 5% | 7% | 3% | 5% | 7% | 3% | 5% | 7% |
| Maintain Purchasing Power | 3.0 | 5.0 | 7.0 | 4.0 | 6.7 | 9.3 | 4.6 | 7.7 | 10.8 |
| Double Real Value in Thirty Years | 5.4 | 7.4 | 9.4 | 7.1 | 9.8 | 12.4 | 8.2 | 11.3 | 14.4 |
| Double Real Value in Twenty Years | 6.6 | 8.6 | 10.6 | 8.7 | 11.4 | 14.0 | 10.1 | 13.2 | 16.3 |
| Double Real Value in Ten Years | 10.2 | 12.2 | 14.2 | 13.6 | 16.3 | 18.9 | 15.7 | 18.8 | 21.9 |

considerable disadvantage of having an abnormally high initial purchase price.

THE TIME PERIOD AVAILABLE for the investment to grow is of great consequence, even more so than most investors realize. A long time period gives you time to make regular contributions to your investment account; it permits the phenomenon of compounding to work in your favor, and it reduces the risks associated with shorter term investing. The power of compounding, combined where possible with tax-deferral, is the most potent weapon available to fight the twin enemies of taxes and inflation which we reviewed in the last chapter. For example, if a generous grandparent gave a child just $1,000 at birth and it was invested in a tax-deferred account at a 10% annual return compounded quarterly, that fortunate individual would receive over $600,000 upon retirement at age sixty-five.

For the sake of simplicity we will from here onwards be looking at investment returns in nominal dollars without the impact of taxes and inflation. You should, of course, relate investment returns to your particular break-even point and to the nominal returns required to produce real growth by referring to Tables 7 and 8.

In order to use the power of compounding most effectively, there are three concepts which need to be understood.

First, since the power of compounding is based upon interest being reinvested to yield interest on the interest throughout the investment period, the frequency of compounding becomes important. Investments may have the return reinvested and compounded annually, semi-annually, quarterly, monthly or even more frequently. Over a long period this makes a big difference. Table 9 shows the value of $10,000 invested tax-deferred for 30 years at 15% annual return compounded at different intervals. In this example, monthly compounding, when compared to annual compound-

TABLE 9

**THE IMPORTANCE OF FREQUENCY OF COMPOUNDING**

$10,000 Invested for Thirty Years at 15% Annual Return

| Frequency of Compounding | Portfolio Value at End of Period | Increase in Value Over Annual Compounding | |
|---|---|---|---|
| | | $ | % |
| Annually | $662,118 | — | — |
| Semi-annually | $766,490 | 104,372 | 15.8 |
| Quarterly | $829,035 | 166,917 | 25.2 |
| Monthly | $875,410 | 213,292 | 32.2 |

ing, produced an additional $213,292 from the original investment of $10,000. This represents a 32% greater return than annual compounding. Even quarterly compounding provides a 25% greater return than annual compounding in this example. This is an important factor to consider when comparing otherwise similar long term interest bearing investments. It is one of the few ways of increasing returns without increasing risk and is a consideration often overlooked by investors.

(2)    The second concept is that the value of a sum at the end of a long period of compounding is highly dependent upon the size and timing of the very earliest investments. For example, a single sum of $20,000 invested at 15% return will be worth nearly $2.7 million after 35 years, whereas $2,500 invested every single year at 15% return will be worth only about $2.2 million. The first investment had $20,000 invested and the second one had a total of $87,500 invested but finished up worth less because it did not have the advantage of a large early investment. In practice, it is difficult for most people to make substantial investments early in life, but the fact remains that this is by far the most effective and least costly way of building wealth.

(3)    The third concept of importance is the realistic amount of time available for the investment to remain compounding. Many people mistakenly assume that the period available will cease upon their retirement. This is not normally so. Part of the cash flow may be used for living expenses, but if the principal is fairly substantial, the portfolio will still continue to compound significantly. A more relevant investment time frame is based on life expectancy. At age 65 men have an average life expectancy of 15 years and women of 19 years. These, however, are only averages, and we do know that the fastest growing age group of the U.S. population is the 85 years and older group. It is very probable that you will be

around spending money well into your 80's. From now until then is the time frame that you should think of for your investments to be compounding.

The I.R.S. requires that, in the case of most tax-deferred retirement accounts, withdrawals must commence at age 70 1/2 based on the overall statistical probability of life expectancy. However, the majority of assets can still remain in the tax-deferred account and those taken out can still be allowed to compound in a taxable account to the extent that they are not required for living expenses. Tax-deferred variable annuity insurance contracts may be held past this age.

In summary, there is generally a longer time period available for compounding than is often assumed. If you are now 50 years of age, for example, you may still enjoy the benefits of 30 years or more of compounding of your assets.

These are the general concepts that you should consider to maximize the power of compounding. Now, let's see what it can do for you. There are at least four scenarios under which you may need to measure the power of compounding. These are:

1. If I invest a single lump sum, what may it become worth in the future? (Table 10)
2. If I invest a constant amount every quarter, what may it become worth in the future? (Table 11)
3. If I need to have a known sum in the future, how much do I need to invest as a lump sum now to achieve it? (Table 12)
4. If I need to have a known sum in the future, how much do I need to invest every quarter to achieve it? (Table 13)

The answers to these questions will permit you to calculate your own personal investment plan to reach your stated objective. Table 10 shows the value of $10,000 invested at different rates of return compounded quarterly over varying

TABLE 10

**THE POWER OF COMPOUND GROWTH OF A SINGLE INVESTMENT**

The Value of $10,000 Invested for Varying Periods at Varying Rates of Return

| Duration of Investment (Years) | Average Annual Rate of Growth, Compounded Quarterly | | | |
|---|---|---|---|---|
| | 7% | 10% | 15% | 18% |
| 5 | 14,148 | 16,386 | 20,882 | 24,117 |
| 10 | 20,016 | 26,851 | 43,604 | 58,164 |
| 15 | 28,318 | 43,998 | 91,051 | 140,274 |
| 20 | 40,064 | 72,096 | 190,129 | 338,301 |
| 25 | 56,682 | 118,137 | 397,018 | 815,885 |
| 30 | 80,192 | 193,582 | 829,035 | 1,967,682 |

TABLE 11

**THE POWER OF COMPOUND GROWTH BY REGULAR QUARTERLY INVESTING**

The Value of $500 Invested Quarterly for Varying Periods at Varying Rates of Return

| Duration of Investment (Years) | Total Sum Invested ($) | Average Annual Rate of Growth, Compounded Quarterly | | | |
|---|---|---|---|---|---|
| | | 7% | 10% | 15% | 18% |
| 5 | 10,000 | 11,851 | 12,772 | 14,509 | 15,686 |
| 10 | 20,000 | 28,617 | 33,701 | 44,805 | 53,515 |
| 15 | 30,000 | 52,338 | 67,996 | 108,068 | 144,749 |
| 20 | 40,000 | 85,897 | 124,192 | 240,172 | 364,779 |
| 25 | 50,000 | 133,377 | 216,274 | 516,024 | 895,428 |
| 30 | 60,000 | 200,548 | 367,163 | 1,092,046 | 2,175,202 |

TABLE 12

**THE SINGLE INVESTMENT REQUIRED TO PRODUCE $1,000 AT A FUTURE TIME**

| Duration of Investment (Years) | Annual Rate of Return, Compounded Quarterly | | | |
| --- | --- | --- | --- | --- |
| | 7% | 10% | 15% | 18% |
| 0 | $1,000 | $1,000 | $1,000 | $1,000 |
| 5 | $707 | $610 | $479 | $415 |
| 10 | $500 | $372 | $229 | $172 |
| 15 | $353 | $227 | $110 | $71 |
| 20 | $250 | $139 | $53 | $30 |
| 25 | $176 | $85 | $25 | $12 |
| 30 | $125 | $52 | $12 | $5 |

TABLE 13

**THE QUARTERLY INVESTMENT REQUIRED TO PRODUCE $1,000 AT A FUTURE TIME**

| Duration of Investment (Years) | Annual Rate of Return, Compounded Quarterly | | | |
|---|---|---|---|---|
| | 7% | 10% | 15% | 18% |
| 5 | $42.19 | $39.15 | $34.46 | $31.88 |
| 10 | $17.47 | $14.84 | $11.16 | $9.34 |
| 15 | $9.55 | $7.35 | $4.63 | $3.45 |
| 20 | $5.82 | $4.03 | $2.08 | $1.37 |
| 25 | $3.75 | $2.31 | $0.97 | $0.56 |
| 30 | $2.49 | $1.36 | $0.46 | $0.23 |

time periods. For example, at a 15% return for 30 years, your $10,000 will become $829,035. You can see, for example, that the 15% rate of return when compared to the 7% rate produces a disproportionately greater return, and by the 30th year, it reaches more than 10 times the value of the 7% rate of return. This is why a few extra percentage points of return are so important over time. From this table you can clearly see the importance of both yield and time, and you can estimate the future value of any sum at any of the illustrated rates of return and times.

Table 11 shows the value of regular quarterly investing with similar variables. This is how most people build wealth. For example, if you want to become a millionaire (before tax) you can open a tax deferred account by the time you are 40 years of age and invest $500 per quarter at a 15% return for 30 years. You will finish up with $1,092,046. If you can only achieve a 7% return, then you would need to invest approximately five times as much each quarter. If you could average 18% annually, which seems somewhat improbable but by no means unprecedented, you could achieve your objective of $1 million in just over 25 years. The second column of Table 11 shows the total amount invested over each period. This again shows how greatly the building of wealth is dependent upon the duration of the investment period. For example, at a 15% return after 10 years, you will get back just over twice what you invested, but over a 25 year period, you will get back more than 10 times your total investment.

Table 12 takes a different view of compounding and shows how much you need to invest today to reach a given sum at a predetermined future date. For example, if you need $1,000 before tax in 20 years, and you can achieve a 15% return, then you would need to invest just $53 now. At a 10% return you would need to invest $139 and at a 7% return, $250. You can, of course, use this table to calculate any value. For example, if you need $25,000 in 20 years and can invest at a 10% return you have to invest now the sum of $139 x 25 = $3,475. That is, $139 for each $1,000.

If you wish to arrive at a given sum after tax, you can simply deduct the tax rate from the yield. For example, a 10% return after a 30% tax will provide an after tax yield of 7%. You simply read off the 7% column from Table 12 and the answer will give you the sum required to produce $1,000 after tax. If you are investing in a tax deferred account, it is a little more complex. First deduct your total contribution from the $1,000 of assets to arrive at the taxable gain.   Then gross it up, (i.e., increase it sufficiently to pay the taxes) since you will have to pay tax on this sum. The figure, when added to your principal of $1,000 will indicate the total gross value of the account required to produce $1,000 after tax.

To take an example, Table 12 shows that to produce $1,000 over 20 years at a 10% return, you need to invest $139. Your taxable gain is $1,000 less your original investment of $139 = $861. Tax at 30% on $861 = $258.3. Gross up 30% tax due as $258.3 x 100/70 = $369. This is the additional sum you need to pay the taxes (Note: the number 70 used in this example is the reciprocal of the tax rate. If the tax rate were, say 40%, then the reciprocal would be 60). The total sum required to produce $1,000 after tax at 30% is therefore $1,000 + $369 = $1,369. If you are in any doubt about a calculation of this type you can very easily check it by working it backwards. In this example we can see that if the total sum before tax is $1,369 then 30% tax on the gain is ($1,369 less $139) x 0.3 = $369. So the after tax sum is $1,369 less $369 = $1,000.

Table 13 varies only in that instead of investing a lump sum now to achieve a future sum, it assumes that you will invest a constant amount quarterly throughout the period. If you are a regular investor, saving and then investing perhaps on a quarterly basis, this table can be of great value to you. For example, if you have a child going to college in 15 years and you can invest at 10% annual return, then you need to invest just $7.35 each quarter for every $1,000 of principal required. You can apply the same approach to tax liability as we discussed earlier but make sure that you include all your contributions to arrive at the total sum invested. If you have only 10 years and can achieve only a 7% annual return, then you will need to invest $17.47 quarterly for every $1,000 of principal required.

These four tables, together with the more detailed tables provided in the appendix, can be used in many different ways to help you develop your own plan. Let's now see how to use them to plan the three hypothetical objectives that we listed earlier in this chapter. They were as follows:

1. FINANCE COLLEGE COSTS OF $20,000 A YEAR FOR EACH OF FOUR YEARS, STARTING IN 15 YEARS TIME — Assume that we need 4 x $20,000 in 15 years after tax at 30%. Having the total sum available will allow us either to prepay all four years to avoid inflationary increases or else to invest the declining balance during the four-year period.

    If we can invest at a 10% return with a 30% tax rate, we shall achieve a 7% return after tax. Table 12 shows us that at an effective yield of 7% over 15 years we shall need to invest now the sum of $353 for each $1,000 required or $353 x 80 = $28,240.

    Alternatively, we can see from Table 13 that we can achieve the same objective by investing $9.55 every quarter for each $1,000 required. We would need to invest a total of $9.55 x 80 = $764 each quarter.

2. TO RETIRE IN 30 YEARS AT AGE 65 WITH A MILLION DOLLARS OF INVESTMENTS — We will assume that this means on an after-tax basis, paying

taxes annually. With this longer time horizon we will assume that a return of 15% annually is possible and that taxes at 33% reduce the after-tax return to 10%. Table 12 shows that an after tax effective rate of 10% and a 30-year time horizon, our investor needs to invest now the sum of $52 for every $1,000 required. Therefore, for $1 million, the sum required to be invested is $52 x 1,000 = $52,000. Alternatively, we can see from Table 13 that at a 10% return for 30 years our investor can invest each quarter during the 30-year period the sum of just $1.36 for each $1,000 required or $1.36 x 1,000 = $1,360 per quarter to produce $1 million at age 65.

If our investor is able to invest regularly in a tax deferred account, the quarterly investment drops from $1,360 to only $674 per quarter which is equivalent to $7.39 per day invested quarterly. This seems to be a reasonable price to pay to become a millionaire! The calculation for this is as follows: To create $1,000 over 30 years at 15% return we need to invest $0.46 per quarter, as shown in Table 13.

Over 30 years, or 120 quarters, the total sum invested is thus 120 x $0.46 = $55.20. The taxable gain is $1,000 less $55.20 = $944.80. Tax at 33% on the taxable gain is $944.80 x 0.33 = $311.78.

Grossing this up for tax at 33% it becomes $311.78 x 100/67 = $465.34.

Thus the total sum required will be $1,000 + $465.3 = $1,465.3 to produce $1,000 after tax.

The cost of this is a quarterly investment of $0.46 x 1.4653 = $0.674 per $1,000.

Thus $1 million will require $0.674 x 1,000 = $674 per quarter.

3. TO PROVIDE AN AFTER-TAX INCOME OF $100,000

A YEAR, STARTING IN 30 YEARS AND LASTING FOR A 20-YEAR PERIOD WHILE MAINTAINING ITS PURCHASING POWER DURING THAT 20-YEAR PERIOD, ASSUMING 5% ANNUAL INFLATION — This may seem particularly ambitious, but if inflation averages 5% per year, then in 30 years $100,000 will be equivalent in purchasing power to $22,000 today.

Let us assume that over this 20-year period a 15% annual return is achievable. A 33% tax rate is assumed, which will reduce the after-tax return to 10% and a 5% inflation rate will further reduce the real after-tax and after-inflation return to 5%. What is the sum of money which when yielding 5% per annum will produce $100,000 and last for 20 years? For this we need to refer to Table 14 which shows how many years principal will last at varying growth rates and withdrawal rates. The assets will be growing at a real rate of 5% per year, and to last 20 years it is possible to withdraw at a rate of 8% per year. This is shown by looking down the 5% column on the table and across the 8% line to read off 20 years. We, therefore, need a capital sum of which 8% is $100,000, i.e. 100,000/0.08 = $1,250,000. This will permit an after-tax income of $100,000 a year and will permit the principal and, therefore, the dollar amount of the yield, to increase with inflation at 5% a year.

To build this amount over 30 years, if we assume a yield of 10% after taxes, Table 12 shows that it will take a single investment now of $52 per $1,000 or $52 x 1,250 = $65,000. Table 13 shows that alternatively, we could achieve the same objective by investing each quarter the sum of $1.36 per $1,000 needed or $1.36 x 1,250 = $1,700 per quarter.

These three examples show how you can calculate the

TABLE 14

**HOW LONG WILL YOUR MONEY LAST?**

The Number of Years That Principal Will Last at Varying Rates of Growth and Withdrawal

| Withdrawal Per Year (%) | Growth Per Year (%) | | | | | | | | | | | |
|---|---|---|---|---|---|---|---|---|---|---|---|---|
| | 3 | 4 | 5 | 6 | 7 | 8 | 9 | 10 | 11 | 12 | 13 | 14 |
| 4 | 46 | | | | | | | | | | | |
| 5 | 30 | 41 | | | | | | | | | | |
| 6 | 23 | 28 | 36 | | | | | | | | | |
| 7 | 18 | 21 | 25 | 33 | | | | | | | | |
| 8 | 15 | 17 | 20 | 23 | 30 | | | | | | | |
| 9 | 13 | 14 | 16 | 18 | 22 | 28 | | | | | | |
| 10 | 12 | 13 | 14 | 15 | 17 | 20 | 26 | | | | | |
| 11 | 10 | 11 | 12 | 13 | 14 | 16 | 19 | 25 | | | | |
| 12 | 9 | 10 | 11 | 11 | 12 | 14 | 15 | 18 | 23 | | | |
| 13 | 8 | 9 | 9 | 10 | 11 | 12 | 13 | 15 | 17 | 21 | | |
| 14 | 8 | 8 | 9 | 9 | 10 | 11 | 11 | 13 | 14 | 17 | 21 | |
| 15 | 7 | 7 | 8 | 8 | 9 | 9 | 10 | 11 | 12 | 14 | 16 | 20 |

many different ways to reach your own financial objective using the information in the tables. The examples given are intentionally ambitious but may easily be scaled down. Approximations may be made for values falling between those shown, or reference may be made to the more detailed tables in the appendixes.

There are two other considerations that you should be aware of when studying the effects of time upon your investment plan.

First, liquidity. Most long-term investments fluctuate in value, whether they are stocks, bonds or real estate. If you need to liquidate a portfolio you should allow a period of several years in which to do so. In this way you can avoid having to sell at a low point in a typical four-year cycle. This means that if a portfolio must be liquidated by a given date, liquidation may need to start well before that date, thus somewhat reducing the time period available for uninterrupted compounding.

Second, tax deferral. How useful is time spent in a tax-deferred account? Are I.R.A.'s and other tax-deferred accounts worthwhile? The comparisons that you see in advertisements claiming the advantages of tax-deferral sometimes conveniently forget that taxes still have to be paid upon withdrawal. Nevertheless, provided that you don't pay significant additional expenses for the tax deferral and that you can accept some lack of liquidity during the time horizon of the investment, they can be very advantageous over long periods of time, whether the contributions are made before or after tax. Table 15 shows the effect of contributing $2,000 a year divided into four quarterly payments of $500 each and invested at a 10% return compounded quarterly, assuming a 30% tax rate. It clearly shows that while there is only a small advantage for a tax-deferred account over a ten-year period, when the period is extended to 30 years in this example there is a very significant advantage of 37% over a regular taxable

TABLE 15

**THE INCREASING ADVANTAGE OF TAX DEFERRAL OVER TIME**

Investment of $500 Per Quarter at 10% Annual Return Compounded Quarterly With a 30% Tax Rate

After-Tax Value at The End of The Period

| Duration of Investment | Regular Taxable Account | Tax Deferred Account | Advantage of Tax deferral |
|---|---|---|---|
| 10 Years | $28,617 | $29,591 | 3.4% |
| 20 Years | $85,897 | $98,934 | 15.2% |
| 30 Years | $200,548 | $275,014 | 37.1% |

account. Once again, time is shown to be a particularly potent tool for building wealth. These then are the various ways in which you can best use time to maximize the return on your investments.

The third factor that we identified as determining the value of an investment at the end of a given period is the average rate of return achieved during the investment period. This depends largely upon how assets are distributed between the various categories of investment, and this will be the subject of the next chapter.

By now you should have clearly stated your own long range investment objective and written it down. Be ambitious. You should also have developed a realistic plan to get you there. You can develop your own plan by using the tables that we have reviewed and the examples that we have discussed and by fully exploiting the maximum time period available to you. Given time, patience and knowledge, it is not too hard to build real wealth.

Now let's move on to construct the ideal balanced portfolio to get you there.

CHAPTER 4

# CONSTRUCTING A
# BALANCED PORTFOLIO

Every type of investment has its season, but every season ultimately ends, only to return again later. In the 1950's stocks did well - in the 1960's housing excelled - in the 1970's precious metals shone and in the 1980's it was stocks again. The 1990's will tell us in due course where is the place to be. At the time, a popular investment category looks as though it will grow forever, but it never does without pause, and the pause may last for many years. Over very long time periods the stock market has done best of all but not without its serious setbacks.

If you examine the performance of the stock market over the past 120 years, you will see that there have been periods of exceptionally high growth at the turn of the century, in the 1920's, in the early 1950's and the 1980's. Both the 1950's and the 1980's produced remarkable average returns of over 17% per year over the course of the decade. However, so far each period of exceptional growth has been followed by a period of correction and consolidation. If you had invested in

August of 1929, when most people were convinced that the market could only go up, it would have taken 15 years and five months just to get your money back. There is no investment for all seasons, and no one can consistently foretell the future and guide you to the best category of investment for the next decade. Many people make financial prophesies for a living, but few if any are truly prophetic. For this reason you need to allocate your assets, whether large or small, across several different categories of investment which complement each other in reducing risk and serve to smooth out year-to-year fluctuations in value.

It has been shown in extensive studies that how you allocate your assets represents the most important investment decision that you will make. It is more important than the individual investments you select within each category. So we need to get it right. Most people's investments represent a hodge-podge of items acquired over the years - which looked good at the time or were strongly pushed by a broker. People tend to buy whatever did well last month or last year or what is a "hot tip" or what looks exotic. There is a better way, by putting together over time a carefully balanced portfolio in which each investment is part of an overall plan.

In this chapter we will discuss how you may develop an optimal portfolio for your own particular needs, balancing the considerations of risk, return, diversification, liquidity, time horizon, stage of life and individual comfort level. We will then suggest how you can manage this portfolio to keep it safe and simple. This will let you accumulate wealth while also allowing you to sleep well at night, knowing that you have a well-thought-out and well balanced portfolio that can prosper in all seasons. First we will examine some of the available choices.

## WHAT ARE THE ALTERNATIVES?

There are basically only three broad types of investment in the world. They are:

1.  FIXED INCOME INVESTMENTS
    You lend money to a person or organization which is, therefore, getting into debt. These are correctly called debt instruments, or more commonly fixed income investments, although the income may not really be fixed. You may lend your money to a private individual, a corporation, a government entity or some other group and it may just be for a few days, as in a savings account or money market fund, or it may be for a long fixed period as in a mortgage or a long-term bond. Examples of so-called fixed income investments include money markets, certificates of deposit, notes, bills, bonds and mortgages. Fixed income investments in which the money is immediately available to the investor and which have a fixed principal are sometimes known as cash equivalents. Bonds may be issued by the Federal Government and its agencies, by state and local governments and by corporations.

    Such a loan is usually, but not always, secured by some asset or power of taxation and is a prime obligation of the debtor to pay off. If a company is heading towards bankruptcy, it must pay off its bond holders before its shareholders who own the company. The bonds of a company, therefore, have less market risk than the shares of the same company and being safer in that respect, they normally earn a lower return.

2. EQUITY INVESTMENTS

If you join with other people to finance a business venture by buying shares in a company, you are then entitled to share in unlimited profits from the enterprise, or your shares may become worthless if the venture fails. The prime obligation of the company is to its creditors, not to its shareholders. As you accept the greater risk of owning a part of the equity or assets of the enterprise, on average over time you are likely to be rewarded with greater returns than those of your more secure creditors. The increased return from owning common stocks rather than "riskless" investments such as Treasury Bills has historically averaged about 6 1/2 percentage points. This is known as the Equity Risk Premium.

3. TANGIBLE ASSETS

You may decide to own some tangible physical thing which you believe is going to become in greater demand and, therefore, will increase in market value. Typical examples of tangible asset investments include gold, silver, rare coins, diamonds and works of art. Such investments are favored when financial assets such as stocks and bonds are out of favor, particularly in times of great uncertainty and in the expectation of high levels of inflation.

It is worth discussing here the position of real estate as this can be confusing. If you own the property itself or part of it with others, you own an equity investment. Also, in some sense real estate can perform like a tangible asset as it is just that. If you own a real estate mortgage, then, of course, you have a fixed income investment. Different types of real estate investments may, therefore, fit into each of our three main categories of investment.

There are many other types of investment that we have not mentioned, such as natural resources, raw land and commodities, but they all fall into one of the three main categories.

If at this stage you are looking for the single ideal investment which will provide safety, liquidity, fixed principal and consistently high and reliable returns, look no further. It does not exist, and if it did it would be in such demand that its price would increase and its yield would decline to the point of ensuring self destruction. There are no "secrets" to investing, it just takes knowledge, patience and discipline, mixed with the uncommon quality of common sense. If an investment looks too good, it probably is.

Now let's take a closer look at some of the more commonly held types of investment within each of these three broad categories.

## FIXED INCOME INVESTMENTS

Treasury Bills are short-term obligations of the United States Treasury for periods of up to one year. They are sold at a discount to their maturity value and pay no interest until they mature at face value. Returns have historically been very low, although in recent years their yield has been above the historical average in relation to inflation. Their chief advantage is absolute security of principal and their chief disadvantage is the probable loss of real value over time, after taxes and inflation. As with all direct obligations of the United States Government, they are generally not subject to state income tax.

Certificates of Deposit are usually obligations of banks for varying periods of up to several years. If the bank is a member of the Federal Reserve Banking System, deposits are guaranteed against loss of principal for values up to $100,000 per account. The yield is fully taxable and there is a real risk of loss of purchasing power over time. As with most fixed income investments, the interest rates may vary from one issue to the next, but the return is fixed during the duration of the deposit.

Cash Equivalent is a term covering highly liquid debt obligations having a fixed principle. Examples are bank savings accounts, bank money market accounts and money market mutual funds.

Short-term bank deposits offer generally low interest rates. If you try to borrow short-term money from a bank and compare this with the same bank's borrowing rate from depositors, you will see the magnitude of the spread. You will have to pay the bank a great deal more to borrow from it than the bank pays you when it borrows from you. Banks are basically money lenders who make their profit primarily by borrowing as inexpensively as possible and lending as expensively as possible.

Money Market Mutual Funds generally offer higher rates than banks, but your deposit is not federally insured. Security of principal is historically very high as the average portfolio maturity can be no more than 90 days and is frequently much less. The share price is fixed and the yield fluctuates daily depending upon market conditions. Taxable funds invest either in the short-term obligations of established companies, known usually as commercial paper, or in short-term obligations of the Federal Government and its agencies. In 1991, the Securities and Exchange Commission (S.E.C.) established strict rules requiring taxable money market funds hold at least 95% of their assets in the highest quality paper having excellent credit worthiness and no more than 5% of their assets in the debt of any one top rated commercial issuer. Those money market funds investing solely in the short-term debt of the United States Government and its agencies not only have superb credit worthiness but also produce income which is generally not subject to state income tax.

Money market mutual funds investing wholly in state and local government obligations produce income which is generally free of federal income tax. These tax exempt money market funds will pay a lower yield but will frequently, but not always, produce a higher after-tax yield for high tax bracket investors.

Money market funds offer a high degree of safety combined with instant liquidity and competitive yields. They are a suitable haven for money which is being accumulated for short-term needs or is being placed there temporarily between long-term investments. Many balanced portfolios will include a small proportion of money market funds to add stability and diversification. There are now more than 500 money market funds to choose among. Together they service more than 20 million investors.

Bonds are the longer term promissory notes of a corporation or government entity. In most cases they provide regular interest payments followed by a return of nominal principal at maturity. The stated rate of interest when the bond is issued is called the coupon rate. However, the market value and, therefore, the yield of the bond, fluctuates throughout its life depending mainly upon current competitive interest rates, the continuing credit worthiness of the issuer and the remaining life of the bond. Of course, once a bond has been purchased at a given price, the yield on that price will not change. The yield will only change if it is sold at a different price.

Bond prices vary inversely with interest rates. As general interest rates move up, the original coupon rate at which the bond was issued becomes uncompetitive and people will pay less for it. The opposite applies, of course, as interest rates decline. The longer the duration of the bond the greater this effect will be. For example, if a bond has an 8% coupon rate and interest rates increase by one percentage point, a ten-year bond will lose 6.5% of its value, whereas a thirty-year bond will lose 10.3%. If interest rates were to increase by four percentage points, the same bonds would lose 22.95% and 32.3% respectively. If interest rates were to decline by the same amount, these losses would be gains. If you hold a bond to its maturity, however, it will always be worth its original or par value in nominal dollars. The advantages of high quality bonds include a predictable cash flow throughout their life, whereas the risks are mainly the credit worthiness of the issuer and interest rate risk if you need to sell the bond before maturity. Foreign bonds not denominated in U.S. dollars also carry an exchange rate risk for U.S. investors.

The initial yield of a bond depends upon its perceived credit risk, its duration and its tax status. Generally, long-term bonds enjoy a higher yield than shorter term bonds as the investor must make a longer term commitment if the bond is to be held to maturity. Municipal bonds issued by state and local governments are usually free of federal tax on their interest, but not on any capital gains. The interest on certain municipal bonds may also be subject to the Alternative Minimum Tax. The credit risk of most bonds is estimated by one or more of the bond rating agencies, such as Moody's or Standard and Poor's Corporation. In the case of corporate bonds, quality may vary from the highest grade, issued by the major corporations of the nation, to low grade speculative "junk" bonds not of investment quality. United States Treasury Bonds obviously have the highest rating as they are backed by the perceived unlimited taxing power of the Federal Government. However, some of the bonds issued by agencies of the Federal Government are not formal obligations of the United States Treasury. Municipal Bonds vary in quality depending largely upon whether they are a general obligation of a state or municipality to repay, using its powers of taxation, or whether the bonds are secured only by the revenue generated by the money borrowed as in the case, for example, of bonds issued to finance an airport or a toll bridge. Such revenue bonds tend to offer higher yields than the generally safer general obligation bonds. In some cases the credit worthiness of cities and even states has become questionable, and the power of taxation may not be an unlimited resource. The credit rating of bonds is sometimes enhanced by insurance or by being underwritten by a major financial institution. States (other than Illinois, Iowa, Kansas, Oklahoma and Wisconsin) normally do not tax the interest on bonds issued in their own state. Therefore, the interest on in-state bonds may be free of federal, state and local taxes to in-state residents, making them particularly attractive to high tax bracket investors.

Finally, there are zero coupon bonds which are bought at a discount and pay no interest until they mature at face value. This can be a convenient way to have a fixed sum available at a future date. However, in the case of taxable zero coupon bonds, although no interest is paid, tax is liable on the imputed interest which is credited to the value of the bond. For this reason, they are most often used in a tax-deferred account.


## EQUITY INVESTMENTS

These may conveniently be considered in three groups, each having different characteristics.

Large Company Stocks are typically represented by such popular market indexes as the Dow Jones Industrial Average and the Standard and Poor's 500 Stock Index. These companies have a high level of capitalization and tend to be widely known to the investment community. They trade mainly on the New York Stock Exchange. Historically they have not been the fastest growing group of stocks, although in the 1980's they were.  They are typically well established companies having a relatively high level of safety of principal, but, as with nearly all stocks, they may show wide fluctuations of value over market cycles.  They offer a relatively low purchasing power risk over extended time periods compared to most fixed income investments.

Small Company Stocks are represented by less well known market indexes such as the Wilshire 4500 and the Russell 2000 stock indexes.  They have lower capitalization and trade over the counter and on the American Stock Exchange.  There are many more of these stocks of smaller lesser known companies and most are not as closely followed by investment analysts as are the larger stocks.  This is the area where investors hope to find undiscovered bargains.  Over long time periods they have, on average, performed better than the larger stocks but with more risk and wider fluctuations in market price.  Some of the smallest companies also may have a higher risk of loss of principal than the larger, well established companies.

International Stocks are usually, but not always, the stocks of larger companies headquartered outside the United States. They are represented by several market indexes, notably the Europe, Australia, Far East (E.A.F.E.) Index provided by Morgan Stanley.  These stocks have often tended to out-perform the U.S. market, and this was particularly evident during the 1980's when the EAFE Index grew at a rate of 23% per year.  In addition to the risks inherent in all stocks, overseas investments not denominated in U.S. dollars have an exchange rate risk.  If the currency in which they are denominated weakens against the dollar, the investor may suffer partial loss of principal.  Conversely, the currency may strengthen against the dollar and provide an additional return.  International stocks do not necessarily move in step with U.S. stock market cycles, and this can provide valuable diversification.

There are many other types of stocks, too numerous to review here. They can represent whatever potentially profitable human endeavor man (or woman) wishes to create.

## TANGIBLE ASSETS

Gold, Silver, Platinum, rare coins, stamps and works of art may possibly have a place in a well diversified portfolio in very small proportions: they may serve as a compensating investment during periods when financial assets are performing poorly. Over very long periods gold has shown little or no loss of purchasing power, although over periods of a single decade it has done so. Most tangible assets produce no regular income and may cost money to store or insure. The spread between the buying and selling price is frequently very great and in most cases, considerable specialized knowledge is a prerequisite to successful investing. Precious metals are the simplest tangible assets to own either by the direct purchase of bullion or by purchasing the shares of companies that mine and process such metals.

## REAL ESTATE

Real estate has a place in a well diversified portfolio as it represents a tangible asset with a regular cash flow and a historically good protection against loss of purchasing power. As with financial assets, real estate values move in cycles and for this reason, and its relative lack of liquidity, it is not a short-term investment. Until the late 1980's, U.S. real estate had enjoyed almost continuous overall growth for at least 40 years, in spite of periodic declines in the rate of growth. Much of the real estate owned during this time was highly leveraged and subject to generally favorable tax treatment. Many of these advantages no longer exist, but on a highly selective basis, real estate investments over the long term may continue to provide a moderate regular cash flow, with rather limited purchasing power risk and the possibility of real appreciation. International real estate, expertly selected, may offer attractive opportunities but as with all international investments, there is the added dimension of currency exchange rate risk.

Equity real estate investments may be made by direct ownership if you have the necessary expertise and management time, or through limited partnerships, master limited partnerships, equity real estate investment trusts (R.E.I.T.S.) or mutual funds which own the shares of real estate companies. Master limited partnerships, REITS and real estate mutual funds all provide very useful immediate liquidity. Generally when reference is made to investing in real estate it refers to these types of ownership of real estate equity.

However, if you wish to own real estate debt instruments, you may purchase mortgage REITS or part of a pool of real estate mortgages. For example, the Government National Mortgage Association (G.N.M.A.) offers investors a mortgage backed security collateralized by a Government guaranteed pool of mortgages. The government carries the default risk and the investor is provided with a monthly interest payment and return of principal over a varying period depending upon the rate of maturity or termination of the mortgages. Alternatively, collateralized mortgage obligations (C.M.O.s) offer mortgage investments for fixed periods of from two to twenty years.

These are some of the alternatives before you. You may at times feel overwhelmed by the diversity of investments that people are trying to sell you. Remember that there are really only three basic categories of investments and within each category there is a limited range of proven and relatively safe investments. The survival of the financial services industry seems dependent upon developing new investment products to tempt the investor, but most represent minor modifications to the existing types of products.

We will now examine just how these different types of investment have performed in the past.

## HOW HAVE THEY PERFORMED?

Every type of investment is subject to market cycles and short-term performance may be more a measure of the stage in the market cycle than of inherent historical performance level. Looking at very long-term performance has the advantage of minimizing the impact of shorter market cycles. On the other hand, it may include periods of an economic environment which appear to be peculiar to that time, such as the Great Depression of 1929 - 1932. However, financial history does tend to repeat itself over extended periods and the very long-term performance record, therefore, has value. The relative performance of an investment over just one decade is certainly no indication of its performance in the next decade. This can be seen by examining a wide variety of investments during the 1970's and the 1980's. The 1970's produced high inflation, a falling dollar and slow economic growth. Investors favored tangible assets such as real estate and gold and to a lesser extent the stocks of those small companies which might have great growth potential. During the 1980's inflation declined, interest rates dropped and the stock market thrived. The results of this are shown in Table 16. During the 70's, with average inflation over 7% and rising to 13.3% in 1979, only gold and small company stocks produced real growth. In the 80's, gold, which had been the best investment, became the worst and financial assets, particularly the stock market,

TABLE 16

**COMPARISON OF INVESTMENT RETURNS – 1970s AND 1980s**

Average Annual Compound Return
(%)

| | Larger Company Stocks (S&P 500) | Smaller Company Stocks | Long Term Government Bonds | Treasury Bills | Gold | Inflation |
|---|---|---|---|---|---|---|
| **SEVENTIES** | | | | | | |
| Average Return: | +5.9 | +11.5 | +6.2 | +6.3 | +22.2 | +7.4 |
| Real Return After Inflation: | -1.5 | +4.1 | -1.2 | -1.1 | +14.8 | – |
| Best Year: | +37.2 | +57.4 | +16.8 | +10.4 | +66.9 | +3.4 |
| Worst Year: | -26.5 | -30.9 | -1.2 | +3.8 | -22.4 | +13.3 |
| **EIGHTIES** | | | | | | |
| Average Return: | +17.5 | +15.8 | +12.6 | +8.9 | +3.0 | +5.1 |
| Real Return After Inflation: | +12.4 | +10.7 | +7.5 | +3.8 | -2.1 | – |
| Best Year: | +32.4 | +39.9 | +40.3 | +14.7 | +91.7 | +1.1 |
| Worst Year: | -4.9 | -9.3 | +4.0 | +5.5 | -32.2 | +12.4 |

performed well. After the high inflation of the 70's and early 80's, interest rates remained high as investors were not convinced that the problem had gone away. In this environment, fixed income investments yielded far higher real returns after inflation than their historical average. Table 16 also shows the wide swings in total return from the best year to the worst year. The losses in the worst year in stocks and gold were, as expected, far greater than in the less volatile fixed income investments.

With clear hindsight, the investor should have been invested in gold during the 70's and then switched to large company stocks during the 80's. If, however, one had tried to time the market by switching from one group to another, there is an almost even chance of being in the wrong investment. If an attempt at timing had driven you into common stocks in the 70's, only to switch to gold in the 80's, perhaps hoping to get on to this bandwagon, you would have lost real purchasing power over a 20-year period. This is the flip side of attempts to time the market between asset categories. However, if you had divided your assets into five equal parts and invested in each category for the entire period, you would have benefited from real growth in every one of your investments and perhaps slept better at night. This is why the wise investor allocates assets across several categories and classes of investment.

If results can vary so much between two consecutive decades, it is obviously necessary to take a longer perspective. Over the past 120 years, nominal returns on stocks have generally trended higher. If you had invested in the market for 100 years from 1871 to 1970, your compound total return would have averaged just under 8% per year. From 1926 through 1990, it would have been around 10%; for the 50-year period, 1941 through 1990, it would have been 12%; while during the decade of the 80's it would have been more than 17%. Part of this increasing trend is due to rising inflation.

The average annual compound total returns for a recent 64-year period adjusted for inflation are as follows:

| Real Inflation-Adjusted Returns Before Tax | |
|---|---|
| Common Stocks | 7.0% |
| Long-Term Corporate Bonds | 2.1% |
| Long-Term Government Bonds | 1.4% |
| Treasury Bills | 0.6% |

This clearly shows the long-term superiority of equity investments over fixed income investments.

Perhaps the most revealing way of comparing historical returns between investment categories is to examine their performance over multiple time periods, to see how the value of $1 invested in each category at the beginning of the period would have grown. This is shown in Table 17 for the period covering five decades from 1941 through 1990. It shows that during the 80's both large company stocks and fixed income investments produced higher than average rates of return. Over the entire 50-year period only large and small company stocks produced real returns of any significance after inflation. The figures are total returns but do not include transaction costs or taxes. The lower half of Table 17 shows the value of $1 invested at the beginning of the period in each category of investment. For example, $1 invested in "safe" long-term government bonds would have grown in line with inflation and be worth $9.03 before tax. By comparison, large company stocks, having greater market risk would have totally overcome purchasing power risk and be worth $289. The more risky small company stocks would be worth the amazing sum of $1,405 from the investment of a single dollar.

TABLE 17

**FIFTY YEARS OF RETURNS**

(1941 through 1990)

| | S&P 500 Index | Small Stocks | Long Term Corporate Bonds | Long Term Government Bonds | Treasury Bills | Inflation (CPI) |
|---|---|---|---|---|---|---|
| **AVERAGE ANNUAL COMPOUND RATES OF RETURN (%)** | | | | | | |
| Last 10 Years | 13.9% | 9.3% | 14.1% | 13.7% | 8.5% | 4.5% |
| Last 20 Years | 11.2 | 13.3 | 9.0 | 8.7 | 7.7 | 6.3 |
| Last 30 Years | 10.2 | 13.5 | 6.8 | 6.2 | 6.5 | 5.1 |
| Last 40 Years | 11.6 | 13.4 | 5.5 | 4.9 | 5.4 | 4.3 |
| Last 50 Years | 12.0 | 15.6 | 4.9 | 4.5 | 4.4 | 4.6 |
| **GROWTH: WHAT $1.0 INVESTED WOULD HAVE GROWN TO** | | | | | | |
| Last 10 Years | $3.67 | $2.43 | $3.74 | $3.61 | $2.26 | $1.55 |
| Last 20 Years | 8.36 | 12.15 | 5.60 | 5.30 | 4.41 | 3.39 |
| Last 30 Years | 18.43 | 44.66 | 7.20 | 6.08 | 6.61 | 4.45 |
| Last 40 Years | 80.64 | 152.94 | 8.51 | 6.78 | 8.20 | 5.39 |
| Last 50 Years | 289.00 | 1,405.70 | 10.93 | 9.03 | 8.61 | 9.48 |

Reprinted by permission of the American Association of Individual Investors, 625 N. Michigan Avenue, Chicago, Ill. 60611

## HOW WELL DO THEY MIX?

The concept of not putting all your eggs in one basket makes intuitive sense as a means of reducing the risk of any venture. In the investment world, broad diversification is an essential feature of all professionally devised investment programs. While the market over time rewards the investor for taking unavoidable risks, it does assume that the investor will be adequately diversified and does not reward him for taking unnecessary risks.

The theory of diversification is basically very simple and a stylized representation of the concept is shown in Figure 2. Asset 'A' increases in value over time but suffers periodic declines along the way. Asset 'B' shows a similar pattern but when asset 'A' is decreasing in value, asset 'B' is increasing. This represents a negative correlation and provides very useful diversification. If the portfolio consists of equal quantities of each asset it will consistently gain in value along line 'C'. If on the other hand assets 'A' and 'B' moved in exactly the same direction at the same time, the two investments would show perfect positive correlation and would not achieve useful diversification.

In practice, when two or more different types of investment are mixed, they are not perfectly correlated either positively or negatively but fall somewhere in between. The extent to which they are correlated is known as the correlation coefficient. A value of 1 indicates perfect correlation, a value of 0 indicates no relationship in either direction and a value of -1 indicates perfect negative correlation as shown in Figure 1. Adding more investments to a portfolio will not necessarily add useful diversification if they are closely correlated. We should be looking for investments having substantially different correlation coefficients to add real diversification.

With this knowledge we can now compare the interactions

FIGURE 2

DIVERSIFICATION IN ACTION

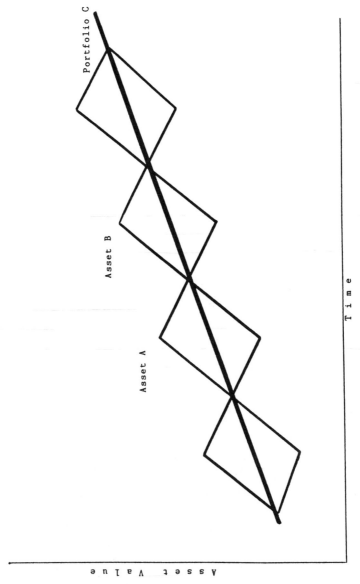

A Hypothetical Example of Two Investments With Complete Negative Correlation

of many different asset categories and asset classes using a numerical measure of correlation.  The degree of correlation varies somewhat over time, but we shall examine the period 1973 to 1989.  This period includes a wide range of economic conditions including both bull and bear markets and periods of widely fluctuating inflation and interest rates.

The comparison is shown in Table 18.  Minor differences between numbers should be ignored.  They are frequently not statistically significant, and in any case, a different time period will produce slightly different values.  If you examine the column headed "large stocks," you will see that small stocks have a 90% positive correlation, therefore, they will generally tend to move together with the large stocks.  By comparison, international stocks, as measured by the EAFE Index, have a correlation of only 56%, which suggests that there is some useful degree of divergence in movement.  As might be expected, long-term bonds have even less correlation with large stocks.  Treasury Bills have almost no correlation, while gold, real estate and inflation all tend to move in the opposite direction to large stocks.  The best correlation with inflation came from real estate and gold, and during the high inflation years of the 70's, these investments produced the highest returns.

Correlation coefficients for a longer period of over 60 years show a greater difference between large and small company stocks.  They also show there to be no statistically significant difference between long-term government bonds, long-term corporate bonds and intermediate-term government bonds.  All longer term fixed income investments tend to move in a similar direction.

The conclusions to be drawn from Table 18 are that, solely from the viewpoint of diversification, a well diversified portfolio should contain some of each of the three basic categories of investments:  equities, fixed income and tangible assets.  The

TABLE 18

CORRELATION BETWEEN INVESTMENT CLASSES

| | Larger Stocks | Small Stocks | International Stocks | Long Term Bonds | Treasury Bills | Gold | Real Estate | Inflation |
|---|---|---|---|---|---|---|---|---|
| Larger Stocks (S&P 500 Index) | 1.00 | | | | | | | |
| Small Stocks (NASDAQ Composite) | 0.90 | 1.00 | | | | | | |
| International Stocks (EAFE) | 0.56 | 0.52 | 1.00 | | | | | |
| Long Term Bonds (U.S. Govt.) | 0.40 | 0.25 | 0.23 | 1.00 | | | | |
| Treasury Bills (one month) | (0.02) | 0.02 | (0.39) | (0.02) | 1.00 | | | |
| Gold | (0.37) | (0.24) | (0.30) | (0.25) | (0.05) | 1.00 | | |
| Real Estate (Single family) | (0.25) | 0.01 | (0.29) | (0.55) | 0.15 | 0.51 | 1.00 | |
| Inflation (CPI) | (0.33) | (0.14) | (0.52) | (0.61) | 0.37 | 0.59 | 0.82 | 1.00 |

Reprinted by permission of the American Association of Individual Investors, 625 N. Michigan Avenue, Chicago, Ill. 60611

Note: A Value of 1.0 indicates complete positive correlation and minus 1.0 (1.0) indicates complete negative correlation. A value close to zero indicates no meaningful correlation.

latter may be in the form of real estate. Within equities certainly both domestic and international stocks should be held and, if possible, both large and small capitalization stocks should be held within the domestic stocks. Within domestic fixed income investments there is no great value in holding several different types of high grade bonds. However, studies have shown that international bonds may only have around 35% positive correlation with domestic corporate bonds and are worth including. Some real estate should clearly be held in a well diversified portfolio as it most closely follows the changes in inflation and helps to offset the negative correlation with inflation of both stocks and bonds.

Correct diversification produces the maximum return for a given level of risk or else the minimum risk for a given level of return. In either case the portfolio takes no unrewarded risk and is therefore known as an efficient portfolio.

To illustrate this effect, we will examine an example. Table 19 shows the average return on various classes of assets from 1973 to 1988. It also shows the standard deviation for each investment class. The standard deviation is a measure of variability and an indication of market risk. The higher the value of the standard deviation the greater the variation around the average figure and thus the greater the implied risk. Generally, but not always, the higher the average return the higher the standard deviation. This is simply a reflection of the general truth that over time unavoidable risk will be rewarded by higher returns. The question to address is, what is unavoidable?

By referring to Table 19 you can see, for example, that if you were prepared to tolerate a very volatile investment in small company stocks you could have obtained an annual return of 16.6% with a high standard deviation of 23.4%. If, however, you wanted less risk in the form of volatility you could, for example, have reduced the standard deviation to

TABLE 19

## THE VALUE OF DIVERSIFICATION

## (1973 - 1988)

| Investment Class | Compound Annual Return | Standard Deviation (Risk) |
|---|---|---|
| Treasury Bills | 8.1% | 0.8% |
| Long Term Corporate Bonds | 8.7 | 11.5 |
| Domestic Stocks, Larger Companies | 10.3 | 16.7 |
| International Bonds | 11.2 | 12.7 |
| Equity REITS | 14.1 | 15.3 |
| International Stocks | 16.1 | 17.2 |
| Domestic Stocks, Small Companies | 16.6 | 23.4 |
| **Diversified Portfolio\*** | **12.3** | **11.5** |

\* Comprising: Treasury bills, 10%; domestic bonds, 20%; international bonds, 20%; larger company stocks, 15%; small company stocks, 5%; international stocks, 15% and equity REITS, 15%.

Based on data from: Asset Allocation, by R.C.Gibson, 1990.

11.5% by investing in long-term corporate bonds but the average return would drop to 8.7%. The most significant fact is that if you had diversified widely across asset classes by holding the Diversified Portfolio as shown, then with the same standard deviation of 11.5% you would have achieved a return of 12.3% instead of the 8.7% achieved with corporate bonds. This would have given you 41% more return (12.3% versus 8.7%) with the same risk level as measured by variability. This is the power of diversification. The choice is yours whether you achieve higher returns at the same level of risk or a lower risk without reducing returns.

There are many other examples of the benefits of broadly diversified portfolios. For example, between 1978 and 1987, growth stock mutual funds enjoyed an average return of 16.2% with a standard deviation of 14.1%. By comparison, during this same period a diversified portfolio of 41.7% international stock funds, 29.1% domestic growth stock funds and 29.2% money market funds would have given virtually the same return of 16.1% but with a much lower standard deviation of 9.9%. You would have reduced the extent of volatility by 30% without significantly reducing the return.

The important principal to understand is that when two or more risks interact to cancel out the effects of each other, then overall risk is reduced, but if two or more risks interact to amplify the effects of each other then overall risk is increased.

So the answer to the question "how well do they mix?" is that to avoid unnecessary and unrewarded risk, they must be mixed, and the less the asset classes are correlated to each other, the better they mix. Broad diversification is essential for any well balanced investment portfolio and is one of our ten basic rules of investing. It can provide additional returns with no additional overall risk as measured by volatility.

Determination of precisely the optimal proportions of each asset class to achieve an efficient portfolio can be achieved using a sophisticated computer program. Many financial planners and investment advisors can provide this service, but you should first be aware of its limitations. It can only be based on past performance and this is most unlikely to be exactly repeated in the future. Calculations using different prior periods will produce different answers. The practical approach for most investors is to build a widely diversified complementary portfolio of both equity and fixed income investments on a global basis, accepting a level of risk which is appropriate for the individual.

## CONSTRUCTING YOUR PORTFOLIO

We will first review the various decisions which need to be made in composing a diversified portfolio and then consider the personal factors which should guide you in determining a level of acceptable risk.

The decision process is summarized in Figure 3 which shows the Investment Pyramid and illustrates the process of building wealth. It shows the seven key management actions that are necessary and the order in which they should be undertaken. The values shown are simply examples and will vary according to individual circumstances.

First the investment objective needs to be set clearly, unambiguously and quantified in terms of dollars and time as discussed in Chapter 3. We have stated the objective of having $1 million (before tax) in 30 years. If this seems too ambitious, reduce it.

Second, a realistic and achievable plan to reach the objective must be established as discussed in Chapter 3. Our plan is to invest $287 per month in a tax-deferred account returning 12% per year, compounded monthly.

Third, it is necessary to decide on appropriate strategic

FIGURE 3
**THE INVESTMENT PYRAMID**
The Process of Building Wealth

Actions

1. Set Investment Objectives

2. Have a Plan to Get There

3. Allocate Into Broad Categories

4. Allocate Broad Categories Into Specific Asset Classes

5. Allocate Asset Classes Into Specific Market Segments

6. Select Individual Mutual Funds

7. Manage Portfolio

Example

30 yrs. $1.0 million*

Invest $287/month in tax deferred account returning 12% pa.

| 60% Equity | 40% Fixed Income |
|---|---|
| 10% Real Estate | 50% Stocks | 30% Bonds | 10% Money Market |

| 10% Real Estate Fund | 20% US Large Company Stks 10% US Small Company Stks 20% Int'l Stocks | 10% US Govt. Long Term 10% Tax Free 10% Int'l. Govt. Bonds | 10% Tax Free Money Market |

| Fund A | Fund B Fund C Fund D Fund E Fund F | Fund G Fund H Fund I | Fund J |

-Buy-and-Hold or Cyclical Timing
-Periodic Fund Upgrading
-Identification of Stage of Market Cycle
-Dollar Cost Averaging
-Occasional Portfolio Re-Balancing
-Monitoring of Fund Performance, Management and Expenses

*Before tax

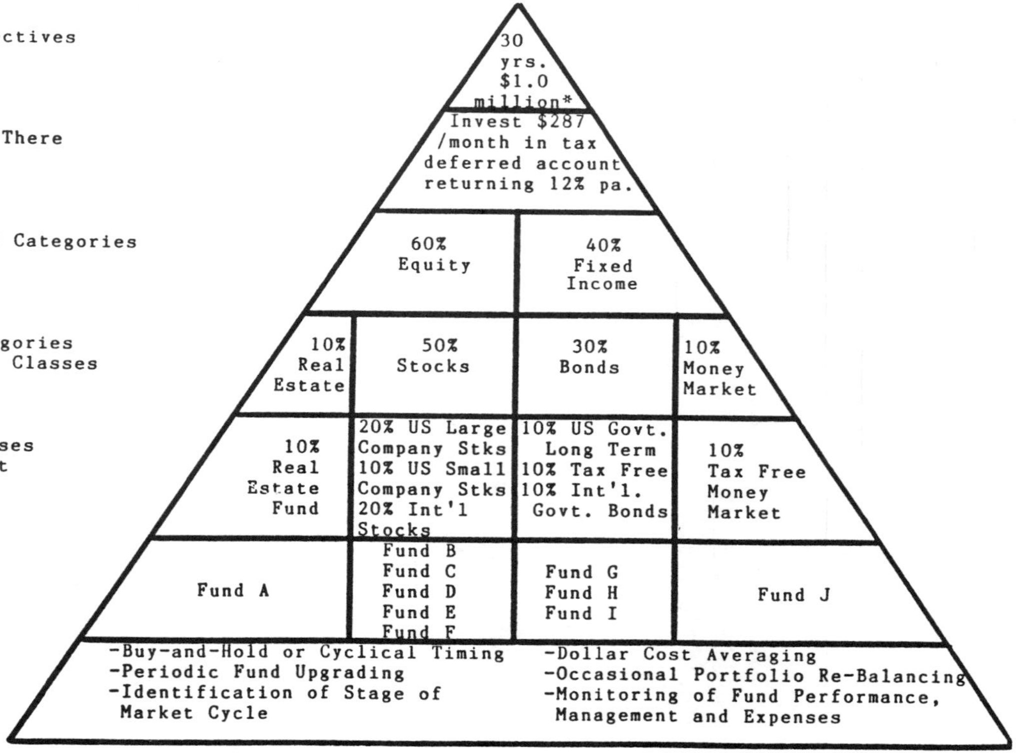

allocation between the three broad asset categories of equities, fixed income and tangible assets. This decision stage is extremely important in achieving the long-term objective. Historically, equity investments have produced considerably higher returns over time than fixed income investments. However, fixed income investments have generally shown considerably less volatility. Two of the major risks faced by investors are purchasing power risk, which is minimized over time by equity investments, and market risk which is less with fixed income investments. The investor placed between the insidious risk of inflation and the less frequent but sometimes dramatic risks of the equity market place must choose a position in which the risks are minimized. A useful generalization is that over the long term, inflation is likely to be the greater threat, and over the shorter term, market risk is likely to be the more significant. The time frame of your investment objective should be very influential in deciding on this split, the longer time frame permitting a greater allocation to equities. In this example we have chosen to allocate 60% to equities (including real estate) and 40% to fixed income investments.

Fourth, these broad categories now need to be broken down into asset classes. For example, equities into stocks and real estate, fixed income investments into bonds, mortgages and money market funds. These decisions may permit further useful diversification and will help to determine the long term levels of return. We have chosen 50% stocks, 10% real estate, 30% bonds and 10% money markets.

Fifth, each asset class needs to be broken down again into the specific types of investment. For example, if 50% of the portfolio is to be in stocks, what type of stocks? This includes, for example, decisions on domestic and international stocks; the company size - large or small; stocks for income or for growth potential and any tactical preference for a particular market segment such as utilities, natural resources or high technology. In the case of fixed income choices the tax level of the investor, for example, may dictate whether taxable or tax-free bonds are most appropriate. There are many different types of specific investment within each asset class and a choice of mutual funds is available for most of them.

Sixth, having clearly defined what is needed, specific mutual funds can now be selected. This will be covered in the second part of this book entitled "Selecting Your Investments."

Seventh, once the correct portfolio is established, it will need to be properly managed. This subject will be addressed in the third part of the book entitled "Protecting Your Investments."

This is an overview of the basic process of creating wealth. The first two steps have already been discussed and you should now have your investment objective and plan to get there clearly thought out and written down. Steps three, four and five will be considered next and cover the important process of allocating assets into broad categories, asset classes and specific types of investment. The last two steps of fund selection and portfolio management will be covered later.

These decisions of asset allocation should be influenced by very individual considerations such as the following:

## STAGE OF LIFE

In the early stages of a career, conventional wisdom assumes that the investor can accept a rather high level of risk, has a long time frame for investment and enjoys a relatively low tax rate. The investor is likely to have heavy family responsibilities with only limited discretionary income for investment. While it is true that principal lost during this period can be made up later, it is also true as we saw earlier that the power of compounding is heavily dependent upon the very early investments made in a person's career. This is the ideal stage at which to possess a high proportion of equities in the portfolio and start the process of compounding, assuming that "The Things To Do Before You Invest" discussed in Chapter 3 have already been provided for.

In mid-career the investor still has the advantage of a long investment time horizon, and if assets have already been compounding for some years, new investments can be exposed to somewhat more risk. A higher tax bracket is likely and careful tax planning becomes necessary. Equities may still comprise a significant portion of the portfolio.

In late career, if a steady income from investments is likely to be needed in retirement it is time to start reducing exposure to volatility and increase the medium and short-term fixed income portion of the portfolio. As the investment time frame becomes shorter the risk of a loss of market value becomes greater. There has never been any 20-year period since 1926 when the stock market has suffered a loss of total return. However, as the time frame is reduced, periods of loss occur with increasing frequency until, over a one-year period, a loss will occur with stocks about 31% of the time and with long-term government bonds about 28% of the time. This effect is shown in more detail in Table 20. For example, if an investor had bought the S&P 500 Index (often used to represent the stock market, particularly the larger stocks) and held it for every possible five-year period, he would have suffered a loss on seven occasions or 12% of the time. However, these results include the period of the great depression of the early 1930's which accounts for four of the seven occasions. The remaining periods were 1937 to 1941, 1970 to 1974 and 1973 to 1977. The point here is clearly that the longer your time horizon, the less the risk from stocks and long-term bonds. If you don't have sufficient time, don't invest in them.

In retirement, the portfolio should be based on safe investments having low volatility if a steady income or possible

TABLE 20

**THE FREQUENCY OF LOSSES OVER VARYING TIME PERIODS**

The Percentage of Holding Periods That Resulted in Losses (1926 Through 1990)

| Holding Period (years) | S&P 500 Index | Small Company Stocks | Corporate Bonds | Government Bonds | Treasury Bills |
|---|---|---|---|---|---|
| 1 | 31% | 32% | 23% | 28% | 0% |
| 3 | 16 | 24 | 13 | 15 | 0 |
| 5 | 12 | 15 | 5 | 10 | 0 |
| 10 | 4 | 4 | 0 | 2 | 0 |
| 20 | 0 | 0 | 0 | 0 | 0 |

Reprinted by permission of the American Association of Individual Investors, 625 N. Michigan Avenue, Chicago, Ill. 60611 liquidation is anticipated. However, to provide some protection against inflation, a portion of the portfolio should remain in lower risk stocks.

## LIQUIDITY

The possible need to turn invested assets into cash at relatively short notice can greatly influence the optimal portfolio mix. If this possibility exists, the anticipated needed sum should be held in cash equivalents such as money market funds or possibly in a short-term bond fund. A need to liquidate most other types of investment may cause loss of principal if the market is depressed. However, in a broadly diversified portfolio, it is more likely that at least some of the assets will be closer to the top of a market cycle. If the investor can afford to lock assets away without the need of sudden liquidity a greater degree of volatility can be tolerated, which will normally result in higher returns. In the case of assets such as real estate, a mutual fund can offer a degree of liquidity, which would be impossible by direct ownership.

## TAX TREATMENT

The current tax laws should not influence basic investment strategy but may affect short-term tactics. For example, in the presence of lower tax on capital gains than ordinary income, it may be desirable to own funds whose objective is primarily capital gains rather than dividend income. At high tax brackets, tax free municipal bonds generally produce a higher after-tax return than taxable bonds having similar duration and credit worthiness and may thus make fixed income investments more attractive. The ability to compound tax-deferred is an obvious long-term advantage, but it should not alter basic investment strategies.

RISK TOLERANCE

The appropriate level of risk for an investor to assume depends both upon his attitude to risk and his financial ability to bear risk.  The two are frequently different.

Attitude to risk should be reflected in the portfolio balance. Discomfort with the level of risk implicit in a portfolio is likely to be unduly worrisome and lead to poor investment decisions. An investor who cannot tolerate the thought of assets declining in value with market cycles, should not hold cyclical investments.

You personally need to assess your own temperament. Are you at heart an aggressive, moderate or conservative investor? Are you a worrier? Are you able to control your emotions when investing?  Which would you rather experience, the loss of principal following a poor investment or the loss of opportunity from not exploiting an investment opportunity?  You need some honest answers to categorize yourself as an investor.

The financial ability to bear risk is perhaps easier to measure.  Again you need to ask yourself a series of questions and receive honest replies.

How long is your investment time horizon?

What is your total level of debt and should you first pay it off?

How large is your emergency cash reserve?

What are your family responsibilities and what is your health status?

What level of job security and income security do you have?

What are your realistic future income prospects?

What is your current level of wealth?  If you are already financially independent, do you need to take the risks associated with aggressively building wealth?  On the other hand, if you have very limited assets, can you afford to take even the modest risks necessary to create real wealth?

An honest consideration of these factors should help you to decide what is the correct type of portfolio for you. Figure 4 shows six different types of portfolio from the very low risk to the speculative and the profile of suitable investors for each type. Decide which description best fits your situation and then refer in the same column to the type of portfolio which may fit that risk level. It is important to realize that at each extreme end of the spectrum, the investor is likely to lose. In the case of the very low risk portfolio, there is a high probability of losing purchasing power, and at the level of speculation, there is a high risk of losing principal. Most investors should make every effort to fit in between, where the probability of creating wealth is greatest. The aggressive portfolio is only suitable for a small proportion of investors who can temperamentally accept and financially tolerate the possibility of significant losses on occasion.

For most people the choice lies within the low, medium or higher risk portfolios. The low risk scenario may suit the retired person living partially on investment income or the person of modest means. The medium risk scenario is a generally good, fairly conservative position for someone with at least ten years to invest and the wish to balance off market and purchasing power risk. This level may well be necessary to achieve returns above your personal break-even point as discussed in Chapter Two. The higher risk scenario is ideal to build real wealth without excessive risk, provided you have the necessary time horizon, no likely needs for liquidity and have the personal qualities of investment knowledge, patience and discipline which make you a successful investor.

We need to look at these three "middle-of-the-road" portfolios in more detail to see how they might be structured. These are simply examples which reflect the broad philosophy that we have discussed. They are not the only alternatives and

FIGURE 4
**LEVELS OF PORTFOLIO MARKET RISK**

Which is Right For You?

| Very Low | Low | Medium | Higher | Aggressive | Speculative |
|---|---|---|---|---|---|
| Can accept little or no market risk; immediate liquidity required. Purchasing power erosion probable. | Can accept low to moderate risk over a 5-10 year time horizon. May be able to maintain purchasing power. | Can accept carefully measured risk & fluctuations in asset value over at least a 10 year time horizon. Can start to build real wealth. | Long time horizon, no need for liquidity. Can tolerate wide fluctuations in asset value. If patient and disciplined, can build a fortune in time. | Long time horizon, substantial assets, good income. No need for liquidity & can accept big losses. Needs patience, discipline and knowledge of investments. | More of a gamble than investment; not recommended unless you wish to gamble and are prepared to lose your shirt. |
| Undiversified portfolio of cash equivalent assets such as money market funds investing in U.S. govt. debt. | Diversified portfolio with majority in shorter term fixed income but some more conservative stock funds & some real estate. | Globally diversified portfolio with a similar proportion of fixed income and equities. Large, small & Int'l. stocks; short, medium & long term U.S. & int'l. bonds. Tax free bonds & money mkts. | Globally diversified, mainly equity portfolio. Higher risk quality stock funds aimed at growth; some aggressive growth & int'l. emerging mkt. funds. Longer term bonds & high-yield tax free bond funds. | Globally undiversified, leveraged high risk portfolio. Mainly aggressive stk. funds incl. non diversified sector funds & U.S. & int'l. small company funds; margin accounts. | |

Lowest                        ------- Return ------->                        Highest

Highest <------ Risk ------ Lowest

may not be the best alternatives for you. Some financial advisors recommend that perhaps 5% of a portfolio should be in precious metals as an insurance against major national or global financial calamity. If you think this is desirable, you may include it in your own portfolio. It is not included in the examples given.

Figures 5 through 7 show examples of low, medium and higher risk portfolios. The proportions shown are those assigned to the portfolios, but it does not imply that they are fully invested at all times. For example, if it is clearly not an appropriate stage of the market cycle to own stocks, part or all of that section of the portfolio may be temporarily parked in a money market fund; it will in due course be invested in stocks. Where separate U.S. and international investments are shown, it may be practical to replace these with a global fund investment. No attempt has been made to define more closely the specifications of the individual funds that would be selected as this will be discussed in detail in Part 2 of this book - "Selecting Your Investments." With the exception of money market funds and possibly Index funds, it is preferable to have no more than 10% of the total portfolio in any one fund. This ensures further diversification of investment objectives and management styles.

You may wish to modify these examples to fit your own particular circumstances, but as presented, they each offer broad diversification ensuring enhanced returns for their given level of risk. Having very carefully constructed a well balanced portfolio matching your unique needs, the next question is how to look after it.

## HOW TO KEEP IT SAFE AND SIMPLE

Having carefully constructed your portfolio based on your

FIGURE 5

**SPECIMEN PORTFOLIO - LOW RISK**

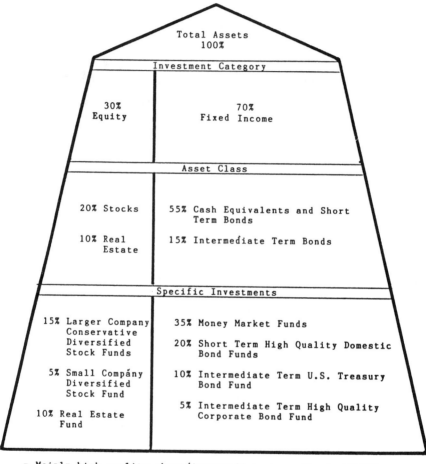

Total Assets
100%

Investment Category

30%
Equity

70%
Fixed Income

Asset Class

20% Stocks

10% Real
Estate

55% Cash Equivalents and Short
Term Bonds

15% Intermediate Term Bonds

Specific Investments

15% Larger Company
Conservative
Diversified
Stock Funds

5% Small Company
Diversified
Stock Fund

10% Real Estate
Fund

35% Money Market Funds

20% Short Term High Quality Domestic
Bond Funds

10% Intermediate Term U.S. Treasury
Bond Fund

5% Intermediate Term High Quality
Corporate Bond Fund

- Mainly high quality short/intermediate term fixed  income
- Small proportion of conservative equity investments.
- No foreign currency risk exposure.

FIGURE 6

**SPECIMEN PORTFOLIO - MEDIUM RISK**

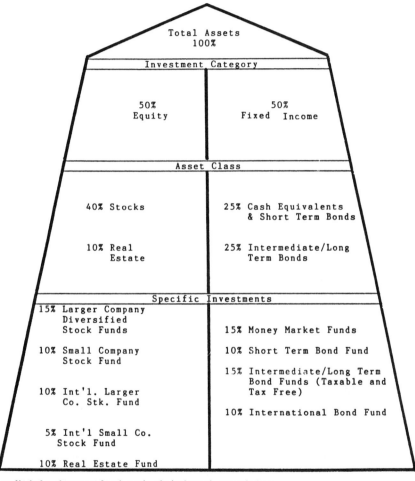

- Widely diversified and globalized portfolio.
- Global funds may replace separate domestic and international funds.

FIGURE 7

SPECIMEN PORTFOLIO - HIGHER RISK

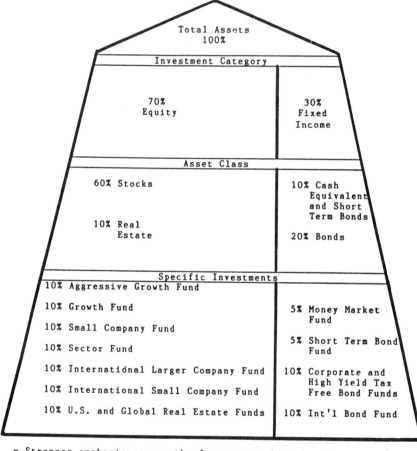

Total Assets
100%

Investment Category

70%
Equity

30%
Fixed
Income

Asset Class

60% Stocks

10% Real
Estate

10% Cash
Equivalent
and Short
Term Bonds

20% Bonds

Specific Investments

10% Aggressive Growth Fund

10% Growth Fund

10% Small Company Fund

10% Sector Fund

10% International Larger Company Fund

10% International Small Company Fund

10% U.S. and Global Real Estate Funds

5% Money Market
Fund

5% Short Term Bond
Fund

10% Corporate and
High Yield Tax
Free Bond Funds

10% Int'l Bond Fund

- Stronger emphasis on growth of assets rather than income.
- Very broadly diversified, but subject to wider fluctuations than
  other portfolios.

current and expected future circumstances, the temptation to fuss with it and make unnecessary changes should be strongly resisted. It is necessary, of course, to review the balance of the portfolio if your financial circumstances have altered or your overall investment objective has changed. Very occasionally it may be necessary to make strategic changes as you approach retirement. Otherwise, leave it alone.

Over the years some investments within the overall portfolio will grow faster than others and this will change the relative proportions. In order to maintain the original level of diversification, the portfolio should be rebalanced to the original allocations every few years, as necessary. When changing the portfolio balance for any reason, it is advisable to do so gradually over a period of time.

A major decision is whether to attempt to time the market. That is, to move assets from the least attractive areas at the time to the most attractive areas; for example, to oscillate between stocks and bonds. This is an intriguing idea, which if it were possible, would create unbelievable wealth. Unfortunately, it is not possible, although this is hard for most people to believe. In fact, most never do. We saw in Table 16 that the star performer of one decade may be among the worst performers of the next decade. The nature of man seems to compel him to believe that it should be possible to jump off one band-wagon as it slows and on to the next as it is gaining speed. This is the premise of most asset allocation mutual funds, many professional money managers and innumerable vendors of financial advice. The hard facts, however, show that it does not work. It simply transfers you from a relatively safe, well diversified portfolio to an undiversified chase for riches. If your choice is consistently wrong, the results will ultimately be disastrous as you continue to back the losers in each consecutive race.

A major study was undertaken over a ten-year period from

1974 to 1983, based on 91 large pension plans whose assets ranged from $100 million to $3 billion. These professionally managed large institutions practiced only limited market timing, with common stocks ranging from 32% to 86% of the portfolio at different times and bonds ranging from 0% to 42%. Even so, over the ten-year period their attempts at timing actually reduced total returns from 10.1% to 9.4%. Other forms of active management reduced it further to 9.0%. The effect on yield of attempted timing ranged from + 0.25% to - 2.68% per year. In the worst case more than a quarter of the total gain was lost by attempting to time the market. This study was continued and the updated results reported in the Financial Analysts Journal for May/June 1991. Once again active asset allocation (market timing) added nothing, and in fact, continued to reduce investment returns. This is not an isolated example. Regular surveys by the Trust Universe Comparison Service show, for example, that throughout the 80's the average of institutional portfolios, most of which practice some form of timing of asset allocation, failed to match the S&P 500 stock index with their equity accounts and failed to match the Shearson Lehman government and corporate bond index with their fixed income accounts.

We should clearly distinguish here between trying to move into the fastest growing type of asset, which is commonly called market timing, or active asset allocation, and trying to move out of a specific asset into cash in anticipation of a cyclical market decline. This is also frequently called market timing. The first approach is a largely futile aggressive pursuit of the highest returns, whereas the second approach is basically a defensive move to avoid anticipated losses. We are speaking here only of the first type of market timing. The second approach can be a conservative risk reduction technique, which will be discussed in Part 3 of this book.

The attempt to jump from one asset class to another in pursuit of maximum growth has never been successfully achieved over extended periods. Roger C. Gibson in his excellent book "Asset Allocation: Balancing Financial Risk" puts this subject forcefully into perspective. If in 1925, a truly prophetic market timer had correctly chosen the best asset class among Treasury Bills, long-term government bonds, long-term corporate bonds, common stocks and small company stocks for the coming year, his investment would have grown by 12%. If he had originally invested one million dollars and had repeated his correct forecasting each year until the end of 1988, his portfolio would be worth $2.65 trillion dollars. Our investor would then own all of corporate America!

However ridiculous this idea may seem, people still believe it is possible and have poured about $5 billion into asset allocation mutual funds, mainly in the past few years, in spite of their rather mediocre performance. Clearly, they are not going to own corporate America.

If you wish to maintain the diversification in your portfolio, you should first of all divide your investments into quite separate portfolios, an equity portfolio and a fixed income portfolio. Keep them completely separate. Have the records of each in a separate book or file and manage each without reference to the other. This will ensure that you benefit from the single most important decision that you have made - the split between equity and fixed income investments. Within the book or file for the records of each separate portfolio, keep separate sections for each class of asset. This will help you avoid slipping away from your established allocation of assets. Only when rebalancing your overall portfolio, or when making very occasional strategic changes, should there be any contact between your portfolios.

In this way, you will keep it simple to maintain your balanced portfolio, and you will keep it safe because you will preserve the risk reduction associated with broad diversification. Let others chase the rainbow. Keeping it simple and safe is the path to successful investing.

**PART TWO**

**SELECTING YOUR INVESTMENTS**

CHAPTER 5

# WHAT YOU NEED TO KNOW
# ABOUT MUTUAL FUNDS

King William the First was crowned as the first king of the Netherlands on September 27, 1815. He introduced a bold new constitution guaranteeing for the first time freedom of worship, freedom of the press and political freedom to all. In 1822, he created the first known Investment Company and by 1840, tired of ruling, he abdicated his throne to his son and retired with the lady of his choice to lead a quiet life, presumably enjoying the fruits of these investments.

The idea of forming a company solely to make investments spread throughout Europe. Many of these early funds were closed-end funds rather than the more popular open-ended mutual funds of today. In 1873, an enterprising Scot named Robert Fleming, after visiting the United States and realizing its huge investment opportunities, set up the Scottish American Investment Trust, one of the very first international equity funds. The first United States open-ended fund was established in Boston in 1924, as the Massachusetts Investors Trust.

Since that time the mutual fund industry has grown to enormous proportions, with more than 3,000 different funds serving about 40 million investors and managing assets worth well over one trillion dollars. It is difficult to comprehend the magnitude of one trillion dollars, but to put it into some perspective, it exceeds the entire gross national product of many major countries such as The United Kingdom, France, Italy, Spain and Canada. The industry has become the nation's third largest financial entity, only exceeded by commercial banks and life insurance companies.

The mutual fund industry is one of the great business success stories of recent times. During the 80's, the industry's assets grew more than ten-fold. The number of funds increased five-fold and the number of accounts increased from 12 million to almost 60 million. These investors are at all stages of life and nearly all income levels. About 25% of mutual fund holders have household incomes below $25,000 and 18% have incomes of over $75,000. Three quarters are college graduates. One quarter of all U.S. households now own mutual funds. Why is this so? What has caused this tremendously wide acceptance of mutual funds as the preferred way of investing? Surveys have shown that the greatest attraction to the investor is their diversification, followed by access to professional management, higher returns, avoiding individual stock selection and ease of investing.

It is a popular misconception that mutual funds are suitable only for the little guy who can't afford to diversify into perhaps 10 to 15 individual stocks or bonds. This myth persists, but like so many broadly held opinions in the investment world, it is wrong. Many knowledgeable money managers advise using mutual funds, at least until an individual portfolio is worth several million dollars. They then only use individual stocks and bonds if the management and transaction expenses are less, which is unlikely, and adequate global diversification can be assured, which is even more unlikely.

In fact, financial institutions controlling millions of dollars are major investors in mutual funds. Banks, business corporations, employee pension and profit sharing plans, insurance companies and foundations all use mutual funds extensively for their investments. Total institutional investment in mutual funds has risen from $6 billion in 1970, to well over $300 billion 20 years later. They now own about one-third of all mutual funds in existence. These professionals know what they are doing.

Like any rapidly growing business in a free enterprise system, the industry has, over the years, learned to meet the needs of almost every possible type of investor. Most funds offer a good service with excellent management and reasonable fees, but some do not. Like everything else, mutual funds have their advantages and disadvantages. The better funds offer an outstanding bargain to the investor and permit him to do things easily that he could never do on his own.

In this chapter we will examine the structure and operation of mutual funds. We will explore their many useful features and how you may use these to the greatest extent possible. We shall address the important question of load versus no-load funds and finally take a good hard look at the important question of fund expenses.

With this information, you will be way ahead of most investors and ready to benefit fully from the smartest investment vehicle of modern times.

## THE NUTS AND BOLTS OF MUTUAL FUNDS

A mutual fund is one type of investment company. It is a public corporation chartered by a state government and having the sole objective of investing in a portfolio of assets. It is owned by its shareholders who together own all the investment assets of the company. It has a board of directors answerable to the shareholders and it issues periodic reports to all shareholders. When you invest in a mutual fund you are buying shares in the company. It normally continues to sell shares throughout the life of the corporation and is therefore known as an open-ended type of investment company. This distinguishes it from an investment company which issues a fixed number of shares and is known as a closed-end fund. Examples of closed-end funds include real estate investment trusts (REITS). The shares of closed-end funds trade on a stock exchange at a market value which may be greater or less than the value of their underlying investments. Throughout this book we shall be discussing investment companies which are open-ended, that is mutual funds.

The company is operated by its officers and staff under the direction of the board of directors. The board may decide to contract out the day-to-day operations to an advisor or management company. In practice it is usually the advisor who sets up the company in the first place in order to create a client for his services. Many management companies operate a wide range of mutual funds, giving rise to families of funds.

Typically, the management company receives a fee for its investment selection and portfolio management activities and for a wide array of administrative services. Management companies often not only manage large families of funds, but they may also be in the brokerage business, the insurance business or money management for individuals, pension funds and other financial institutions.

There are some management companies such as the Vanguard group of funds which are not engaged in other activities and do not necessarily act as their own advisor. They carefully select an outside advisor who appears to be the best qualified to manage a particular fund.

For reasons of security, mutual funds do not themselves hold the assets of the company. By law they are required to place them with a custodial bank whose employees are bonded by an insurance company. They are also required to have a transfer agent, often a bank, which transfers shares, distributes dividends and maintains shareholder records.

The distribution system for mutual funds varies widely. Most load funds are bought retail from the sales people of brokers, from financial planners or from insurance agents after mark-ups have been added along the distribution chain. If you know what you want and do not particularly care to support a selling organization to sell you what you already know you want, then you may very simply buy a no-load or low load fund directly from the fund "wholesale" or without distribution mark-ups. The choice is yours. The term "load" refers to an initial sales charge normally used to support the distribution costs of a fund.

Any mutual fund sold in the United States, whether its assets are domestic or international, is subject to very rigid control by the federal Securities and Exchange Commission (SEC). The Securities Act of 1933, the Securities Exchange Act of 1934, the Investment Advisors Act of 1940 and particularly the Investment Company Act of 1940, all serve to control the activities of United States investment companies and require full disclosure of information to shareholders. The SEC enforces these Acts and protects the interest of shareholders. In addition to these federal statutes, almost every State requires a fund to comply with their regulations before it can be sold in that state. An investor buying offshore funds which are not sold in the United States should be aware that very few other countries have such firm regulatory control of investment companies and shareholders interests may be less well protected.

Nevertheless, an investor cannot be adequately protected

unless he reads the fund prospectus. The law requires that many features of the fund must be revealed in the prospectus and that a copy of the prospectus must be supplied before an investment is made. The prospectus will tell you right up front what are the expenses of the fund. It will also state the objective of the fund. Read this carefully. Is this what you want done with your money? Is the fund leveraged? Is it diversified? Is it too aggressive or too conservative for you? It will report its historical performance, which may not be repeated in the future. The section on risks may scare you until you have read a number of prospectuses. Every possible risk seems to be listed, but now is the time to be aware of all the downsides. It will inform you on many other subjects such as portfolio turnover (which costs you money), the fund's advisors, the frequency of distributions and administrative matters such as the purchase and sale of shares. Read the prospectus and compare it with that of other funds having similar objectives.

You are also entitled by law to receive upon request and free of charge a "Statement of Additional Information" also known as Part B of the prospectus. This lists the securities of the fund, the directors, their occupation and fees received from the fund. It also provides the audited financial statements and details of anyone owning more than 5% of the fund. You should also read the fund's most recent report to shareholders but remember that opinions expressed here may not always be entirely objective. We shall see later on that there is almost essential additional information, not contained in the prospectus, which you can get from readily available reference sources before you buy a fund.

The value of a share in a mutual fund is normally calculated at the end of each business day. It is the value of all assets held, less expenses and liabilities, divided by the total number of shares issued. This is known as the net asset value or NAV. In the case of a no-load fund this is the fund price that you will see in the newspaper on the following day. In the case of a load fund, a "bid" and an "asked" price is quoted. The higher "asked" price is what you would pay if you bought the shares and the lower "bid" price is what you would receive if you sold the shares. The difference is the sales commission or load.

Figure 8 explains what you can learn when looking up the price of a fund in a newspaper. First, look up the fund family such as Fidelity, Vanguard or Dreyfus. Then find the abbreviated name of the specific fund. Read across the columns and find, in the case of a load fund, the bid and asked price, or in the case of a no-load fund the single NAV followed by the letters "NL". Next appears the change in value since the previously reported value. Don't ignore the little letters which may appear immediately after the fund name, they are generally bad news. The letter "p" means that there is an ongoing charge against the NAV to help support the management company's cost of distribution. This is known as a 12b-1 charge which refers to the SEC regulation which permits it. Here is an exception to the general rule of the SEC protecting the investors interests. The letter "r" refers to a redemption charge or back-end load which is paid whenever the fund is sold or it can refer to a contingent deferred sales charge which only applies if the fund is sold within a certain time period. The first of these charges is simply a somewhat hidden sales charge whereas the second one does not affect the long-term investor, but may penalize the trader making frequent switches which in turn can disturb the fund for the remaining investors.

Once you have purchased shares in a fund there are several ways in which you may profit. First, the fund is likely to receive dividends and interest payments from their investments. Second, the assets held by the fund may increase in market value. Third, the fund may sell some of its assets at a price which is higher than it paid for them. All of these changes in value, whether positive or negative, are instantly reflected in the price of the fund shares. When a fund periodically distributes either ordinary income or capital gains to shareholders, the assets of the fund are reduced by the same amount and the NAV declines accordingly. For this reason, such distributions do not increase your net worth, but they may increase your tax liability.

FIGURE 8

How to Read Newspaper Fund Tables

■ The first column is the abbreviated fund's name. Several funds listed under a single heading indicate a family of funds.

■ The second column is the Net Asset Value (NAV) per share as of the close of the preceding business day. In some newspapers, the NAV is identified as the sell or the bid price—the amount per share you would receive if you sold your shares (less the deferred sales charge, if any). Each mutual fund determines its net asset value every business day by dividing the market value of its total assets, less liabilities, by the number of shares outstanding. On any given day, you can determine the value of your holdings by multiplying the NAV by the number of shares you own.

■ The third column is the offering price or, in some papers, the buy or the asked price—the price you would pay if you purchased shares. The buy price is the NAV plus any sales charge. If there are no initial sales charges, an NL for no-load appears in this column, and the buy price is the same as the NAV. To figure the sales charge percentage, divide the difference between the NAV and the offering price by the offering price. Here, for instance, the sales charge is 7.2 percent ($14.52 − $13.47 ÷ $1.05; $1.05 ÷ $14.52 = 0.072).

■ The fourth column shows the change, if any, in net asset value from the preceding quotation—in other words, the change over the most recent one-day trading period. This fund, for example, gained eight cents per share.

■ A "p" following the abbreviated name of the fund denotes a fund that charges a fee from assets for marketing and distribution costs, also known as a 12b-1 plan (named after the 1980 Securities and Exchange rule that permits them).

■ If the fund name is followed by an "r," the fund has either a contingent deferred sales charge (CDSC) or a redemption fee. A CDSC is a charge if shares are sold within a certain period; a redemption charge is a fee applied whenever shares are sold.

■ A footnote "t" indicates a fund that habitually reports the previous day's prices, instead of the current day's.

■ A "t" designates a fund that has both a CDSC or a redemption fee and a 12b-1 plan.

Reproduced by permission of the Investment Company Institute.

*(Handwritten annotations in margins:)*

offering price = buy price = asked price ( = NAV + any sales charges )
NL for no load funds appear in this column.

NAV/share of preceding day (no load fund)
or
sell or bid price (amt/share received if you sold your shares) (load + no load fund)

abbreviated fund's name →

change in NAV fr. preceding day (i.e. change in value/share fr. preceding day)

p = following abbreviated fund name = 12b-1 charge (an ongoing charge against NAV for marketing + distribution costs)
r = " " " = contingent deferred sales charge, CDSC, or redemption fee or back-end load.
t = " " " has both CDSC or redemption fee.
= 12b-1 plan + CDSC or redemption fee.

Nearly all mutual funds are constituted under Subchapter M of the Internal Revenue Code which means that they distribute to shareholders each year at least 97% of the income from dividends and interest and not less than 98% of net realized capital gains. By so doing, the fund does not pay tax on these sources of revenue and it does not, of course, pay tax on its unrealized capital gains. The concept is that the fund acts as a conduit between the investments and the shareholders. The distributions received from such funds are fully taxable to the investor when received except ,of course, in the case of tax-free income funds. The fund will report to the shareholder each year just what part of the total distributions is investment income, which is treated as ordinary income for tax purposes and what portion is capital gains. If you purchase shares in a fund just before a distribution, you will in effect have a portion of your investment returned to you on which you will then pay tax. This is not smart. Check the date of the next distribution before buying.

When you sell the shares of a fund, you become liable for tax on the undistributed capital gains which the fund has been accumulating. In a fund which does little buying and selling, and thus has a low turnover ratio, this gain may be substantial. All the time you hold the fund you are enjoying some degree of tax deferral. This is yet another advantage of holding a fund over as long a period as practical. The trader never enjoys this benefit. On some occasions a fund may have a net realized capital loss to carry forward. This is an obvious advantage to a new investor as it can be used to offset future capital gain tax liability.

In considering the nuts and bolts of mutual funds, there are many useful fund services that should be considered, although they vary considerably among funds. The prospectus will describe these and tell you, for example, whether there is a minimum required initial investment and any minimum for subsequent investments. If there is, it is usually lower for IRA accounts. Some fund families such as 20th Century Investors Inc. have no minimum, while others intended mainly for large institutions may have a million dollar minimum. Many offer payroll deduction plans and facilitate regular monthly investments. Nearly all funds offer automatic reinvestment programs in which your distributions immediately go back to work. This is both a convenience and an investment advantage, but you are still liable for any taxes due on the distributions. Usually you can arrange for automatic withdrawals from funds, or in the case of money market funds you may write checks from your account.

Buying and selling funds is a simple matter described in the prospectus. It is very simple to switch between funds of the same family, and in some cases, this can be done by a telephone call. However, increasingly funds are limiting the number of switches that can be made in a given time in order to discourage hyperactive traders. This is in the interests of the remaining shareholders. Some funds offer special services, for example, Benham Capital Management Group, a no-load family, operates an open order service for their variable price funds. This means that within a 90-day period, they will arrange for you to buy their shares when the price sinks to a pre-determined level or to sell their shares when they reach a pre-determined higher price level. This is not a service that most funds offer, but it illustrates the fact that in this highly competitive market, many convenient services are available, usually at no additional cost.

Nearly all funds have an 800 telephone number which lets you speak to a representative of the fund. These are usually knowledgeable and helpful people who can answer any questions about a fund but will positively not offer advice on whether to buy or sell a fund - that is your decision. After you have read the prospectus and other literature on the fund, if you have any questions call up the fund's representatives, that is why they are there.

If you own and trade a lot of different funds and want the ultimate convenience of a single statement, you may want to purchase many no-load and low load funds through a discount broker such as Charles Schwab. This costs a small fee which could otherwise be invested, but it is far cheaper than buying a load fund. In some cases you may in this way purchase less than the minimum investment required by the fund as the broker is able to provide the necessary minimum.

## HOW TO EXPLOIT
## THE BENEFITS OF MUTUAL FUNDS

Having a useful investment vehicle such as a mutual fund and knowing how to use if effectively are two different things.

Your investments need to be run as a business and you are the manager. Act as a manager, not as an amateur. Find the most able fund managers, select the best, hire them and if necessary, fire them. Don't try to use your limited time acting as an amateur stock picker. You most likely don't have the time, knowledge, temperament, skills or qualifications of an investment analyst. Just as you don't try to be your own dentist, don't try to be your own investment analyst unless you are one. Modern fund managers have huge data resources, sophisticated analytical techniques and the ability and time to interview the CEO of almost any company they wish to invest in. With all these resources the professional still finds it hard to select the best stocks. Your solution is simple; hire the best managers and reduce your paperwork and record keeping enormously by receiving regular consolidated statements from each fund family that you invest with. This will give you the time to manage your investment business. No hot tips, no brokers calling you up, no piles of paperwork.

We have discussed the importance of diversification, but you must still use it in practice. When you buy a single stock, about 70% of its fluctuation in price is due to factors related directly to the company and only about 30% is related to the overall market. The unnecessary risk involved in owning a small number of stocks is frightening and quite avoidable if you invest in a diversified fund. The prospectus will tell you whether or not it is diversified. If for example it only owns the stock of companies that mine gold, then it is not diversified. It is much safer than buying the stock of one or two individual gold mining companies, but you are not using the available benefits of a diversified fund.

To illustrate the practical importance of diversification, let's suppose you had owned all the 30 stocks of the Dow Jones Industrial Average for the 10 years ending January, 1990. On average, they would have increased in value by 424% during this time. If you had chosen to buy just two individual stocks instead of the entire group, you might have bought Westinghouse Electric and Merck which gained 635% and 543% respectively; or you might have chosen Bethlehem Steel and Navistar International which actually lost 12% and 42% of their value respectively. At the time, picking the future winners was not easy. By investing in a properly diversified fund you virtually eliminate the individual company risk, which means that for a given level of risk you can expect higher returns.

There are times when the stock market may be entering a dangerous phase of its cycle. If you plot the performance of a single stock to detect important trends, you will most probably produce rather meaningless charts with no clear trend line. Most individual stocks are just too volatile. However, if you do the same with a fund that owns perhaps a hundred stocks, it is much easier to detect a longer term trend. This may permit you to move out of the market during dangerous periods. We will be discussing the methodology later. If you succeed, you will further reduce risk and increase returns. Of course, in a no-load fund it costs you nothing to do this; there are no shareholder transaction costs such as the brokerage commissions that you would pay on individual stocks.

We have already seen in Chapter 4 that to have a well-diversified portfolio, you are going to have to invest in the world economy, most just that of any one nation. Now as the manager of your business you have a problem. How are you going to know where to invest, when to invest, what are the economic prospects or how to read the various company annual reports in each country? Most of all, you don't know how business is done, how safe it is, what are the accounting standards used or many other important things. Caveat Emptor - let the buyer beware. You are about to enter a mine field.

Remember that as a manager you don't have to acquire all these skills yourself, but you do have to find and use the most successful experts having the best track record. There are now many international stock funds available but only a relatively few with a good long-term record. We shall be discussing how to find the very best funds. If you need to diversify into international bonds or real estate there are funds which specialize in these areas. Evaluate them and use them. Now you are really exploiting the benefits of mutual funds. You are in a different league from your friendly neighborhood broker.

In managing your business you will have special needs. For example, you may want to own the whole of a given market, in which case you can simply buy an index fund. You may want to defer taxes, in which case you can put your funds into an IRA account or you can own a suitable fund in a tax-deferred annuity. If this does not meet your needs, you can own a stock fund which makes no distributions and, therefore, causes no tax liability until you sell it. The Copley Fund is such a case. If you prefer to pay no federal taxes on income, you may purchase a tax-free bond fund or money market fund. If you want to diversify among a large number of guaranteed mortgages to reduce the risk of a single mortgage, you may quite easily do so with a Ginnie Mae Fund in which the mortgages are guaranteed by an agency of the federal government. If you need any one of many special services, there is usually no difficulty in finding a good fund which will offer it and usually free of charge.

You can now manage your investments in a manner which would be quite impossible without mutual funds and would have been difficult even with mutual funds just a few years ago. This is the modern way of investing and these are just a few examples of how to exploit the benefits of mutual funds. The mutual fund industry is still in its infancy. Your challenge is to be a good enough manager to benefit from what it offers now and what it will offer in the future. This will enormously increase your chances of winning the money game.

## LOAD VERSUS NO-LOAD FUNDS

There are two types of expenses which investors may incur in owning mutual funds. They are shareholder transaction expenses and operating expenses. Transaction expenses may include a sales load or charge on the purchase price, a sales load on reinvested dividends, redemption fees (paid to the fund distributors) when you sell the fund and exchange fees when you switch funds. One or more of these fees will be charged by a load fund; none will be charged by a true no-load fund. Operating expenses are primarily the cost to the shareholders of operating the fund, and although they can be minimized, they cannot be eliminated. Shareholder transaction costs, on the other hand, are a different story. There is no need whatever to pay any type of transaction cost and doing so merely reduces the amount of your money which is put to work for you. The transaction expenses you pay to own a load fund are used to pay the fund's distribution and selling costs.

At the front of every prospectus under the heading of Annual Fund Expenses, you will find a list of shareholder transaction expenses. A no-load fund will have "none" written against each item. It will also show here a list of operating expenses. The upfront load at the time of purchase cannot exceed 8 1/2% of the offering price by federal law and is usually less. It also usually decreases as the size of the investment increases. A redemption fee is usually much less and may typically range from 1% to 2%. Perhaps the most pernicious transaction cost is that levied on reinvested distributions where no selling expenses are incurred but a load is still charged. This is only practiced by a relatively few funds, and they are obliged to reveal it in the prospectus.

In recent years a new type of load fund has appeared which typically charges an initial load of 1% to 3%. These so called low loads have been added to a number of previously no-load funds. Low load mutual funds are frequently bought directly from the fund, as are no-load funds. Fidelity Investors was one of the first fund families to introduce the concept of directly sold funds bearing a low sales load.

If you invest $1,000 in a fund having an 8.5% load, the commission comes off the top and only $915 is actually invested ($1,000 less $85). This means that you have not just lost 8.5% but that your investment will have to grow by 9.3% before you get back your original $1,000. Furthermore, as the load forms part of your cost of the shares, it is not tax deductible as an expense at the time of purchase.

The true cost of paying a sales load at varying levels for varying periods is shown in Table 21. It assumes that $10,000

TABLE 21

**LOAD VERSUS NO-LOAD FUNDS**

Value of $10,000 Invested at 12% Per Year Compounded,
After an Initial Load

| Duration of Investment | Initial Load | | | |
|---|---|---|---|---|
| | 0% | 3% | 5% | 8.5% |
| 1 Year: | $11,200 | $10,864 | $10,640 | $10,248 |
| Cost of Load: | $0 | $336 | $560 | $952 |
| 5 Years: | $17,623 | $17,094 | $16,742 | $16,125 |
| Cost of Load: | $0 | $529 | $881 | $1,498 |
| 10 Years: | $31,058 | $30,127 | $29,505 | $28,418 |
| Cost of Load: | $0 | $931 | $1,553 | $2,640 |
| 20 Years: | $96,463 | $93,569 | $91,640 | $88,263 |
| Cost of Load: | $0 | $2,894 | $4,823 | $8,200 |
| 30 Years: | $299,597 | $290,609 | $284,617 | $274,130 |
| Cost of Load: | $0 | $8,988 | $14,980 | $25,466 |

is invested at a 12% annual compound return and that there is only an upfront load with no load on reinvested distributions and no back-end load or redemption charge. The results are most revealing. With an 8.5% load, compared to a no-load it has cost you $1,498 after five years; $2,640 after ten years; $8,200 after 20 years and an amazing $25,466 after 30 years. This is what it has cost you to have a salesman sell you a fund rather than you selecting your own no-load fund. You have to decide whether his or her advice is worth it. Remember that the person selling you the fund may not be offering truly expert advice on funds, is certainly not offering impartial advice, and often has only a narrow selection of funds from which to choose. You, however, can buy any no-load fund that you please. With the amount of money you have saved after even one year, you could afford to buy reference information and a good no-load fund newsletter for a year and still have useful change.

There are issues other than cost which help determine whether a load or no-load fund is better. Quite obviously if load funds, on average, produced better results, they would be worth it. This is not the case, they do not produce superior performance. The load charge does not go to the fund advisor to provide him with extra resources, it goes to the distribution chain and helps to pay for the cost of the sales force. For example, one national brokerage firm pays its brokers 34% to 42% of the commission for selling their own in-house mutual funds but less than this for selling third party funds. Which do you think the broker would prefer to sell you? Do you believe you are really getting expert and impartial advice?

If you have paid a significant upfront load on a fund and shortly thereafter you need to sell it, you face a dilemma. Most people tend to hold on to the fund and this significantly reduces their flexibility. There is another side to this argument, however. In a true no-load fund, it costs nothing to sell out and short-term market timers may disturb the fund by frequent trading, forcing the fund manager to sell large numbers of shares at what he may judge to be the wrong time. Some funds have had to hold additional cash to meet these demands, which is not necessarily in the interests of the longer term shareholders. To discourage short-term trading some no-load funds impose a short-term deferred contingency sales charge which means that a redemption fee is charged if the shares are sold within a given period of time after purchase. Some no-load funds charge a small fee of this type which is paid into the fund itself and not paid to the fund advisor. This seems a fair way of protecting the interests of the shareholders. Other funds simply limit the number of switches which may be made in the course of a year.

There seems very little reason to buy load funds when there are so many good no-load funds available directly from the sponsor. It is basically a question of whether you wish to buy "wholesale" directly from the sponsor or retail at the end of a distribution chain. However, sales loads are not the only expenses which may be incurred, and it is necessary to select funds also having low overall operating expenses. There are many true no-load funds having low operating expenses and, all else being equal, such funds should be preferred. Over time, probability favors these funds over those which take an initial, repeated or final slice off your principal.

Many of the true no-load fund families belong to the "100% No-Load Mutual Fund Council." There are almost 30 members of this association and here you will find some of the time honored names in the industry such as Acorn, Benham Management, Century Investors, United Services Advisors, Value Line Funds and many others. A complete list of members is provided in Appendix B. Not only do members offer funds free of all loads, but they are also free of 12b-1 charges within their operating expenses, as they rightly view these charges as a type of ongoing load used to promote the fund.

There is also an association of no-load funds known as the "Mutual Fund Education Alliance" which comprises fund families offering funds directly to the public having "little or no sales charges or commissions." Some of them do, however, charge 12b-1 fees. This association contains respected names such as Financial INVESCO Funds, Scudder, T. Rowe Price and Vanguard. A complete list of members is provided in Appendix C.

Before buying any fund satisfy yourself that any share-holder transaction charges are in your best interests. With more than 3,000 funds from which to choose, there are plenty of other good games in town.

## THE QUESTION OF OPERATING EXPENSES

Whereas sales loads are totally avoidable and may occur only once or twice while a fund is held, operating expenses are continuous and unavoidable. They represent the cost of operating the fund and the profit of the management com-pany. Fortunately, they are visible to the investor and should be scrutinized in the prospectus and a recent annual report before a fund is purchased. They are detailed in the first few pages of every fund prospectus and examples are shown of the total cost of these expenses per $1,000 invested over given time periods. There are several different types of expenses that you should understand.

Management expenses in most cases include the fees paid to the advisor or management company plus the expenses born directly by the fund. Typically, the advisor will be paid a fee for providing the fund with investment advisory services and a varying level of administrative service and support. The advisor has a contract with the fund which frequently reduces his fee as a percentage of the assets of the fund as the fund grows in size. The advisor may or may not receive a fee based on performance. The annual fee may be in the range of 0.5% to 1% of fund assets.

2.      Administrative expenses are usually those expenses of the fund not borne by the advisor and may include Director's fees, legal, accounting, custodial and shareholder services expenses.

3.      Distribution expenses, or 12b-1 plan fees, is also an item to look for.  In 1980, the SEC permitted funds to use shareholder's assets to pay for marketing, promotional and distribution expenses. These were previously all paid for by the fund distributors and not by the shareholders. These expenses may include commissions to banks, financial planners and stockbrokers and also many advertising and direct mail promotional expenses. Fees charged to shareholders may range from 0.1% to 1.25% annually.  They are most frequently, but not always, associated with load funds.  Many funds which have redemption fees tend also to have 12b-1 charges.  Some funds for legal reasons have adopted 12b-1 plans but do not use them, so check not whether a fund *may* charge a 12b-1 fee but whether it *actually does*.  Effective July 1993, new S.E.C. rules limit 12b-1 charges to 0.75% but allow in addition an annual service fee of 0.25%, making a maximum distribution fee of 1.00%.  Funds claiming to be no-load will be limited to a 12b-1 charge of 0.25%.

These fees really constitute a continuous load charge, and it is for this reason that members of the 100% No-Load Fund Council do not levy them. If you pay a 12b-1 fee as part of a fund's operating expenses you may be providing a steady ongoing income to the salesman for as long as you own the fund. At the time that 12b-1 fees were approved, the SEC was persuaded that they would increase sales of the funds, which would lower their operating costs, which in turn would benefit the shareholders. A recent study of 612 funds has shown that this is not so, and that in general, funds charging 12b-1 fees have higher operating expenses than those that do not. Other studies have shown that they produce lower total returns than funds without 12b-1 fees.

Together these expenses make up a fund's stated operating expenses. In total they may range anywhere from around 0.25% to more than 3.0% of assets annually. One fifth of all equity funds have expenses greater than 2.0%. At the lower end of the expense range, the investor is clearly getting a bargain, but at the higher levels he is suffering a real and continuous burden on his net return. Most operating expenses are between 1.0% and 1.5% for stock funds and somewhat less for fixed income funds. International funds frequently carry higher expense levels than domestic funds.

Just as there is no need to pay shareholder transaction expenses such as sales loads, there is no need to pay high operating expenses. If you are managing your investment business efficiently you will be paying no loads, or at worst only low loads. For domestic diversified larger stock funds you need average no more than about 1% total operating expenses. For domestic bond funds you need to average no more than about 0.7%. This will eliminate a lot of funds but only in this way do you reach the gems. In many cases you can purchase good general funds and index funds having expense levels well below these levels.

For example, if you wish to buy the whole market as reflected by the S&P 500 index, you may do so from the Vanguard Group with no load and operating expenses of about 0.25% per year or $25 per $10,000 invested. To own the whole market and have someone else do all the paperwork for such a low charge is really using the advantages of mutual funds. For a similar expense level you may take your pick of a range of bond funds or a small stock index fund. Many other no-load fund groups offer funds with low operating expenses. Examples include Dodge and Cox, Fidelity Spartan Funds, Lindner, Mutual Series and Nicholas.

If you invest $10,000 at a 10% annual compound return before expenses, at a level of 0.5% annual expenses, after 10 years it will be worth $24,782; at 1.0% expenses it will be worth $23,674 and at 3% expenses it will be worth only $19,671. You can increase investment returns by accepting higher risk or by reducing expense levels. The good business manager does the latter.

There is another aspect of fund expenses which is rarely considered, and this is the fund's own transaction costs. They have to buy and sell shares or bonds and this costs them money. The prospectus will tell you the portfolio turnover ratio. A 100% turnover ratio means that during a stated period, usually a year, on average every investment has been traded. More aggressive funds generally have higher portfolio turnover ratios. If you bought individual stocks or bonds you would also have a portfolio turnover ratio and you should match the fund's rate to a level that you are comfortable with. It is then a question of examining the cost to you as a shareholder of the fund compared with the cost to you if you bought individual investments. In both cases you ultimately have to pay the costs. Funds are not required to report these costs separately in the prospectus, and they are reflected directly in the fund's NAV rather than being itemized as a separate expense. In addition to the considerable bid-asked spread in a transaction, there are also the direct brokerage costs. Surveys have shown that funds have very low brokerage costs ranging from 4¢ to 8¢ per share with an average of 6.4¢. As an example, Fidelity Magellan in the year ending March 1988, had a portfolio turnover ratio of 101% and its brokerage commissions cost 0.25% of its net assets. You would need to own about $500,000 of each individual stock in your portfolio to come close to matching the typical transaction costs of a mutual fund. If you owned the stocks directly, a round trip of buying and selling say $10,000 of a single stock might cost you 2% at a discount broker. A round trip of $500 of a single stock might cost 3.2% and a round trip of $100 per stock might cost around 8.4%. Each example will vary, but in this example, provided that the fund turnover ratio is similar to what you would incur as an individual, you have saved yourself from 1.75% to more than 8% of the value of your portfolio each year. Even if the saving is only a part of this amount, it should more than pay for all the fund expenses and give you all the benefits of a mutual fund at no cost. Now you are well on your way to winning the money game.

You may sometimes hear it said that fund expenses are unimportant if the fund has a high performance level. This argument is fallacious, as in reality it is very hard to know the future performance of a fund when you buy it, irrespective of its past performance. The factors which can be much more reliably forecast are its expense levels and its risk level. These tend to be more consistent, whereas its performance contains an element of chance. It is, therefore, wise to control the controllable.

CHAPTER 6

# HOW TO MANAGE RISK

There is a time in the life of every investor when he must face up to a reality called risk. Risk tends to be forgotten in bull markets and remembered too late in bear markets.

There is no such thing as a riskless investment, it is just a question of which type of risk you prefer to be exposed to. If you do nothing and put your money in a shoe box, you are deciding to be exposed to purchasing power risk and perhaps to the risk of theft. Risk is all a matter of probabilities and a thorough understanding of risk will reduce the probability of you needlessly suffering from its.

This chapter will address how you can recognize, measure and control risk. It may get a little heavy at times but in the great words of Albert Einstein *"everything should be made as simple as possible, but not simpler."* Try to stay with it, as it is your money on the table as the wheel of fortune spins.

## RISK AND REWARD

The dictionary defines risk as *"the possibility of loss, injury, disadvantage or destruction"* and that fairly well describes the hazards to which your money might be exposed.

FIGURE 9

**AREAS OF RISK AND REWARD**

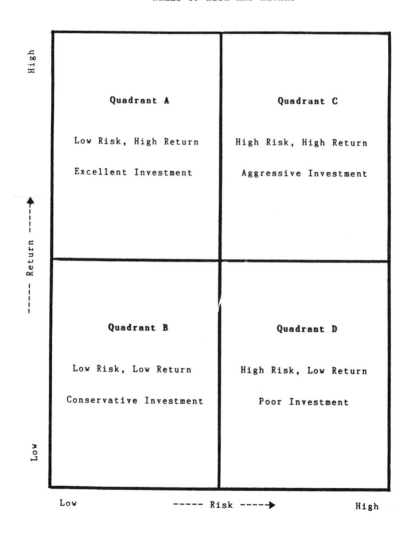

As the manager of your investments, you will decide to which of these hazards your money will be exposed and to what extent. As a broad generalization, the greater the risks, within certain limits, the greater the likely return. The objective of the smart investor is to achieve relatively high returns with as little risk as possible.

This situation is shown schematically in Figure 9. If your investments are in quadrant "A" of the figure you are enjoying high returns with low risk. This is a rare bargain. It may be possible with excellent diversification, good fund management and low expenses. However, be skeptical. If an investment looks too good to be true, it probably is.

If you are in quadrant "B", you have a conservative stance which is fine if that is your objective. As with all the quadrants, if you can be in the top left corner you will get a better risk/reward ratio than, for example, in the lower right corner.

Quadrant "C" is more aggressive, seeking higher returns and accepting higher risks. This may be quite appropriate for the knowledgeable investor with a very long time horizon and a suitable risk tolerance. Extremely high risk is frequently not rewarded and should be avoided. It may be approaching the level of speculation, and in the words of Mark Twain, *"There are two times in a man's life when he should not speculate, when he can afford it and when he can't."*

Quadrant "D" exposes you to high risk and low returns and should be avoided. The market does not demand this and the chances are that someone is shifting the odds in their favor and against yours. This may be the result of poor portfolio construction, poor investment selection or high expenses and transaction costs. Whatever the reason, you need to move out of this quadrant.

If we draw a straight line from the bottom left corner of quadrant "B" (low risk/low return), to the top right corner of quadrant "C" (high risk/high return), we will find that most types of investments in an efficient market are positioned close to this line. This effect is shown schematically in Figure 10. There are several important caveats to this figure. First, it is measuring reward in nominal dollars, not considering inflation. If it did, Treasury Bills would not necessarily be considered low risk. Second, the relative risk and returns shown are only examples. As we have seen previously, different types of investment will perform quite differently over different time periods and risks will vary widely with market conditions. Third, it does not take into account different tax liabilities which may exist. With all these limitations, it still indicates where various types of investments may frequently belong on the risk/reward line.

We begin to see why it is meaningless to rank mutual funds simply on the magnitude of their returns without considering the risks that they are taking with your money. To have any true meaning, returns must be measured on a risk-adjusted basis and we shall explore how to do this later. For now, just realize that when the press declares that a certain specialized sector fund gave the highest return last year or last month, you should not be surprised; they probably took the greatest risks and had the good luck to succeed. There may be other funds which did almost as well and took much less risk. Put another way, on a risk-adjusted basis such a fund may not have been the highest performer. That privilege more probably fell on a well managed, diversified, low expense, middle of the road, unexciting fund, such as a good growth or growth and income fund.

When we speak of return, we know what we mean and how to measure it as total return. When we speak of risk it has many different forms. We will take a look at the most common types of financial risk which you may encounter. In practice, several of these are interrelated.

FIGURE 10

**RISK AND REWARD**

Generalizations Based on Past Performance

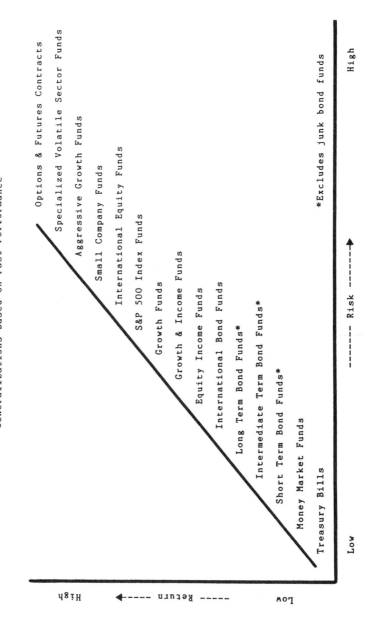

Options & Futures Contracts
Specialized Volatile Sector Funds
Aggressive Growth Funds
Small Company Funds
International Equity Funds
S&P 500 Index Funds
Growth Funds
Growth & Income Funds
Equity Income Funds
International Bond Funds
Long Term Bond Funds*
Intermediate Term Bond Funds*
Short Term Bond Funds*
Money Market Funds
Treasury Bills

*Excludes junk bond funds

Low ------- Risk -------> High

High <----- Return ----- Low

## THE TYPES OF RISK

### LOSS OF PRINCIPAL

The most serious risk is obviously loss of principal. This may be permanent or temporary. If you own just one single stock and the company becomes bankrupt, you have probably lost all your money forever. In this case it is no use reading from the academic literature that on average, over time high risk produces high rewards. In your case you have just lost the money game. This, of course, is virtually impossible in a well managed diversified mutual fund due to the many different stocks that are held. More likely is a temporary loss of principal due to wide fluctuations in value reflecting normal market cycles. This *will* happen (not *may* happen) with stocks, bonds and most other longer term investments. The greater the volatility the greater the risk if you need to liquidate your assets. Extreme volatility should be avoided because it is unnecessary and takes a great deal of catching up. For example, in 1990, when the S&P 500 Index declined by 3.1%, there were several funds that declined by more than 30%. That means they had to increase in value by 43% just to get back where they were. An important and obvious rule of investing is - don't lose money.

Loss of principal can be rapid, total and spectacular as in the case of the total failure of a company, or it may be gradual and insidious and continuous as in the case of inflation. Either way it is a permanent loss of principal.

### LOSS OF INCOME

Another form of risk is the possibility of loss of income from an investment. This may be partial as in the case of a company lowering its dividend or total when a bond defaults and is unable to make its obligatory interest payments. Once again, broad diversification in a well managed mutual fund, which in turn is part of a broadly diversified portfolio will largely control such risk.

## PURCHASING POWER RISK

This has already been discussed in Chapter 2 and identified as a major risk for the investor in Treasury Bills and other so-called "riskless" investments. We saw in Table 18 that the best long-term protection against erosion of principal by high inflation has been investment in real assets such as real estate and gold, and that the investments most susceptible to the effects of inflation have been long-term bonds. Stocks fell in between. In times of high inflation or anticipated high inflation, interest rates rise, which inevitably reduces even the nominal value of bonds and is likely to have a similar effect on stocks. Purchasing power risk is the greatest hazard for conservative investors who want a "riskless" investment and sacrifice return in a futile attempt to avoid risk. It may appear at times as though inflation is on a downward trend and that purchasing power risk is unimportant. Experience over the last 50 years has shown that brief periods of low inflation are inexorably followed by periods of higher inflation. Perhaps one day the United States economy will enter long periods of deflation such as it experienced in the 19th Century and early 20th Century, but this would represent a major change in a long-term trend. Don't count on it, and even a low 3.5% inflation rate will still halve the purchasing power of your money in 20 years.

## DEFAULT RISK

This is very simply the risk that someone to whom you lend money will not pay it back. It occurs in fixed income investments and the probability is related to the credit worthiness of the borrower. It can largely be avoided by investing only in high quality bonds and achieving broad diversification through a mutual fund.

During the late 80's, many low quality corporate bonds were issued by highly leveraged corporations that were overburdened by debt. Ignorant or greedy investors bought up huge quantities of these "junk bonds," attracted solely by their high current yields without reference to the level of risk. Many investors were surprised when they lost all or a part of their investment. Remember, if it looks too good to be true, it probably is.

The highly respected debt rating agencies such as Moody's and Standard and Poor's do an excellent job for the discerning investor. Standard and Poor's rates high quality investment grade bonds as AAA, AA, or A; triple A being the highest quality. BBB is considered an intermediate investment grade bond while BB, B, and CCC are increasingly speculative with declining perceived ability to bear the risks to which they are exposed. Moody's has a similar rating system by which investment grade bonds are rated Aaa, Aa, A and Baa. Ratings below this level (e.g. Ba, B, Caa, Ca and C) again indicate increasingly speculative characteristics. These ratings are valid only at the time that they are issued and may change with time. For example, in times of economic hardship a municipality's obligatory expenses may rise and its ability to collect taxes may decline. In recent years, investors in the municipal bonds of New York City, Philadelphia and the State of Massachusetts have seen their bond ratings decline, causing a drop in market value. Similarly, in hard times the sales and profit of a corporation may decline while its accounts receivable may dramatically increase, together causing a risk of default on debt. An investor in a bond mutual fund can easily determine the likely default risk of the bonds comprising the fund by checking what proportion of each rating the fund owns.

## LIQUIDITY RISK

This refers to the potential difficulty of liquidating an asset due to a shortage of willing buyers. In the case of directly owned investments, particularly real estate, works of art and small parcels of some bonds this may be a real problem. Almost anything can be sold at some price, so liquidity risk usually translates into a partial loss of principal upon liquidation. The owner of mutual funds avoids such problems, as the shares can be sold back to the fund on any business day at their current market value. This is a major advantage of funds in general and real estate funds in particular.

## REINVESTMENT RISK

This concerns the probability of being unable to reinvest the interest or dividends from an investment at a level comparable to the original investment. For example, the yield to maturity of a bond is calculated on the assumption that future interest can be reinvested at the current yield, but that may not be so. In the case of stock and bond funds there are interesting implications. As a stock fund rises in value its dividend yield will normally purchase fewer new shares and when the market value of the fund declines the investor can purchase more shares of lower value. This produces a desirable effect similar to dollar cost averaging which will be discussed later. A similar situation occurs with bond funds. Reinvestment risk may be minimized by purchasing growth stock funds which focus on capital appreciation rather than dividends or by purchasing zero coupon bonds which provide no cash flow but automatically compound interest payments at a predetermined and fixed rate, adding them to the principal.

## INTEREST RATE RISK

This term refers to the possibility that either the value of an investment or the cash flow from it will be adversely affected by changes in interest rates. An investor in a money market fund who is dependent on the interest payments to live on will find that as short-term market interest rates decline, so will his income. A money market fund has very little risk of loss of principal but a major risk of a partial loss of income from the fixed principal. Conversely, a bond fund may show loss of principal not when interest rates decline but when they rise. As with many forms of risk, you have a choice. You may choose stability of principal or stability of income. You can't normally have it both ways. Perhaps the only exception is individual fixed income investments held until maturity. You can, however, with care and knowledge, balance different investments partially to compensate each other. For example, a fund investing in the utilities industry will tend to change in value in the opposite direction to the change in interest rates. Utilities tend to borrow so much money that their operating costs are strongly affected by the cost of the money they borrow. On the other hand, companies with high cash reserves or banks who are lending money will often benefit as interest rates rise. A combination of such investments will provide another dimension of diversification.

Interest rates tend to move in cycles. Money is a commodity and like all commodities its short-term price depends upon supply and demand. When everyone wants to borrow, there is a shortage and the price goes up. In times of economic contraction there are fewer investments made and the demand for money subsides. However, this simple approach is complicated by two facts. First, that the federal government is a huge borrower and is unconstrained by market discipline, and second, that the Federal Reserve Board determines the supply of money and in several ways it directly influences interest rates. The difficult task of the Federal Reserve is to keep interest rates low enough to maintain economic growth and prosperity while containing the growth of the money supply sufficiently to avoid higher inflation or the fear of it. As soon as investors suspect higher inflation, the yields on long-term debt will increase in order to compensate the investor. The yield on a bond is basically an inducement to the investor a) to tie up his money for a given period b) to accept a predicted level of inflation with return of principal in nominal dollars (i.e. not adjusted in value for reduced purchasing power) and c) to accept the credit risk of the borrower. Put another way, the yield on a bond is a function of liquidity risk, purchasing power risk and credit risk. In total they determine the bond's yield, changes in which lead to interest rate risk.

Changes in interest rates drive the entire economic machine. As interest rates fall, real estate prospers due to cheaper mortgages. Stock prices generally increase due to lower borrowing costs, bond prices increase and yields on fixed principal investments such as money markets fall. Rates of inflation also tend to fall. In a well diversified portfolio of funds, moderate changes in interest rates should constitute a manageable risk, as those parts of the portfolio that are adversely affected should be offset by those parts which are favorably impacted.

## BUSINESS RISK

This is the financial risk associated with one business or organization. It is a significant risk for anyone unwise enough to invest in only a small number of stocks. More than 40% of stock market investors own five or fewer stocks and they are greatly at risk. Business risk is also known as diversifiable risk because it can be reduced to insignificance by adequate diversification. It is sometimes known as unsystematic risk as it does not apply broadly across the entire market in a systematic way, but is limited to a particular business or industry. Because it is an avoidable risk the investor is not rewarded for taking it. It is, therefore, your task as manager of your investments to ensure that you are adequately diversified.

About three quarters of the risk of owning a single stock is due to business risk. It is your job to reduce this to near zero. This is a simple matter with diversified funds. Conventional wisdom has maintained that owning 10 to 15 stocks will ensure adequate diversification but recent research has suggested that it may take at least 80 stocks to virtually eliminate business risk. With most diversified funds this is still no problem but there are a few funds such as Janus 20 which hold only a smaller selection of stocks. Generally this is yet another type of risk that can readily be managed by the use of broadly diversified mutual funds.

## MARKET RISK

This is the uncertainty of investment returns attributable to market cycles. It applies, for example, not just to one stock or industry but to the entire market or a large portion of it. It is also known as systematic or undiversifiable risk. When most people speak of the risks of investing, it is market risk to which they refer.

The first thing to realize about market risk is that unlike permanent loss of principal due to inflation, default or bankruptcy, if you ignore market risk for long enough the problem will go away. Market cycles have their highs and lows. Most cycles have a total duration of four to five years. If you don't need liquidity for at least another five years, you can afford to sit it out and let the market correct itself. As we discussed earlier, there are still good reasons to be concerned about market risk. In a major recession it may take a very long time to regain the loss. For example, if you had bought the entire stock market in August 1929, it would have taken you 15 years and eight months just to match the return on Treasury Bills, and if you had bought in December 1972, it would have taken 12 years and five months. You never really know when this type of decline will occur. An investment that avoids such a loss can grow safely and at a modest rate and still beat the performance of a fund which has suffered this type of a decline. If your investment horizon is less than about five years, you should be extremely cautious in being exposed to market risk and invest only in funds that have low volatility. For this it may be necessary to emphasize cash equivalents and short-term bond funds.

For most investors, unless you have a very long time horizon, price volatility is an extremely important aspect of risk. We need to study this further and learn how to measure it.

## HOW TO MEASURE RISK — RISK-ADJUSTED RETURN

For the purposes of this discussion we shall assume that risk is the amount of fluctuation over time in the total value of an asset. This is a generally held assumption, but remember that of all types of risk the most serious is always the permanent loss of principal.

In the financial academic world, much has been written on risk and how best to measure it. We shall attempt to keep this discussion as simple as possible, but no simpler, avoiding complex mathematical formulas. Remember that you are the manager of your investments, and you need to use your limited time effectively. This may not be by crunching out masses of

138                    *BUILDING WEALTH WITH MUTUAL FUNDS*

numbers. It is sufficient to understand the concepts and then look up the necessary statistical data in a reference source.

## THE CONCEPT OF BETA COEFFICIENT

The commonest way of expressing the market risk within the domestic stock market is by use of the beta coefficient. This measures not the total risk or price fluctuation of the market, but the historical risk of a single stock or mutual fund in comparison to the entire market.

The total domestic stock market is normally assumed to be represented by the S&P 500 index, which is a capitalization weighted index of industrial, financial, utility and transportation stocks traded on the New York and American stock exchanges and in the over-the-counter market. Typically, the 20 largest companies in the index represent over a quarter of the weighting. It is generally used as a benchmark by money managers against which to compare the performance of their portfolios.

By definition, the S&P 500 index has a beta of 1.0. If an individual stock or fund historically increases or decreases in value to the same extent as the index it also has a beta of 1.0. If, however, the market increases or decreases by, say 10% and the fund in question changes in value by 20%, it would be said to have a beta of 2.0. If it moved only half as much as the index, its beta would be 0.5. A money market fund, which has a fixed principal, shows no price fluctuation and, therefore, has a beta of zero. A beta value thus shows not how volatile a fund has been in absolute terms but how volatile relative to the market. The beta of a given stock may fluctuate widely over time, but a diversified equity fund normally has a more stable beta value. This is a great advantage in the process of both measuring and predicting a level of market risk. Beta values should not be used to compare the market risk of funds which are not closely related to the general stock market. For example, a high risk gold fund may have a low beta. That is not because it has a low market risk, but because its market risk is not closely related to that of the general stock market.

Figure 11 shows how the beta coefficient may be used. The horizontal axis shows increasing beta values of from 0.0 to 2.0 while the vertical axis measures total return. The horizontal line "A" to "F" shows a so-called "riskless" return on Treasury Bills. This will, of course, vary with changes in interest rates. The example shown assumes a yield of 6.8% which was a recent five year average. Historically, equities have returned a greater yield to reward investors for greater risk. This is known as the Equity Risk Premium. Over the long term this has averaged between six and seven percentage points. Our example shows a value of 6.3% being the actual value for the same five year period. It is represented by the line "B" to "E". We now know that the market has a beta of 1.0 so we may draw a vertical line "G" to "C" to join a beta of 1.0 to the total market return. The lines meet at point "C". Now we know two facts. First, that at point "A" as there is no fluctuation in a "riskless" investment, the beta will be zero and second, that at point "C" it will be 1.0. It has been shown that the straight line "A" - "C" - "D", known as the market line, will permit us to relate beta to total return. We can now read off all other relationships. For example, a beta of 0.5 in this example gives an expected return of 10%, while a beta of 1.5 provides an expected return of 16.2%. Earlier, in Figures 9 and 10, we had related risk and reward in a general way. Now we may measure it quantitatively using beta values. For example, aggressive growth funds will normally have a beta of more than 1.0, whereas growth and income funds and equity income funds, being less volatile and more dependent upon steady income will typically have betas well below 1.0. Beta is widely used as a convenient and simple measure of market risk, but it can only be used intelligently for funds that are broadly diversified.

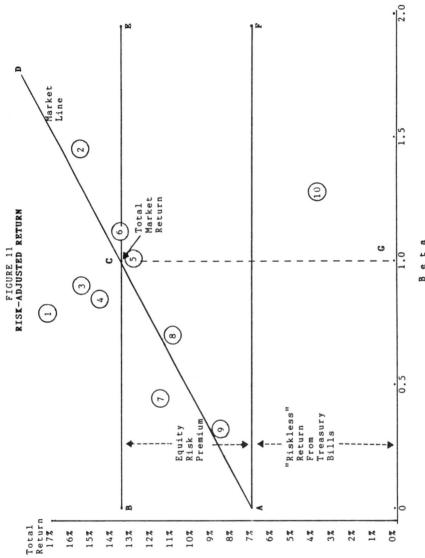

FIGURE 11
RISK-ADJUSTED RETURN

(Numbers in circles represent the funds listed in table 22)

RISK-ADJUSTED RETURN

If we now examine several specific funds, each having known betas, we might expect that their total return would be such that it would be on the market line. A fund with a beta of 1.0 has an expected return in this example of just over 13%. This is not necessarily its actual return. If it were, selecting the best fund would be a rather simple matter of deciding on your chosen beta and receiving an assured commensurate return. This is not the way it works. At any given level of risk, different funds will give different returns at any point in time. The best funds, other things being equal, are clearly those which provide not just the greatest absolute returns but the greatest returns for a given level of risk. This is known as their risk-adjusted performance and is the correct way of comparing fund performance. It allows you to measure return per unit of risk, and this is an important concept to understand. Nearly all the lists of the best performing funds published in the general press are unadjusted for risk. If they were so adjusted, the list would be rather different.

Each circled number in Figure 11 represents the actual five-year average annual compound total return and beta of a fund. We showed empirically in Figure 9 that the upper left quadrant of a risk/return graph was the preferred position to be. Now we can quantify this. Fund #1 in Figure 11 has a beta of 0.77 which would lead to an expected return of just under 11%. The actual return at this level of risk was far better, at 16.97%. On the other hand, fund #10 with a beta of 1.24 had an expected return of almost 14% but only actually returned 3.5%.

If you draw a line from point "A" on Figure 11 to each of the circled numbers, you will discover that the steeper the angle of the slope, the greater the risk-adjusted performance. Where the slope points downwards, as with fund #10, the investor has suffered market risk without receiving even the rewards of a riskless investment.  If you compare funds #2 and #3, their returns are quite similar but fund #2 has been exposed to a level of risk considerably greater than the total market risk to achieve its return, whereas fund #3 has been exposed to a much lower risk and has achieved similar returns.  Looking at these funds on an unadjusted basis, you would have no particular preference for one or the other, but on a risk-adjusted basis, fund #3 is much preferable.

When comparing hundreds of funds, it is not practical to plot their position on a graph, so a simple formula is used as follows:

$$\text{Risk-Adjusted Performance} = \frac{\text{Total Return Less Riskless Return}}{\text{Beta}}$$

For example, fund #1 has a total return of 16.97%, the riskless rate of a Treasury Bill during the period was 6.81% and the beta of fund #1 was 0.77.  Its risk-adjusted return was therefore:

$$\frac{16.97 \text{ less } 6.81}{0.77} = \frac{10.16}{0.77} = 13.19\%$$

Using this simple formula we can now compare the risk-adjusted performance of all the funds in Figure 11.

Table 22 shows the results.  The first column lists the funds which were shown in Figure 11 and includes the S&P 500 index and Treasury Bills.  The annualized five-year returns are shown in the next column followed by the same values after subtraction of the riskless rate of 6.81%.  This value, divided by the beta, provides the column of risk-adjusted performances.  As a matter of convenience these are then expressed in comparison to an index fund representing the S&P 500 Index.  This is more realistic than using the actual S&P 500

TABLE 22

COMPARATIVE RISK-ADJUSTED RETURNS OF SELECTED FUNDS USING BETA COEFFICIENT

| Diversified Domestic Equity Fund | Annualized Five Year Total Return (to 1/1/91) | Return less Riskless Rate | Beta | Risk-Adjusted Performance* | Risk-Adjusted Performance Compared to S&P 500 Index Fund | Ranking Un-Adjusted | Ranking Risk-Adjusted |
|---|---|---|---|---|---|---|---|
| Strong Opportunity | 16.97% | 10.16% | 0.77 | 13.19% | 7.22% | 1 | 1 |
| AIM Constellation | 15.48% | 8.67% | 1.43 | 6.06% | 0.09% | 2 | 6 |
| IAI Regional | 15.29% | 8.48% | 0.88 | 9.64% | 3.67% | 3 | 3 |
| Janus | 14.43% | 7.62% | 0.85 | 8.96% | 2.99% | 4 | 4 |
| 20th Cent. Select | 13.33% | 6.52% | 1.08 | 6.04% | 0.07% | 5 | 7 |
| S&P 500 Index Fund | 12.78% | 5.97% | 1.00 | 5.97% | 0% | 6 | 8 |
| Copley Fund | 11.62% | 4.81% | 0.43 | 11.19% | 5.22% | 7 | 2 |
| Mutual Shares | 11.01% | 4.20% | 0.68 | 6.18% | 0.21% | 8 | 5 |
| Lindner Dividend | 8.51% | 1.70% | 0.29 | 5.86% | (-0.11%) | 9 | 9 |
| Stein Roe Capital Opportunities | 3.56% | (-3.25%) | 1.24 | (-2.62%) | (-8.59%) | 10 | 10 |
| | | | | | | | |
| S&P 500 Index | 13.13 | 6.32 | 1.00 | | | | |
| Treasury Bills (riskless rate) | 6.81 | 0% | 0% | | | | |

* Total return less riskless rate, divided by beta. Also known as the Traynor ratio, it measures comparative return per unit of market risk.

Index as the latter does not include the unavoidable costs and transaction expenses inherent in operating a fund. Note that on this basis, five of the ten funds would have outperformed the index fund. Finally, you may compare the performance ranking on an unadjusted basis with that after adjusting for risk. While there are some similarities, it is interesting to see for example that AIM Constellation fund drops from #2 to #6 while the Copley fund improves from #7 to #2.

A risk-adjusted return is simply a means of comparing the total return per unit of risk for different funds. It is not the actual return, and it does not mean that the fund having the highest risk-adjusted return is necessarily the right fund for you. It does mean that you should not accept a fund that exposes you to unnecessary risk to achieve its return. Table 22 shows an interesting comparison between Strong Opportunity fund and AIM Constellation. Both delivered high returns of 15% to 17%, but Strong Opportunity achieved these returns with about half the risk (beta) of AIM Constellation and thus achieved about twice the risk-adjusted return. Similarly, both the Copley fund and Mutual Shares achieved around 11% return — but Mutual Shares exhibited higher risk in achieving it, making the Copley fund the better performer per unit of risk.

These are simple examples of how you may use risk-adjusted performance to avoid unnecessary risk in achieving whatever level of return you select. Some investors will take the position that they don't care abut the level of risk provided that they are adequately rewarded for it. In this case, remember that past high performance does not necessarily signify future high performance, but past high risk is most likely to indicate future high risk. You can only tell in retrospect whether the high risk was rewarded with high returns.

Finally, on the question of beta, it is necessary to refer to recent academic studies reported by professors Fama and French at the Center for Research in Security Prices in the

Graduate School of Business of the University of Chicago. They have produced evidence that during the period 1963-1990, probably in contrast to earlier periods, the simple relationship of beta to average returns did not exist. In other words, increasing risk was not necessarily rewarded by increased returns. They found that this simple relationship was complicated by several other factors such as company size, market valuation and leverage. Further studies will be required to clarify this challenge to the conventional wisdom which has been generally accepted by the professional investment community for many years.

Although beta is the most widely used measure of market risk there are others that can be used to great advantage.

## ALPHA

This is not strictly a measure of risk but is a measure of a fund's performance due to factors other than its level of market risk. It is, therefore, an expression of risk-adjusted performance. For a single stock it is the business, or unsystematic, risk associated with a company or industry. However, in a diversified mutual fund it is one way of measuring the effectiveness of portfolio management, given a certain level of risk. It is calculated by comparing the actual return to the expected return.

For example, an alpha of 5.0 simply means that over a given period the performance has averaged 5% per annum more than would be expected by its beta value. It is, in a way, the value added by the stock selection and management skills of the advisor. All means of measurement have their limitations and this is no exception, but as a broad generalization, the best managed diversified funds with reasonable operating expenses tend to have a positive alpha, while the lower performing funds of a given risk level tend to have a negative alpha. Alpha values are calculated from beta coefficients and, like beta, can only be used effectively with well diversified stock funds and not with, for example, highly specialized sector funds. Small differences in alpha value are of little significance but large differences may well be. As an example, the top three performing funds in Table 22 had an average positive alpha of 0.6, while the bottom three had an average of -7.5.

## R-SQUARED

This is the percentage of a fund's price movements that are explained by movements in the market, as defined by the S&P 500 index. Index funds attempting to match the S&P 500 index will have an R squared ($R^2$) close to 100 while sector funds will tend to have low $R^2$ values. This is not so much a direct measurement of risk as a measure of diversification across the domestic stock market. If a broadly diversified fund has an $R^2$ very close to 100, you may be paying relatively high expenses to achieve the performance of an inexpensive index fund. $R^2$ is calculated as the square of the correlation coefficient.

## RETRACEMENT

The shortcomings of risk measurements such as beta are that they measure fluctuations in value, whether gains or losses. Increasing asset values are not a risk for investors yet they influence beta coefficients just as much as do decreases in value. In practice an investor is only concerned about exposure to loss, not to gain. One simple means of measuring the historical exposure to loss is to measure retracement, or declines from a previous high. This is a technique frequently used in highly leveraged and volatile investments but can equally well be used in an unleveraged mutual fund portfolio.

Retracement should be measured over a period of several years and can simply be the sum of the percentage weekly or monthly declines, if any, from the previous high, divided by the number of periods. But you do not need to start crunching numbers to use such a measure. It has all been done for you. Morningstar Mutual Funds, a publication of Morningstar Inc., is probably the ultimate source of data on thousands of mutual funds and is most likely available at your local library. It contains all the risk measurements that we have discussed and a great deal of other valuable information. Morningstar Mutual Funds uses a risk measurement based on the concept of retracement. They measure monthly fund returns in relation to Treasury Bill returns, add together the amounts by which the fund trails this measure and divide this by the period's total number of months. The resultant number, the average loss statistic of a fund, is then compared to those of other funds to generate a comparative risk rating. Measures such as this are more meaningful than a simple beta coefficient. They measure the historical record of loss rather than of total volatility.

Several other simple measures can be used effectively to measure historical losses. The percentage of years with negative returns, the average loss in negative years and the percentage of years that returns were less than a money market fund are all useful measures when compared to a suitable index or to a group of funds having similar objectives. This type of information is readily available in some of the more sophisticated newsletters such as the L/G No-Load Fund Analyst newsletter.

## STANDARD DEVIATION

The beta coefficient measures just part of a fund's volatility, that attributable to market risk. It does not measure it in absolute terms but only compared to the performance of the S&P 500 index. To answer the question "how volatile is my diversified domestic stock fund compared to the S&P 500?" — it is a good measure. However, to answer the question "How volatile is my investment in absolute terms?" — you need to use the measure of standard deviation. This will measure total volatility from all causes.

If you plot the monthly gains and losses of a stock fund, you will find that with most funds the changes are usually no more than about 5% positive or negative with a few more positive values than negative. Occasionally you may find the variation as much as 10% and very occasionally even more. The values will deviate from the mean, with most of them clustered close to the mean and fewer and fewer values as you move further away from the mean.

This effect is shown in Figure 12, which represents a normal distribution curve forming a typical bell shape. The mean value is represented by the central vertical line passing through the middle of the bell. Invariably in such a situation, 68% of all values will fall within one standard deviation of the mean and 95% will fall within two standard deviations. The width of the bell-shaped curve depends upon the magnitude of the standard deviation. A highly volatile fund would show a broader, flatter curve and a less volatile one having a lower standard deviation would be taller and narrower. But in all cases, 68% of values will be within one standard deviation, and 95% will fall within two standard deviations. Three standard deviations, although not shown in the Figure, include 99.7% of all values on every occasion.

The use of standard deviation, like most measurement techniques, does have some limitations. It only has meaning when compared to the average that it relates to. Also it is based on the assumption of a normal distribution, that is equal fluctuations on each side of the mean. This is not strictly

FIGURE 12

STANDARD DEVIATION OF THE STOCK MARKET

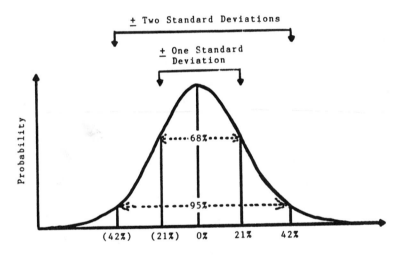

Annual Fluctuation

Notes:
-The annual standard deviation of the domestic stock market has averaged approximately ±21%, assuming a normal distribution. This means that 68% of the time it will be within 21% of its mean and 95% of the time it will be within twice this range.

-Numbers in parenthesis indicate negative values.

correct for the stock market, which exhibits a general long-term upward trend. In spite of these limitations, standard deviation is widely used by professional money managers and permits generally valid comparisons which cannot readily be made in other ways.

The numerical value of a standard deviation increases over time as the possibility exists for wider fluctuations to occur over increased time periods. Most commonly, standard deviations are quoted as either monthly or annual values. Over the period 1926 to 1990, the average annual standard deviation for the domestic stock market was 21% (over a shorter time period it may be closer to 20%). Figure 12 shows along the horizontal axis a gain or loss of 21% within one standard deviation and 42% within two standard deviations.

What does this mean in practice? It means that about two-thirds of the time (68%) the annual fluctuations of the stock market will not exceed plus or minus 21%. It may, of course, be very much less. One hundred dollars of typical stock will stay within the limits of $79 and $121 two-thirds of the time on an annual basis. Likewise, it will stay within the range of $58 and $142, 19 times out of 20 on an annual basis. In fact, over an extended period the losses will be less and the gains will be greater due to the long term upward trend of the market. The historical volatility of stocks, bonds and Treasury Bills can be directly compared using standard deviation, as shown in Table 23. It shows the maximum volatility that has been experienced at two different frequencies for different types of investment. The greatly increased volatility and risk of common stocks compared to Treasury Bills is the reason that investors are rewarded with an Equity Risk Premium which may almost double the return received on Treasury Bills, as we saw in Figure 11.

TABLE 23

**AVERAGE VOLATILITY OF STOCKS, BONDS AND BILLS**

Historical Annual Fluctuations of $100 Invested

|  | Two Years Out of Three (One standard deviation) | Nineteen Years Out of Twenty (Two standard deviations) |
|---|---|---|
| Common Stocks* | $79 - $121 | $58 - $142 |
| Long Term Government Bonds | $92 - $109 | $83 - $117 |
| Treasury Bills | $97 - $104 | $93 - $107 |

*Actual losses will be less and gains will be greater to the extent of the upward trend of the market.

RISK-ADJUSTED RETURN
USING STANDARD DEVIATION

Just as we could adjust returns for comparative market risk
or volatility expressed by beta, so we can now adjust for total
volatility of all types using standard deviation. The resulting
number is sometimes known as the Sharpe ratio named after
Professor William Sharpe, Nobel prize winner and professor at
Stanford University. The formula is similar to that used
previously:

$$\text{Total Risk-Adjusted Performance} = \frac{\text{Total Return Less Riskless Return}}{\text{Standard Deviation}}$$

Now, we are measuring total volatility due to all causes and
are not just comparing it to a specific market index. We can
broaden our choice of funds for comparison, and don't have to
stick to the market as represented by the S&P 500 index.
Table 24 shows a selection of 13 funds including aggressive
growth, growth, growth and income, equity income, international equity and specialty sector funds together with United
States Government bond funds, international government
bond funds and municipal bond funds. They can all now be
compared directly using risk-adjusted returns. Table 24 shows
that of all these funds, the highest risk-adjusted performance
during the period came from fund #3, MFS Worldwide Government Trust, an international government bond fund which
provided a return of 16.44% with a monthly standard deviation
of only 2.27%. This fund took far greater risk than the other
bond funds listed but much less than the stock funds. Among
the stock funds, the international funds performed well and
produced higher returns than the aggressive growth fund (#10
Founders Special), and did so with considerably lower risk.
When an equity fund has a monthly standard deviation ap-

TABLE 24

RISK-ADJUSTED RETURNS OF SELECTED FUNDS USING STANDARD DEVIATIONS

| Name of Fund | Annualized 5 Year Tot. Return (to 1/1/91) | Standard Deviation (monthly) | Risk-Adjusted* Performance | Ranking Un-Adjusted | Ranking Risk-Adjusted | Type of Fund |
|---|---|---|---|---|---|---|
| Vanguard Specialized Health Care | 19.22% | 4.44% | 2.80% | 1 | 2 | Equity, Sector |
| T R Price Int'l Stk | 18.28% | 5.19% | 2.21% | 2 | 4 | Equity, Int'l. |
| MFS Worldwide Govt Trust | 16.44% | 2.27% | 4.24% | 3 | 1 | Bond, Global Govts. |
| Janus Venture | 15.92% | 4.39% | 2.08% | 4 | 6 | Equity, Small Company |
| Scudder Int'l | 15.88% | 4.91% | 1.85% | 5 | 7 | Equity, Int'l. |
| Vanguard Energy | 15.48% | 4.15% | 2.09% | 6 | 5 | Equity, Sector |
| Janus | 14.43% | 5.37% | 1.42% | 7 | 9 | Equity, Growth |
| Financial Ind Income | 13.03% | 4.98% | 1.25% | 8 | 11 | Equity, Income |
| S&P 500 Index Fund | 12.78% | 4.39% | 1.36% | 9 | 10 | Equity, Growth & Income, Index |
| Founders Special | 12.03% | 7.36% | 0.71% | 10 | 12 | Equity, Agg. Growth |
| Stein Roe Managed Municipals | 10.56% | 1.34% | 2.80% | 11 | 2 | Bond, Municipal |
| T R Price Short Term Bond | 7.63% | 0.52% | 1.58% | 12 | 8 | Bond, Corporate Short Term |
| 20th Cent US Govts | 7.35% | 0.78% | 0.69% | 13 | 13 | Bond, US Government Short Term |

* Total return less riskless Treasury bill return (6.81%), divided by the standard deviation. Also known as the Sharpe ratio, it measures comparative return per unit of total risk, as measur' by volatility.

proaching six or more, it is generally difficult for it to compete on a risk-adjusted basis with the many funds that produce good returns with lower levels of risk.

On the other hand, a low standard deviation in no way implies a good risk-adjusted return. Fund #13, Twentieth Century U.S. Governments, had the lowest standard deviation of all the funds but also had the lowest risk-adjusted return due to its low total return. Although very safe, this type of fund is likely to provide a return below your break-even point as we defined it in Chapter 2 and almost certainly below the level required to meet your financial objective as discussed in Chapter 3. However, the top half of the funds in Table 24 on a risk-adjusted basis would have been more likely to have met your objectives and to have done so without unnecessary risk, if they were part of a well diversified portfolio. It is significant that although fund #11, Stein Roe Managed Municipals, had a good but not excellent total return and a low but not very low standard deviation, the combination elevated it from #11 to #2/3 on a risk-adjusted basis. This, together with its tax advantaged character, made it one of the best investments.

## HOW TO AVOID UNNECESSARY RISK

We can now pull together much of what we have learned about risk and develop a specific list of key actions to help avoid unnecessary risk. Some of these actions were outlined in the "Ten Basic Rules of Investing" in Chapter 2 and others have been discussed in Chapters 4 and 5. We are now in a position to add our new knowledge to these earlier considerations.

First, we will list the key actions, and then we will review each item in turn. They are as follows:

1. Understand the various types of risk and how to measure them.

2. Accept only the unavoidable risks at a level most appropriate to your particular circumstances.
3. Select your investments in accordance with your time horizon.
4. Diversify investments by category (e.g. equity and fixed income) and asset class (e.g. bonds and money markets within fixed income). Maintain separate portfolios for each category.
5. Diversify by specific market segments (e.g. domestic and international stocks).
6. Diversify by fund objectives (e.g. growth or income for stock funds) and investment style (e.g. value or growth for stock funds).
7. Select individual funds on a risk-adjusted basis.
8. Get out of the market when it becomes exceptionally risky.

These actions, when taken together, will give you an exceptional advantage in managing risk.

1. UNDERSTAND THE VARIOUS TYPES OF INVEST-MENT RISK AND HOW TO MEASURE THEM

These have been covered earlier in this chapter, and we now know the main types of risk, several of which are virtually eliminated in a well diversified mutual fund. We have warned against permanent loss of principal over all other types of risk and have identified volatility as being synonymous with most types of risk. We have discussed beta, standard deviation and retracement as different ways of measuring volatility and risk, each having its own particular uses.

2. ACCEPT ONLY THE UNAVOIDABLE RISKS AT A LEVEL MOST APPROPRIATE TO YOUR CIRCUM-STANCES

We have concluded that you cannot avoid risk, but you can decide the types of risk to which you will be exposed. Which is the greatest threat to you? Purchasing power risk, default risk, interest rate risk, or market risk? The short-term investor should avoid market risk and interest rate risk as he does not have the time to ride out the inevitable market cycles. He is obliged to accept purchasing power risk by investing in cash equivalents and short-term debt obligations in which the principal is stable. The same may be true for the investor of very limited means living off investment income. He may not be able to accept the risks associated with higher returns in stocks or even bonds. On the other hand, the very long term investor can accept market risk but not purchasing power risk. Only the very wealthy investor should consider accepting default risk with any significant portion of his assets. The lesson of junk bonds should not be forgotten.

You established your risk tolerance in Chapter 4; now you can refine it further by establishing what types of risk that lets you accept.

3.  SELECT YOUR INVESTMENTS IN ACCORDANCE WITH YOUR TIME HORIZON
    This is one of our ten basic rules of investing outlined in Chapter 2. We showed in Table 20 the frequency of losses over different holding periods. There is about a 31% chance of loss in stock values in any one year but this declines to 12% over five years, 4% over 10 years and near 0% over any 25-year period. The position of long-term government bonds was rather similar. This is an important consideration. If you are a long-term investor not needing to liquidate your investments for many years, you have the great advantage of a steadily declining cumulative risk. We can now express this concept using standard deviation.

TABLE 25

THE EFFECT OF DURATION OF INVESTMENT ON RISK-ADJUSTED PERFORMANCE

| | Investment Period (Years) | | |
|---|---|---|---|
| | 1 | 4 | 16 |
| Annualized Standard Deviation of S&P 500 Index | 20% | 10% | 5% |
| Average Annual Range 2 Years out of 3 (one standard deviation) | 80% - 120% | 90% - 110% | 95% - 105% |
| Average Annual Range 19 Years out of 20 (two standard deviations) | 60% - 140% | 80% - 120% | 90% - 110% |
| Annualized Total Return | 12% | 12% | 12% |
| Return Per Unit of Risk (12%/Standard deviation) | 0.6 | 1.2 | 2.4 |

Table 25 shows the annualized standard deviation of the S&P 500 index for varying periods. At one year it is about 20%, but for a four-year period, the annualized rate drops to 10% and in 16 years it is only 5%. These losses and gains are not, of course, eliminated by extending the investment period to 4 or 16 years, but the average annual range becomes narrower. Thus, after 16 years the investor will still have experienced the losses or gains of one year, but on average the annual gains or losses become less. Table

25 assumes an annualized total return of 12%, and dividing this by the level of risk (standard deviation) shows the return per unit of risk. This increases progressively as the time period increases, growing from 0.6 at one year to 2.4 at 16 years.

The obvious conclusion is that the longer your investment period the better value you stand to get from the market. If you may need to liquidate your investments within a year or two, you are getting much poorer value, and you should limit your investments to cash equivalents or short-term bonds.

4.  DIVERSIFY BY INVESTMENT CATEGORY AND AS-SET CLASS
    The fundamental key to risk management and the most important aspect of diversification is the prime allocation of assets into different broad categories of investments as equity, fixed income and tangible assets. Next in impor-tance is allocation into asset classes such as stocks, real estate, bonds, money markets, etc. We discussed this in Chapter 4, illustrated the process in Figure 3 and presented specimen portfolios in Figures 4 through 6. We empha-sized the importance of keeping quite separate portfolios, at least for fixed income and equities and not trying to be in the ideal place all the time with all your assets. You may finish up in the wrong place at the wrong time and lose the money game.

This prime level of diversification is one of the most important decisions you have made.

5.  DIVERSIFY BY SPECIFIC MARKET SEGMENTS
    We showed in Figure 3 that having decided, for example,

p. 82

to hold 50% stocks it was then necessary to diversify the stock holdings into market segments such as large company domestic stock funds, small company domestic stock funds and international stock funds. The reason for this became evident when we looked at the correlation coefficients in Table 18. Remember that diversification towards an efficient portfolio reduces risk without sacrificing returns. This is how to manage risk.

6. DIVERSIFY BY FUND OBJECTIVE AND INVESTMENT STYLE

The final level of diversification addresses the particular type of fund, its investment objectives as stated in the prospectus and its investment style. For instance, our example in Figure 3 just states that 20% of the portfolio is in large company domestic stocks. Now at this level we decide what type of large company domestic stock fund to select. Should its objective be aggressive growth, growth with income or primarily equity income? Or should you invest in a non-diversified sector fund such as a utility company fund?

The answer is that the investor should not be limited to any one of these types of fund but may choose several. Each type tends to do better under different economic conditions and at different stages of the market cycle. During the early stages of a bull market, aggressive growth and growth funds may do best, whereas later in the cycle growth and income or equity income funds may excel. In an environment with declining interest rates, a utility fund may perform at its best. You cannot and should not invest in every type of fund, but you should invest in more than one. Even a fairly conservative portfolio can accommodate some higher risk within a diversified selection.

The second factor to address is the investment style. There are many different styles of investing and the style of your investment managers can provide another useful means of diversification - if their styles are different. Suppose you plan to invest in two growth funds, one of your funds could be a fund that emphasizes growth above all else. It will tend to buy expensive stocks with high price/earnings ratios and low dividend yield but with high earnings growth. These tend to be the "hot" stocks that everyone wants and they may or may not continue to grow fast. Such funds will often have rather high turnover ratios and, therefore, high fund transaction expenses as they frequently buy and sell the stocks of the moment.

In contrast, the other fund may be value oriented and seek out unpopular stocks with good fundamental strengths but which are selling at a low price, perhaps below their book value, and are providing above average dividend yield. The investment manager sees more merit in these stocks than does the general investing public and so he buys them cheaply. They are often in unglamorous industries, but given good judgment and time, they may thrive and ultimately become popular high priced "hot" stocks. At this time the manager would sell them at a substantial profit. This approach is known as value investing and represents one important style.

There are other important styles of management. Some funds stay fully invested at all times, while others increase their cash holdings if they anticipate a market decline. They are not always right. Others will invest only in companies with strong balance sheets, large cash flows, high market shares or simply perhaps a perceived outstanding ability of a company management. Yet others may specialize in merger and acquisition candidates, while some may rotate the type of stock held in anticipation of perceived investor enthusiasm. Some types of stock become fashionable for a while, based often on investor emotion and over-reaction.

An indication of fund style may be obtained from the prospectus but also from shareholder reports and published interviews with fund managers. You may also look up a fund in a good fund reporting service such as Morningstar Mutual Funds. From this you can examine for each fund its turnover ratio, $R^2$, P/E ratio, price/book value ratio and the major industries and size of companies in which the fund is invested.

This is often a better approach, as quite frequently the title of a fund, or even its prospectus, does not adequately reflect its nature. It may, for example, provide no clue as to whether it invests primarily in large, medium or small capitalization companies or whether its style of investing is mainly value investing, growth investing or a blend of both. The interaction of these variables can be expressed in a simple matrix format. An example is shown in Table 26. This type of format has recently been adopted by Morningstar Mutual Funds, which allocates each domestic equity fund in their universe of funds into an appropriate box in the matrix. This is not based on the title of the fund, or even its description in the prospectus but rather upon the actual quantifiable analysis of its portfolio.

Small company funds are those having a portfolio median market capitalization of less than $1 billion; medium sized are those between $1 and $5 billion and large sized are those above $5 billion. Likewise, the investment style is based upon actual measurement of the relative price/ earnings ratio and the price/book value ratio of each fund.

Generally, the more conservative growth, growth and income, and equity income funds fit into the upper left hand part of the matrix, while the more aggressive growth and small company funds generally fit into the lower right hand part of the matrix. The middle ground is occupied mainly by general growth funds, the more volatile growth and income funds and the tamer small company funds.

Table 26 shows, for each box, the percentage distribution of all equity funds to that box and the typical relative historical risk level associated with the funds in that box. For example, small cap growth funds account for about 10% of all funds in the Morningstar universe of funds. They have shown a risk level 25% above the average for all equity funds.

By contrast, the opposite corner of the matrix shows that the large cap value investing funds also account for about 10% of all funds, but they have shown about 21% less risk than the average of all funds.

This type of matrix can be extremely useful in helping to assemble a balanced portfolio of funds to meet your own specific requirements. If you place your funds within such a matrix, it permits you to see the degree of diversification by both company size and investment style. It serves to warn you immediately if you have too great a concentration of funds having similar characteristics. It also clearly shows the historical risks associated with each category. Best of all though, this type of matrix gives you a visual overview of your portfolio based on objective measurements.

TABLE 26

**INVESTMENT STYLE MATRIX**

|  | VALUE INVESTING | BLEND | GROWTH INVESTING |
|---|---|---|---|
| LARGE CAP. | FUNDS: 10.2% (1)<br><br>**RISK: 0.79** (2) | FUNDS: 17.3%<br><br>**RISK: 0.82** | FUNDS: 12.7%<br><br>**RISK: 0.91** |
| MEDIUM CAP. | FUNDS: 14.6%<br><br>**RISK: 0.83** | FUNDS: 8.7%<br><br>**RISK: 0.97** | FUNDS: 12.8%<br><br>**RISK: 1.12** |
| SMALL CAP. | FUNDS: 7.5%<br><br>**RISK: 1.05** | FUNDS: 5.5%<br><br>**RISK: 1.09** | FUNDS: 10.1%<br><br>**RISK: 1.25** |

(1) Percent of stock funds qualifying for category
(2) Market risk level. 1.00 = the average Morningstar risk
    for equity funds.

Source: Morningstar Mutual Funds, May & June, 1992.

The combination of diversification across both fund objectives and management styles will add a valuable further level of stability and risk reduction.

7.  SELECT INDIVIDUAL FUNDS ON A RISK-ADJUSTED BASIS
    We have discussed this fully earlier in this chapter. You are now able to make these important comparisons using beta coefficient and standard deviation. The use of risk-adjusted performance will do much to avoid unnecessary risk for whatever level of return you seek.

8.  GET OUT OF THE MARKET WHEN IT BECOMES EXCEPTIONALLY RISKY
    There are times in the stock market cycle when an unusual level of risk exists. At such times when the market is grossly overvalued, risk can be very greatly reduced by withdrawing to the safety of a money market fund until at least a normal level of risk exists. We shall discuss this further in Chapters 11 and 12. The longer term cyclical market timing that we shall describe may be practiced, not primarily to enhance returns, but rather to reduce risk. If this can be achieved with even partial success, it will avoid the greatest fluctuations in value and, therefore, very substantially reduce overall risk.

These then are the key actions you should take to reduce risk in your portfolio. Taken together the use of these techniques will put you ahead of the great majority of amateur investors and not a few professional money mangers.

Having now acquired these skills it is time to turn our attention to the interesting task of shopping for specific mutual funds.

CHAPTER 7

# THE INCREDIBLE CHOICE OF FUNDS

By providing funds to satisfy almost every conceivable investment need, the mutual fund business has grown to become a flourishing more than one trillion dollar industry, serving one quarter of all households in the United States.

Gone are the days when a mutual fund was either a general stock fund, a bond fund or a money market fund. Today's investor has developed broader and more sophisticated requirements, and the industry has been quick to meet the need. This evolution is still continuing — in five or ten years there will be types of funds as yet unheard of.

Most of the innovations meet real investment needs while a few may satisfy mere whims of the moment. Examples of useful innovations might include a wide selection of index funds offering investments in entire markets, whether they be the world, the U.S.A., or a specific industry or commodity. Funds investing in the bonds of governments around the world or in global real estate investments have added new and useful possibilities for investing. The emergence of funds investing solely in other mutual funds meets the needs of some indecisive investors. Most of these innovations would be largely unavailable to the investor in individual stocks. On the other hand, the so-called asset allocation funds seemed to arise out of investor's emotional reaction to the 1987 stock market crash and have yet to prove their worth as a real and useful innovation.

There are now more than 3,000 funds from which to choose, so you may need a little help. In this chapter we shall review some, but not all, of the types of funds available. These are your building blocks, and you need to understand how each building block fits into the overall structure of your diversified portfolio. Later on, in Chapter 14, we will show you where to find current information on the best funds within each of these various types.

## THE CLASSIFICATION OF FUNDS

This may follow several paths. We are not considering here the so-called closed-end funds which trade on the stock market, usually at a premium or at a discount to their net asset value. They add yet another unnecessary element of risk. We have discussed load versus no-load funds and have indicated a preference for true no-load funds or at worst low load funds. This is an important distinction and most of the examples given in this book will be of no-load funds. Another means of classification is as diversified or undiversified. Whereas the diversified funds own stocks broadly positioned across the market, undiversified funds are strongly focused on one or a few types of stock. They are frequently sector funds and may concentrate on one industry, one commodity such as gold, or on one foreign country. Undiversified funds are taking a larger risk by putting all their assets into one narrow area. If this is the area of choice at the time, they will do very well, but if not — look out! These funds frequently appear both among the best performing funds and also among the worst.

Another way of classifying funds is by whether they are invested in equities, including stocks of all types, or whether in fixed income investments such as bonds. As we have seen, this is an important and very basic distinction.

A simple classification of funds and their objectives is shown in Figure 13. This shows just the principal types of funds and relates them to each other. You can compare money market funds having a fixed principal and fluctuating yields with bond funds, where the principal will also fluctuate in value and with equity income funds, whose main function is to provide dividend income but which may also provide modest capital growth. Then you can make the comparison with growth and income funds which tend to be middle-of-the-road funds providing both some dividend income and some capital gain. Finally the international stock, growth, small company and aggressive growth funds all have the prime objective of capital growth with income as a secondary consideration. Aggressive growth funds may adopt more risky techniques such as leverage and trading options in an attempt to achieve maximum capital gains.

The values shown for returns are annualized total returns over a ten-year period and will, of course, vary over different time periods. Relative risk is the typical standard deviation for the type of fund and will also vary somewhat over time.

These are the main choices for your portfolio, and we will now examine each type in further detail, starting with the various types of equity funds.

## TYPES OF EQUITY FUNDS

The principal types of equity funds are analyzed in Table 27. Our earlier consideration of mutual funds in Chapter 5, and of risk in Chapter 6, now lets us characterize a fund type

FIGURE 13

### THE CHOICE OF MUTUAL FUNDS

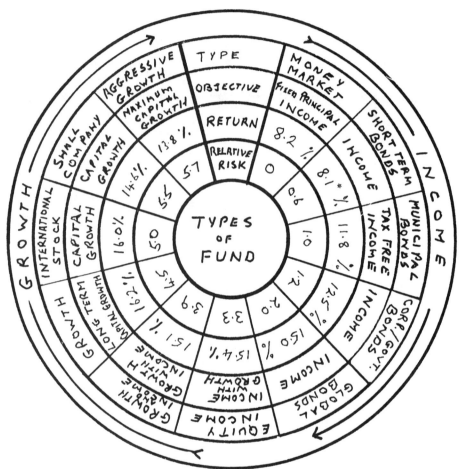

*   "Return" values represent total returns over a recent ten
    year period except for Short Term Bonds which represent
    a five year period.

    "Relative Risk" values represent average monthly standard
    deviations for a recent three year period.

    Additional types of funds exist which are not reflected
    here.

    All values will change somewhat over different time periods,
    especially total returns. These reflect historical values
    as of mid 1992.

TABLE 27

**AN ANALYSIS OF EQUITY MUTUAL FUNDS**

| Type of Fund | Alpha | Beta | Standard Deviation (%) | Turnover Ratio (%) | Expenses (%) | P/E Ratio | Total Return (%) |
|---|---|---|---|---|---|---|---|
| Aggressive Growth | 1.8 | 1.19 | 5.7 | 147 | 1.85 | 24.6 | 13.8 |
| Growth | 0.4 | 1.01 | 4.5 | 102 | 1.34 | 21.6 | 16.2 |
| Small Company | (0.1) | 1.14 | 5.5 | 89 | 1.44 | 23.7 | 14.6 |
| Growth & Income | (0.8) | 0.85 | 3.9 | 76 | 1.26 | 18.5 | 15.1 |
| International | (5.8) | 0.77 | 5.0 | 71 | 1.72 | 20.6 | 16.0 |
| Equity Income | (1.4) | 0.74 | 3.3 | 69 | 1.16 | 17.4 | 15.4 |
| Specialty (Sector): | | | | | | | |
| Financial | 0.2 | 1.12 | 6.1 | 151 | 2.00 | 13.3 | 16.4 |
| Health | 23.1 | 1.15 | 6.1 | 75 | 1.33 | 25.4 | 25.8 |
| Nat. Resources | (4.8) | 0.65 | 4.6 | 94 | 1.71 | 20.2 | 10.1 |
| Technology | (0.8) | 1.25 | 6.9 | 158 | 1.55 | 25.7 | 12.1 |
| Utilities | 3.0 | 0.51 | 3.1 | 42 | 1.33 | 14.5 | 15.7 |
| S&P 500 Index Fund | (0.2) | 1.00 | 4.2 | 23 | 0.22 | 18.3 | 17.7 |

Based on data from Morningstar Mutual Funds, as of May 1992. Total Return is for a ten year period annualized. Values in parenthesis are negative. All values will change somewhat over different time periods, especially total returns.

rather easily and succinctly with a simple set of numbers. Remember, however, that the numbers are just a series of snapshots of a given time period and will vary somewhat over different time frames. Experience shows that risk levels and expense levels tend to remain fairly constant over time, whereas total return can vary widely. The time period chosen included the crash of 1987, as well as a bear market at the beginning and towards the end of the period. Remember that these are average numbers representing both the good funds and the very poor. In the next chapter we shall discuss how to pick the best funds. If you manage to only pick funds in the top third, your performance will be substantially above the average values shown here.

The first column of Table 27 reveals the very mixed quality of funds, as many types show an average negative alpha. If you simply picked a fund with a significantly and consistently positive historical alpha, you would most likely do better than the average. For example, the extremely high alpha value for specialty health funds is reflected in its very high total return.

Beta and standard deviation are again averages and a wide range of values exists within any fund type. For example, in the case of growth funds, individual betas range from less than 0.5 to more than 1.2; the former being lower than the average for any type of equity fund and the latter being higher. Remember that beta can only usefully be used to compare diversified general domestic funds and not international or specialty funds. In this regard, standard deviation is a more useful measure.

The expense ratios are high in many cases and for a portfolio of domestic diversified funds, there is no need to average more than about 1.0%, particularly if you include some index funds.

The price/earnings ratios are measures of how expensive the shares in a fund are in relation to the earnings of the company. The more aggressive funds tend to buy shares at higher market values, as they are popular and sought-after shares.

Total return figures should be treated with caution and should not be considered necessarily representative of future performance.

At the bottom of Table 27, the Vanguard S&P 500 index fund is shown as a benchmark for comparison. It has been hard to beat.

The table does not include the so-called hybrid funds, such as balanced funds and asset allocation funds, which hold both stocks and bonds. We concluded in Chapter 4 that it was preferable to manage your equity and fixed income portfolios quite separately and not attempt to mix them.

Overall, what Table 27 should tell you is that unless you are truly prophetic and can forecast the economic and financial conditions of the future, you should diversify across several types of fund, mainly using diversified rather than sector funds and choosing the better quality funds in each type. It also shows that the more aggressive types of fund are not always the winners over a 10-year time period. During this particular time period the conservative, low risk utility funds out-performed the higher risk aggressive growth funds, and the conservative equity income funds slightly out-performed the more volatile small company funds. The unexciting index fund out-performed every type of fund except the specialty health funds. Now we will take a closer look at each of these various types of funds.

Aggressive Growth Funds seek maximum capital gain and in attempting to achieve this, they may take unusually high risks. They are likely to buy volatile stocks and trade them actively using, in some cases, options and leverage. They may not be broadly diversified. They have a low current income of around 1% and a less stable principal than most types of fund.

They are not for the faint of heart, for those requiring liquidity, or for anyone who cannot or should not assume above average risk. Aggressive growth funds may, however, fulfill a useful role in balancing the risk level of an overall portfolio, particularly for investors having a long investment time horizon. The best stage of the market cycle to own aggressive growth funds is in the early stages of a strong bull market when they may out-perform all other types of fund.

Small Company Funds seek growth through investing in companies with low market capitalization. These smaller companies are more volatile than most and may pay little or no dividends. Income is not a significant contributor to total return, and the principal value of the funds may fluctuate considerably. Historically, the value of small company stocks has grown faster with more risk than that of larger company stocks, which makes intuitive sense when you think about it.

If all the stocks traded on the New York Stock Exchange are divided into ten groups, according to their size as measured by market capitalization, it has been shown that as you move progressively from the largest capitalization group to the smallest, both the total return and the standard deviation will fairly consistently increase. During the period 1926 to 1987, the largest capitalization stock group had an average annual compound return of 9.1% and an annual standard deviation of 19.4%, whereas the smallest capitalization group had values of 15.5% and 46.0% respectively.

This situation has caused investors to seek small company stock funds in the hope of achieving spectacular returns, but the other significant fact to consider, and one that is rarely mentioned, is that this higher-than-average performance has only occurred at certain times and for unknown reasons. From 1926 to 1963, the return from small company stocks was similar to that from larger stocks. Then from 1964 to 1983, small stock values increased an amazing 26 times compared to only a four fold increase in the S&P 500 index. Since that time, throughout the remainder of the 80's, they have consistently underperformed the market leading to widespread disenchantment but eternal hope. Based on their more recent performance it looks as though they may re-emerge as performance leaders in the 90's.

Their long-term performance over the last decade certainly does not justify including small company stocks in your portfolio, but there may still be good reason to do so. First, it provides useful diversification with an average $R^2$ value lower than that of most general types of domestic funds. Second, one day they will start another long period of rapid growth relative to the market, and this may well already have started. Third, although the average performance has been poor in recent years there have been winners. Remember that all funds of a given type are not necessarily similar in performance or risk. Small company funds such as Founders Frontier and Janus Venture have comfortably out-performed the total market over the past several years.

Growth Funds invest for long-term capital growth rather than income. Principal value fluctuates significantly. They generally invest in medium to large-sized companies which may be well known household names. Their focus is often on blue chip companies whose long-term earnings growth may exceed that of the market, and as they trade less often than the more aggressive funds, their turnover ratio and expense ratio tend to be lower.

High quality growth funds belong in the portfolios of most long-term investors as they tend to reward the investor adequately for the level of risk assumed. They are particularly appropriate during the first part of a bull market. There are several hundred funds which may be classified as growth funds and their levels of risk and return vary widely. No-load growth funds that have performed well in recent years in relation to the level of risk assumed include among others, Gabelli Asset, Gabelli Growth, IAI Regional, Janus, T. Rowe Price Capital Appreciation and the Lindner Fund.

Growth and Income Funds are the most popular types of equity funds and account for about $100 billion of assets. They seek both long-term growth of capital and current dividend income. The funds tend to invest in well established companies having significant and reliable dividends. Some of the assets may be in utility companies, convertible bonds and regular bonds to enhance income. This permits them to have some lower yielding growth stocks while still achieving the objective of the fund. Compared to the more aggressive funds, growth and income funds tend to have lower risk, lower expenses, lower turnover and lower market value as defined by price/earnings ratios and price/book value ratios.

Some growth and income funds almost certainly belong in your equity portfolio, unless you want an overall portfolio of extremely high or extremely low risk. These are the classic middle-of-the-road equity funds. They will be out-performed during the initial stages of a bull market but will come into their own when the market is going nowhere in particular, which is what it does most of the time.

If you should want a no-load growth and income fund which has the lowest expenses, the lowest turnover ratio and has been in the top one-third of all growth and income funds for much of the past decade, you could select Vanguard Index Trust 500 Portfolio, which passively manages the stocks in the S&P 500 Index. Other growth and income funds that have performed somewhat comparably, but with slightly lower betas, include Founders Blue Chip and Fidelity Growth and Income Fund, the latter being a low load fund.

International Funds are those funds which invest totally in markets other than the United States. However, sometimes global funds are included within the classification of international funds. Global funds, as their name suggests, may invest in any country of the world, including the United States. International funds may have the world excluding the United States as their investment universe, or they may be constrained by the fund's objective to invest only in a given continent, region or single country.

The advantages of broad international investing are that it adds excellent diversification, the markets may move in different cycles and there are more investment opportunities, frequently with less competition than in the domestic market. It has also historically offered good risk-adjusted total returns. The disadvantages include the added exchange rate risk as well as local market risk , and perhaps psychologically, the investor may be uncomfortable with investments in markets of which he may know little.

Overall, there is no reason to limit your investments to one country of the world such as the United States when you can profitably invest in them all. International stock funds belong in all well diversified portfolios. This type of fund has become increasingly popular in recent years, and we are beginning to see fragmentation of the type, not only by geographical area but also, for example, by company size and general aggressiveness. This trend will doubtless continue. International funds are the subject of Chapter 9.

Equity Income Funds invest in companies having rather high dividend yields, as their prime objective is the production of income, with any capital appreciation being incidental. They may also own a small proportion of bonds. They are exposed to relatively low levels of risk, but nevertheless, both principal value and income will fluctuate. There are two particular advantages to funds which rely mainly on dividend income. First, dividend yield is a much less volatile component of total return than is price appreciation and second, over time a company's dividend will increase, leading to further income growth. This compares favorably to a fixed income investment such as a bond, where the initial coupon rate is fixed and the interest payments do not increase over the life of the bond. This, of course, is why a bond is called a fixed income investment.

Many investors do not realize that over extended time periods the total return on stocks has been about half due to capital appreciation and half due to income. The capital appreciation component has shown a fairly high standard deviation of well over 20%, whereas the income component has shown a standard deviation of only 1.3%. On a risk-adjusted basis the income component is obviously a better proposition. Equity income funds exploit this advantage.

This type of fund belongs in most diversified portfolios, whether they are heavily weighted towards equities or fixed income investments. They can add a little spice to an essentially fixed income portfolio, or serve as an element of relative stability in a mainly equity portfolio. Their fairly low typical turnover ratio and expense ratio may permit very efficient operation. A good equity income fund such as Financial Industrial Income Fund has been turning in a positive return for each of the past ten years and has averaged well over 15% annual compound return during that period.

Specialty Funds are a mixed bag of undiversified funds which focus on a specific industry or other narrow area of investment. They are also known as sector funds as they represent one particular sector of the market They present the considerable risk of investing in one narrow field, but if you wish to do so, they will diversify you within your chosen area. There is an appropriate fund covering almost every area, whether it be in restaurants, computers, transportation, bio-technology, electronics, real estate or whatever. The most favored investment areas are financial service companies, the health industry, natural resources, precious metals, technology and utilities. Natural resources and precious metals, both being tangible assets, are only poorly correlated with the stock market and thus provide useful diversification. Utility companies have a relatively low risk and provide a higher level of dividend income than most. The health sector is one that has performed very well since the mid-80's and a specific focus on this area would have provided about a 20% annual return. If you are an aggressive investor, some of the more volatile sectors such as technology can provide you with an exhilarating and perhaps profitable ride.

These funds do not belong in every portfolio, but they may have a place either as a stake in tangible assets through real estate, precious metals and natural resources or else as the more aggressive part of an equity portfolio using sectors such as technology, health or financial services. Watch out for high expense levels and very high turnover ratios.

Index Funds are those funds which seek to match the performance of a well known market index. Such funds may, for example, represent the domestic stock market, small company stocks, domestic bonds or international stocks. They offer an inexpensive and very simple way of investing in an entire market. These funds are the subject of Chapter 10.

Social Responsibility Investing (SRI) involves the introduction of social, environmental and political idealism into the investment decision-making process. It basically expresses a wish to be doing good while financially doing well.

This market segment has grown rapidly, increasing more than ten-fold in value since 1984. Church organizations, certain pension funds and some individuals are seeking investments in companies which meet their definition of social responsibility. This may, for example, exclude companies involved in armaments, nuclear power, tobacco, alcohol, gambling and environmental pollution. In the past, they have nearly all been opposed to investing in South Africa. They may favor Third World investing in certain types of projects and investing in companies whose labor relations they believe to be correct. Surveys have shown that individual social responsibility investors are typically women, baby boomers and school teachers who live in the North East or North West, probably have a college education and have inherited wealth. Their investment alternatives are tracked by the Social Investment Forum in Minneapolis.

The mutual fund industry, as always, has been quick to fill this market niche with specialized funds which seek to direct investment assets either towards or away from certain types of endeavors depending upon their social viewpoint. These SRI funds should not be confused with bona fide sector funds such as environmental services or pollution control, which are considered by many to be promising areas of investment in their own right.

SRI funds include Calvert Social Investment Fund, Dreyfus Third Century Fund, Pax World Fund, the New Alternative Fund and the Parnassus Fund. Two of the oldest and more financially successful no-load SRI funds are Pax World Fund and Dreyfus Third Century Fund, both of which have been in existence for more than 20 years. SRI is not new.

Some investors may consider social responsibility investing as the application of unnecessary constraints on the investment decision-making process, while others find it a comfortable way of nurturing both their principal and their principles.

Fund of Funds are mutual funds that invest solely in other mutual funds. This concept has some merit if you are an indecisive investor seeking broad diversification or if you just want the ultimate convenience of one-stop shopping. Naturally, most fund families offering such funds invest in other funds within their own family. This type of fund can incur a double layer of expenses, which is unnecessary. At least two good no-load fund families offer such funds without any additional charge over that associated with the underlying funds. Vanguard Star Fund is invested solely in a range of Vanguard equity and fixed income funds while T. Rowe Price offers two funds, Spectrum Growth and Spectrum Income, which each invest solely in the appropriate funds within the T. Rowe Price family.

## TYPES OF FIXED INCOME FUNDS

The general nature of fixed income investments was discussed in Chapter 4. Here we will consider money market funds and several types of bond funds as a practical means of achieving a diversified fixed income portfolio.

You may, of course, buy individual bonds rather than bond funds, but small parcels of bonds bought retail are expensive. Usually it is necessary to buy at least $25,000 to $50,000 of a single bond to buy and sell it at a reasonable price. Small lots of bonds may be difficult to sell and the bid-asked spread may be unusually wide. You will also need to shop from broker to broker as there is no fixed price for a bond. However, if you hold the bonds to maturity the problem of selling does not occur and you are assured of repayment of principal, whereas a bond fund has a continuous existence with a fluctuating net asset value. Funds do offer an extraordinary degree of diversification together with expert selection of the bonds. They also monitor their portfolio on an ongoing basis to ensure that the bond quality remains satisfactory and that the weighted average duration of the portfolio is likely to optimize returns, consistent with the fund's objectives.

There are many different types of bonds from which to choose, and unless you are knowledgeable in a given field of bond investing, you are probably better off in a well-managed no-load bond fund which has a good track record and low expenses.

premium = a sum above the nominal or par value of a
thing; of higher price or cost; great value or esteem;
a bonus, gift, or sum additional to price, wages,
interest, or the like.

The principal types of bonds funds are shown in Table 28. Total returns during this ten-year period averaged around 11-13%, except for global bond funds which were higher at 15%. The municipal bonds produced tax advantaged returns similar to those of taxable bonds. This represents outstanding value, particularly on a risk-adjusted basis. Standard deviations are much lower than those of an average equity fund, indicating lower volatility of price.

The column showing average bond maturity in years is, in fact, a measure of interest rate risk. When interest rates rise, bond values decline and the extent of decline increases with the remaining duration of the bond. This effect is shown in Table 29. For example, you can see that a bond having an 8% coupon, in the presence of a two percentage point rise in market interest rates, will decline in price by 18.9% if it has 30 years to maturity. It will only decline by 5.1% if it has three years to maturity and only 1.9% if it has just one year to maturity. This is why shorter term bond funds are more stable in price as interest rates change. A consequence of this is that shorter term bond funds also miss most of the possible capital appreciation when interest rates fall. Well managed funds will, to some extent, extend maturities as interest rates fall and shorten them as rates rise. The significant opportunities for both capital gains and losses, in addition to interest income, means that bond funds must be compared and evaluated on a basis of total return and not solely on the level of current income.

Money Market Funds were discussed in Chapter 4. They are a safe and convenient place to put money while awaiting an investment opportunity, and they may have a place to add stability to an otherwise volatile portfolio. Most offer convenient services, such as writing checks against their accounts and switching by telephone between a money market and other funds within the same family.

TABLE 28

AN ANALYSIS OF BOND MUTUAL FUNDS

| Type of Fund | Alpha (%) | Standard Deviation (%) | Turnover Ratio (%) | Expenses (%) | Average Maturity (Years) | Income (%) | Total Return (%) |
|---|---|---|---|---|---|---|---|
| Municipal Bonds: | | | | | | | |
| National | (1.2) | 1.0 | 66 | 0.80 | 19.5 | 6.6 | 11.8 |
| Single State (excl. California & N.Y.) | (1.2) | 1.0 | 24 | 0.67 | 21.9 | 6.6 | 12.7 |
| Corporate Bonds: | | | | | | | |
| General | (0.8) | 1.3 | 133 | 1.06 | 11.2 | 8.5 | 12.9 |
| High Quality | (0.2) | 1.2 | 99 | 0.80 | 11.6 | 7.9 | 12.5 |
| Government Bonds: | | | | | | | |
| General | (0.6) | 1.3 | 201 | 1.13 | 12.7 | 8.1 | 11.6 |
| Mortgage | 0.5 | 1.1 | 148 | 0.99 | 14.9 | 8.2 | 12.4 |
| Global Bonds | 0.7 | 2.0 | 226 | 1.58 | 7.0 | 8.9 | 15.0 |

Based on data from Morningstar Mutual Funds, as of May 1992. Total Return is for a ten year period annualized. Values in parentheses are negative. All values will change somewhat over different time periods, especially total returns.

**TABLE 29**

THE EFFECT OF CHANGES IN INTEREST RATES ON THE VALUE OF A BOND

(8% Coupon)

| Bond Duration (Years to maturity) | Change in Interest Rates | | |
|---|---|---|---|
| | 1% | 2% | 4% |
| Rise in Interest Rates | | | |
| 1 | (0.9%) | (1.9%) | (3.7%) |
| 3 | (2.6%) | (5.1%) | (9.8%) |
| 5 | (4.0%) | (7.7%) | (14.7%) |
| 10 | (6.5%) | (12.5%) | (22.9%) |
| 20 | (9.2%) | (17.2%) | (30.1%) |
| 30 | (10.3%) | (18.9%) | (32.3%) |
| Fall in Interest Rates | | | |
| 1 | 1.0% | 1.9% | 3.9% |
| 3 | 2.7% | 5.4% | 11.2% |
| 5 | 4.2% | 8.5% | 18.0% |
| 10 | 7.1% | 14.9% | 32.7% |
| 20 | 10.7% | 23.1% | 54.7% |
| 30 | 12.5% | 27.7% | 69.5% |

Values in parenthesis are negative.

Although the principal value of a money market fund is fixed, the yield will fluctuate. The yield is a function of four factors - current short-term market interest rates, the credit worthiness of the borrower, the expenses of the fund and the tax status of the investments.

Short-term interest rates have fluctuated widely over recent years based partly on the expected inflation level. They reached a peak of 12% in 1982 and have been on a generally declining trend since then.

The credit worthiness of the borrower is of importance, but due to the very short-term of the debt and the stringent requirements of the SEC, the default risk is extremely low. Some money market funds remove even this risk by investing only in the short-term obligations of the United States Government.

The expenses of the funds may vary widely and should be scrutinized. They must be clearly shown at the front of the prospectus. Some money market funds have total expense ratios of over 2%, whereas others are less than 0.3%. You are getting about the same level of service in both cases, but the higher expenses are removing maybe 30 to 40% of your gross investment income. You cannot afford high expenses in a low yielding investment such as a money market fund. Sometimes, due to competitive pressures, a money market fund management will absorb part or all of the expenses of a fund for a period of time. This may represent good value - while it lasts. In any case, there is no need to accept total expense levels of more than 0.5%. A good benchmark for comparison of funds is the Vanguard Money Market Reserves, Prime Portfolio.

The tax status of a money market fund can be of great significance. Tax-free money market funds invest in the short-term obligations of states and local governments and offer a lower gross income, but if you are in a high federal tax bracket, you may well be better off on an after-tax basis. It is easy to calculate this using the following formula:

$$\frac{\text{Tax Free Yield x 100}}{\text{100 Less Marginal Tax Rate}} = \text{Taxable Equivalent Yield}$$

For example, if you are in a 31% tax bracket and the yield on a tax-free money market fund is 5%, then the yield on this fund is equivalent to the yield of a taxable fund yielding,

$$\frac{5}{\text{100 Less 31}} \text{ x } 100 = 7.24\%.$$

If you are in a 15% tax bracket, your taxable equivalent would be,

$$\frac{5}{\text{100 Less 15}} \text{ x } 100 = 5.88\%$$

You can maximize money market returns by periodically checking which is the better type of fund for you. At the highest tax it will frequently, but not always, be the tax-free fund. While these funds are free of federal income tax, remember that they may be subject to state taxes. Similarly, money market funds that invest exclusively in the obligations of the federal government are free of state income tax in most states.

Short Term Bond Funds have characteristics between those of money market funds and general bond funds. If you seek a little higher yield than money market funds offer and can tolerate a relatively small fluctuation of principal, a short-term bond fund, either taxable or tax-free may be just right for you. Table 28 showed them to have the lowest standard deviation of any type of bond fund and a duration typically of around two to three years. Table 29 shows how this short duration will minimize fluctuations of principal value due to changing interest rates.

On a risk-adjusted basis, short-term bond funds, either taxable or tax-free, can be attractive as a conservative part of your total fixed income portfolio, or as a temporary parking place for money while awaiting other investments. You only have to put up with the possibility of rather minor fluctuations in value of the principal. Examples of good quality no-load short-term bond funds would include Fidelity, T. Rowe Price, Scudder and Vanguard shorter-term bond funds, investing in both corporate and government debt; Federated Short-Intermediate Government Trust, investing solely in United States Government debt; or Vanguard Municipal Bond Fund Short-Term Portfolio as a tax-free bond.

Municipal Bond Funds have portfolios of debt instruments issued by states and local governments and are generally not subject to federal income tax on their income distributions. Municipal bonds are also frequently free of state and local taxes for residents of the state in which they are issued. For this reason several families of funds now offer municipal bond funds limited to the bonds of a single state, to provide income substantially free of tax for in-state residents.

For high tax bracket investors, municipal bond funds have provided a very attractive element of a fixed income portfolio. For example, during the ten-year period ending June 1992, 199 taxable bond funds tracked by Morningstar Mutual Funds had an annualized return of 12.60%, while 168 tax-free funds had an annualized return of 11.71%. At a 30% marginal tax rate that 11.71% is equivalent to 16.73% before tax (excluding any tax on net capital gains). Residents of most high tax states would have benefited even more if they had owned in-state bond funds. Using the same numbers, at a 35% total tax rate, the before-tax equivalent would have been 18.0%. On a risk-adjusted basis this represents outstanding value.

Municipal bond funds may be classified by bond duration,

by credit risk and by tax status. As we saw in Table 29, the longer the duration the greater the price volatility. As an example, within the Vanguard Group there are short-term, limited-term and long-term municipal bond funds. The short-term fund has a weighted average maturity of one to two years and a recent standard deviation of 0.28%. The limited term has a maturity of from two to five years with a recent standard deviation of 0.52%, while the long-term fund has a maturity of 15 to 25 years with a recent standard deviation of 1.73%. As duration increases, so does the typical total return and, of course, so does the risk.

The default risk of the bonds in a fund is indicated by their credit rating, as determined usually by Standard and Poor's or Moody's rating services, as discussed in Chapter 6. In the case of Standard and Poor's rating, the highest rating is AAA, followed by AA and A. All of these indicate good quality investment grade bonds. Next comes BBB, which is still considered investment grade but which may reflect less capacity to pay interest and to repay principal than the higher rated grades. This is followed by BB, B, CCC, CC and C, which are increasingly speculative. Moody's rating service uses Aaa, Aa, A and Baa for investment grade bonds, again in declining order of quality, and Ba, B, Caa, Ca and C for increasingly speculative bonds. Their investment grade bonds are further differentiated by a number from one to three, one being the highest quality and three the lowest. Many bonds are un-rated, not necessarily because they are of poor quality but because the issuer has not incurred the expense of having them rated.

Some bonds that would otherwise have lower ratings are insured against default, and the rating attached to such bonds is then measuring the credit worthiness of the insurer. Insured bonds usually have a AAA rating, but, in reality, the ability of an insurance company to pay up in the event of really extensive nationwide bond defaults has never been challenged and is perhaps questionable. Most municipal bond funds invest predominantly in good quality investment grade bonds with perhaps a few carefully selected un-rated bonds.

The "high yield" municipal bond funds, of which there are about 20, invest in somewhat lower grade bonds and have produced a generally higher total return. Typically they will hold about 20% of un-rated bonds, 20% of BBB rated bonds, a few lower grades and the remainder A rated bonds. Before investing in any bond fund you should find out from the fund or from a fund rating service just what proportion of each grade of bond the fund currently holds. This is not necessarily specifically included in the prospectus.

The tax status of municipal bond funds has already been discussed. Remember that it is only the interest payments that are free of federal tax, and frequently, this applies also to state income tax for in-state residents. Municipal bonds are now one of the very few tax-free sources of income. Do not confuse tax-free and tax-deferred investments. The latter merely delays the painful process, whereas the former eliminates it.

Corporate Bonds are subject to many of the considerations discussed under municipal bonds with two important exceptions. First, they are secured by the assets and future earning ability of the corporate issuer, rather than by the taxing ability of states and municipalities. Second, the interest income is fully taxable.

The credit worthiness of corporate bonds is rated by Standard and Poor's and Moody's in the same general way as municipal bonds and the same considerations apply. However, whereas a typical general municipal bond fund holds nearly all investment grade bonds, a general corporate bond fund tends to be of lower quality with more B rated bonds. There are, however, high grade corporate bond funds which contain virtually only investment grade bonds. In recent years these higher grade funds have performed at least as well as the lower grade somewhat riskier funds.

At the lower end of the market are the junk bonds, more correctly known as high yield corporate bonds. These comprise mainly low grade speculative and un-rated bonds leading to the rather high standard deviation seen in Table 28. Their high risk has not typically been rewarded by high total returns. In fact, they have performed far worse than the highest quality corporate bond funds, because their higher yield has been offset by a high default rate. Do not take unrewarded risk.

The choice between corporate or municipal bond funds of comparable quality and maturity should be determined by comparing after-tax returns. This can be determined by using the simple formula shown under the discussion of tax-free money markets. The only difference here is that while money markets have a fixed principal, in the case of bonds there may be capital gains as the result of falling interest rates and these will be taxed. Since this will apply equally to both corporate and municipal bonds and cannot be anticipated, the comparison may be made just on the interest income.

Government Bonds Funds invest only in the debt instruments of the federal government and its agencies. These may be Treasury Bills, with maturities of from 90 days to one year, notes with maturities of one year to ten years, bonds with maturities of 10 to 30 years or mortgage debt guaranteed by a federal agency. All of these underlying fixed income investments are guaranteed by the full faith and credit of the United States Government. This does not mean that the funds themselves are guaranteed by the government, and it certainly does not mean that the market value of the bonds is guaranteed. It does mean that the underlying investments of the fund are guaranteed against default risk but not against interest rate risk.

The interest from direct debt instruments of the federal government is not subject to income tax at the state and local government level. In states having high levels of tax this is an important advantage over corporate bonds. You should compare the current after-tax total return of high quality corporate bond funds with that of government bond funds of similar maturity.

Many government bond funds are known as Ginnie Mae (GNMA) funds which have the majority of their assets in mortgage pools issued by the Government National Mortgage Association, (A United States Government corporation within the Department of Housing and Urban Development), and guaranteed by a federal agency such as the Veterans Administration. Funds may also hold similar securities issued by the Federal National Mortgage Association (FNMA or Fannie Mae) or by the Federal Home Loan Mortgage Corporation (FHLMC or Freddie Mac), both of which are supervised by the government but are not agencies of the federal government.

Government mortgage bonds provide generally higher returns than bonds issued directly by the United States Treasury, but their interest is not exempt from state and local taxes. In periods of lower interest rates, homeowners may repay or refinance the underlying mortgages of GNMAs at lower interest rates. As a result, the investor's yields may decline with those of mortgage interest rates. This is a risk not shared by other types of bond fund.

International Bond Funds are a relatively new innovation of the mutual fund industry, developed during the 80's. There are now more than a dozen such funds, but unfortunately, most of them are load funds. However, Fidelity, T. Rowe Price and Scudder offer no-load funds and doubtless more will emerge. The Fidelity and Scudder funds are really global bond funds, whereas the T. Rowe Price fund is a true international bond fund. Most such funds tend to have high expense ratios of well over 1% which, for a fixed income fund, represents a fairly high percentage of an average likely return.

On the other hand, during the ten years ending February

1992, international bond funds produced an annualized return of over 15%, beating every other type of taxable fixed income investment. In addition, they generally had the relative safety of a fairly short maturity.

However, during much of this time period they had the benefit of a generally falling dollar value. This may prove to have been an unusually prosperous time in the life of these young funds.

The principal countries invested in have been the United States, Canada, the United Kingdom, Japan and France, with smaller commitments to many other countries. Most of the holdings are issues of national or provincial governments together with a few major banks, utilities and general large corporations.

International bond funds are likely to continue to present a greater risk than domestic bond funds because of the additional exchange rate risk, and they may continue to have relatively high expense ratios. However, if a suitable fund can be found, the segment offers good long-term diversification within a fixed income portfolio and should be included on a rather limited and selective basis.

CHAPTER 8

# HOW TO PICK THE BEST FUNDS

Now we come to one of the most interesting and difficult challenges that the investor faces - how to choose the best funds. We know by now that we want to buy a particular type of fund and there are hundreds from which to choose. Does it matter which we choose? It most certainly does. If you had bought $10,000 of the Fidelity Magellan Fund and held it for ten years, selling it in early 1992, your $10,000 would have been worth more than $100,000. If, however, you had bought the 44 Wall Street Fund at the same time, your $10,000 investment would have been worth about $3,000. Yes, it does make a difference.

The successful investor is skeptical and does not always accept conventional wisdom. In this case, conventional wisdom says that you should identify a fund having objectives similar to your own, which has performed well over recent years ,and that you buy it and live happily ever after. As one well known mutual fund service says, "assuming careful selection on his part at the start and success in matching management objectives to his own, the investor should enjoy freedom from worry and detail for many years to come." This would be nice, but in this chapter we shall challenge some of the more comforting thoughts and look at the real difficulties and best approaches to fund selection.

There is no easy way to select the best fund and there is undoubtedly no certain way, but the probability of success can be greatly increased through a little careful study. We will consider the more important criteria which, when used together, will put you ahead of the game.

## FIRST DO THE SIMPLE THINGS

1.  MAKE SURE THAT YOU KNOW WHAT YOU ARE LOOKING FOR
    By now you should know a lot about the risk level, objectives and operating efficiencies of the fund that you are looking for. Don't be an impulse buyer.

2.  STUDY THE PROSPECTUS AND A GOOD FUND REPORTING SERVICE
    Study the fund prospectus, annual report and all other information available from the fund distributors. Then look up the fund in a good fund reporting service such as Morningstar Mutual Funds, which you will probably find in your local library. This will provide important information not contained in the prospectus. For example, it will include a great deal of useful information on the risk level and nature of the investments held and many aspects of the fund's historical performance. If you have further questions, ask the fund.

3.  PARTICULARLY, CHECK THE FUND OBJECTIVES AND RESTRICTIONS

From the prospectus, make quite certain that the fund objectives and restrictions are appropriate for you. Is this what you want done with your money?

4. PRACTICAL MATTERS

Is the fund registered for sale in your state? If not, they ought not to send you the prospectus. Is it quoted in the Wall Street Journal or Barrons? If not, it may have less than 1,000 shareholders and you should probably avoid it. Does it offer the services you want? Can you make telephone switches within the fund family? Can you make automatic withdrawals if you wish to? Does it severely limit your right to buy and sell with whatever frequency you choose? Are fund representatives helpful on the telephone? You will not need all the services that a good fund offers, but make sure that it offers the ones that you need.

Check when the next distribution from the fund is due. If it is just after you buy the fund, you will in effect get back part of the money that you just invested and will then be taxed on it as income. This is not a smart way to win the money game. If the fund has recently experienced a period of loss for good and proper reasons, does it now have a tax loss to carry forward? If so, that could reduce future tax liability on fund distributions.

5. FUND MANAGEMENT

You are entrusting your money to a single manager, several managers, or a committee, depending upon the fund. Most often it is a single manager. The manager is constrained in his choices by the provisions of the prospectus. However, within these limitations he has wide discretion. What do you know about him? First, find out from the fund the name of the manager and how long he or she has been managing the fund. That is the length of history you have with which to judge the fund. What his predecessor did is irrelevant. If the fund won't tell you who is managing the fund and how long he has been there — be cautious, there are plenty of good funds that will. Also ask the fund if the manager has recently given published interviews or written articles. These may give useful insights into his investment management style. Publications that present interviews or commentary about fund managers include the Mutual Fund Investment Report published by Wiesenberger and Morningstar Mutual Funds published by Morningstar, both likely to be at your library, and the Journal of the American Association of Individual Investors. The Mutual Fund Sourcebook, published annually by Morningstar, provides a useful profile of every fund manager that has one available. Among newsletters some of the most comprehensive analysis of fund managers is provided by the L/G No-Load Fund Analyst.

The style of the manager can be detected somewhat by examining the fund statistics in, say, Morningstar Mutual Funds. This will tell you the fund turnover ratio. Is he a heavy trader? It will tell about the companies the fund has invested in. For example, their average price/earnings ratio, price/book ratio, five-year earnings growth, return on assets, percentage of debt and the median market capitalization. This will give you a good feel for his style. Is he a high roller, churning the portfolio and buying high valued small company stocks having rapid growth and using extensive debt, or just the opposite?

If you like the management style, and either by luck or by skill he has produced good performance, you then have to wonder how long he may stay there. If you intend to buy and hold the fund, this is important. Studies have shown that if the manager is the primary owner of the management company or has a material interest in it, he is much more likely to remain in charge of the fund than if he is an employee of a large firm. It could also be argued that an employee, who may readily be fired for short-term poor performance, is more likely to follow the crowd right or wrong than is the owner-manager who has a longer time perspective.

Some of the no-load or low load fund families with a manager having a material interest in the business include Acorn, Evergreen, Gabelli, Mutual Series, Nicholas, Pennsylvania Mutual, Strong Funds, Twentieth Century Funds, and many of the Vanguard Funds. The case of Vanguard is unusual, as it hires outside management companies to manage many of its funds. Often the fund manager is an owner or part owner in the outside management company.

Studies by Morningstar of their entire universe of over 1,000 funds have shown the importance of the length of tenure of a fund manager. They divided all their funds into five groups based on the tenure of the manager; the shortest period being less than two years and the longest more than ten years. As the length of tenure increased, so did the risk-adjusted return and the assets of the fund, while the expense ratios and turnover ratios decreased. There are, of course, exceptions to this generalization, particularly in the case of already proven managers who are new to a fund. Quite clearly the need to have a time tested and outstandingly successful manager running your fund is of overwhelming importance.

6.   PAST PERFORMANCE

It is certainly true that past performance does not necessarily indicate future performance, and we shall be
discussing this in considerable depth a little later on. At
this point, just check to see that the fund you are
considering has had reasonable performance over the
past one, three and five years, or as long as the current
management has been in place.   Compare it to the
appropriate index, such as the S&P 500 Index, the
Wilshire 5,000 Index, representing the total domestic
quity market, or the EAFE Index for international equity
funds.   Details of the more commonly used market
indexes are given in Appendix D. You may also compare
its performance with a group of funds having similar
objectives.  Comparisons of this type are readily available
in some of the information sources described in Chapter
14.  One of the most convenient is the Lipper Mutual
Fund Performance Averages reported periodically in the
Wall Street Journal and weekly in Barrons at the end of
their section on mutual funds. Another good source is the
table entitled "Performance Summary by Investment
Objective" in the summary section of Morningstar Mutual
Funds. In this way you may compare the performance of
both equity and fixed income funds against their peers.

At this stage, the purpose of checking past performance
is to ensure that you are not looking at one of the funds
which is steadily declining into oblivion.  This happens
with some equity funds and for some reason investors
tend to stay with the fund. Occasionally, funds ultimately
close down and may even be investigated by the SEC as
happened with a fund family that lost a substantial part of
their investor's money over the years. Each of their funds
had negative alphas in the double digits.  More often,

funds that fail never die, they simply change their name or get merged with another fund. Remember that funds such as these are all included in the average fund performance figures, and just by avoiding them, you will significantly increase your probable rate of return.

7.   RISK
     We learned in Chapter 6 how to recognize the different types of risk, how to measure relative stock market risk or volatility using beta and how to measure absolute risk or volatility using standard deviation. We also learned how to compare risk-adjusted performance. We saw in Table 26 the historical risk of funds having different investment styles (such as "value" and "growth") and how this related to company size.

     In selecting an individual fund for your portfolio, you need to ensure that, at least in the past, the fund has given good performance per unit of risk accepted, when compared to its peers. If you are considering several funds, look up their total return, subtract the riskless Treasury Bill rate and divide by the standard deviation to arrive at a comparative risk-adjusted return. A simpler alternative is to look up its comparative risk level in a good mutual fund data source such as Morningstar Mutual Funds. All the work has been done for you. Don't accept risk without reward.

8.   ASSET CONCENTRATION
     You should not try to second guess the stock picking prowess of the fund manager. Remember that you are managing your portfolio, and he is managing one of your chosen funds, or at least one that you are considering. However, there are some broad considerations to look at.

Is he or she concentrating the assets of the fund in a few industries or areas of greatest promise and if so, is this simply and convincingly justified in the shareholder's information? Is he, on the other hand, holding hundreds of stocks across all industries, resulting in an $R^2$ of close to 100 and a beta close to one? If so, are you really buying an index fund, but one which is being actively managed, causing unnecessary expenses?

9.  FUND SIZE

Much has been written on the effect of the size of the fund on its performance. Once a fund enjoys a period of stellar success, more investors pour money into it, and it may grow from a few hundred million dollars in assets to several billion. For a bond fund this may not matter and it permits some economies of scale and lower expenses. However, for a stock fund it may make it harder to respond rapidly to changing market conditions. For example, if the Fidelity Magellan Fund, with assets of around $12 billion, wanted to invest just 1% of its portfolio in a promising small company, it could not. There just would not be that much stock to buy, and even if there was, it would immediately bid up the price of the stock. Similarly, if it wished to liquidate a small company stock holding, it would depress the price of that stock. On the other hand, a fund with assets of, say, $50 million could probably invest or divest 1% of its assets in a company fairly readily.

There can be no finite rule, but a fund investing in small company stocks has a greater advantage in being small. A growth and income fund investing in larger and more stable companies can probably accommodate larger assets without any problems. Many of the better funds recognize when they are growing too large, and in the interests of the shareholders, they temporarily close the fund to new investors. Sometimes, as in the case of the Sequoia Fund, an excellent growth fund may remain closed for years.

Probably it is unwise to invest in a fund with assets of less than $10 million, and if you want the fund to be fairly nimble in the marketplace, it should be no greater than $1 billion in assets. If you want to see your fund attempt to time the market or actively exploit smaller aggressive stocks, you may want to limit its size to around $500 million.

10. TURNOVER RATIO

A fund cannot trade without it costing you money as a shareholder. There is nothing inherently wrong with a high turnover ratio, provided that the extra performance from trading significantly exceeds the cost. All the time that a fund holds an appreciating stock there is no tax liability on the capital gain. As soon as it sells it at a profit a realized capital gain is recorded which will be passed on to you, the shareholder, as a tax liability. A fund with a very low turnover ratio is providing some tax deferred gain, just as though you owned a single stock and kept it to appreciate while only paying tax on the dividend until such time as you decided to sell it.

A turnover ratio of 100% means, of course, that during a 12-month period, on average the fund has replaced every stock or bond in its portfolio. The average turnover ratio for all equity funds is close to 100%, with some of the aggressive growth stocks and sector funds having the highest ratios of around 150%. The true index funds have some of the lowest ratios of frequently less than 20%. Taxable bond funds average around 150% turnover, while tax-free bonds are traded much less frequently and average about half as much.

If a fund under consideration has a turnover ratio above the average for its type, satisfy yourself that you are prepared to pay for it.

11.  EXPENSES
We discussed in Chapter 5 the question of expenses and concluded that whenever possible the shareholder transaction expenses, or different types of loads, should be zero. If this should be impractical on any occasion, then so-called low load funds should be used. These typically have upfront or back-end loads of 1% to 3%.

The total annual expense ratio charged to the shareholder depends largely upon the type of fund and the particular family of funds. Higher expenses don't mean either better performance or better service. Generally, aggressive equity funds have higher expenses while growth and income funds and equity income funds are somewhat less. Among fixed income funds, international bond funds tend to be the highest and municipal bond funds the lowest. The fact that a fund has no sales load does not necessarily mean that its operating expenses are low. Occasionally, a fund will be a no-load to get your business and then exploit you with an unreasonable expense level. The 44 Wall Street Fund has no initial sales load but has had total operating expenses greater than 9% annually. The difference between fund families is significant. The Vanguard group is the low cost standard by which others should be judged. Most of the large fund families are publicly traded or are part of large insurance companies or brokerage houses. Vanguard, on the other hand, is owned by the shareholders of its mutual funds. For this reason it manages its funds at cost.

In summary, currently for equity funds the average expense ratio is around 1.4%, but your average need not exceed about 1.0% and the Vanguard average is around 0.45%. For taxable bond funds, the average is around 1.0%, but your average need not exceed about 0.7% and the Vanguard average is around 0.36%. For tax-free bond funds, the average is around 0.75%, but your average need not exceed about 0.5% and the Vanguard average is 0.25%. For money market funds, the average is around 0.75%, but your average need not exceed 0.5% and the Vanguard average is around 0.28%.

12. ALPHA VALUES

There is no single measurement with which to assess the merits of a mutual fund or its management, but alpha values as we discussed in Chapter 6 are an approximate measure of the value added by management in a diversified fund. They are not infallible and close comparisons should not be made, but a fund having a significant positive alpha value is much more likely to have performed well, within its type, than one with a significant negative alpha. This simple distinction is often overlooked in the eternal and sometimes frantic search for the "best" fund.

We saw in Tables 27 and 28 that the great majority of all classes of funds, both equities and fixed income, had average negative alpha values. The better performers usually, but not always, have positive alpha values. To illustrate this, we averaged the alpha values of the top five and bottom five funds over a recent three-year period from the more than 1,500 funds tracked by the Mutual Fund Performance Report, a publication of Morningstar Inc. The top performing five funds showed gains of over 30% and had an average alpha of plus 14.8%, whereas the bottom five funds averaged a loss of 16.5% and had an average alpha of -19.5%.

You won't find the value of this measure discussed in the literature issued by the funds or by their trade associations for obvious reasons. There is even a tendency to discount its value at times. However, when used together with the other selection criteria, it can be a powerful tool to separate the extraordinarily good or bad from the commonplace.

These are the simple things that you can do to screen a fund. Most of these considerations apply to both equity and fixed income funds. For many fixed income funds this may be all that is needed, and you may now conclude your selection. For equity funds, due to their much higher volatility, there are other considerations which we shall shortly discuss. However, already you have applied more knowledge, common sense and selectivity than the great majority of investors. Not only have you selectively reduced the number of remaining funds to manageable proportions, you have also enormously increased your chances of profitable investment without unnecessary risk. This is the way to build wealth.

## THE FALLACY OF PAST PERFORMANCE

Almost always, when you read something about mutual

funds, you will see the statement that past performance does not necessarily indicate future performance. Having said that, the author invariably proceeds to discuss past performance as an indication of what the fund may do in the future. Never do you see the statement "therefore, we will not discuss past performance." Why this almost universal inconsistency? Which is correct, that past performance is useful or useless in anticipating future performance? Is there something to be learned from past performance, or do we just look at it because it is the only type of performance that we have? Is this just another manifestation of man's deep seated belief that somehow there must be a way of seeing the future?

The more sophisticated analysts may tell you that in general the past performance provides no prediction of the future, but the way they look at it is different. It may be just the past three years or five years or ten years performance that they think important. More thoughtful analysts look at fund performance separately, both in up and in down markets rather than continuous performance over many years. Is this really any different? Have they found a real truth?

In this section of the chapter we will attempt the difficult task of looking at this matter objectively. We need an answer in order to proceed with our task of picking the best funds.

Financial academics generally believe that the movement of stock prices is a random event in which the movements in one period are quite unrelated to movements in other periods. In other words, the past is no indication of the future. Statistical analysis of stock price movements over more than 60 years supports this theory, with possible minor exceptions. The academic view is also that the market is efficient; that every stock is, by definition, fairly priced at market value, as the information upon which the price is established by the market is freely available to all.

These theories, if true, suggest that stock picking is non-sense, as everything is fairly priced, there are no bargains and future prices are totally chance events unrelated to past prices. If this were completely and convincingly true, we could dispense with all forms of stock selection. Thousands of money managers and hundreds of newsletter editors would be otherwise employed. As it is, people pay large sums of money for their advice. They are frequently wrong, but rarely in doubt.

On the side of the financial services industry there is perhaps equally strong evidence. For example, the Value Line Survey, since 1965, has weekly been classifying groups of stocks according to their probability of beating the market over the next six to twelve months. The stocks in their highest rated group have on average almost invariably beaten the average of the stocks in the lower rated groups. Can this be due to chance?

Several studies have suggested that mutual fund managers cannot consistently out-perform the market, and we constantly see evidence of this. But what of the very few great managers who for decades have consistently beaten the market - names like Peter Lynch, John Neff and Sir John Templeton. Are their outstanding long-term track records entirely due to chance?

Let us leave the debate and focus back on the selection of our funds. It is useful to know of this dichotomy of opinion, but we have practical decisions to make. Conventional wisdom s ys, seek funds with outstanding past performance over severa years. If this is useful, then a top performing fund over the past one year or five years or ten years should also appear on the top performing list of funds during most other periods chosen. If it just appeared at the top during one of several time periods would that perhaps just be due to chance? So if we examine, say, the past six months, twelve months, five years and ten years, we might expect the top performing funds to appear at each, or most, of these time periods. Does this really happen? Table 30 shows the recent top ten growth funds for these time

TABLE 30

**THE TOP TEN GROWTH FUNDS FOR DIFFERENT TIME PERIODS**

| Three Months | One Year |
|---|---|
| American Pension Inv. Growth Trust (1) | Phoenix Capital Appreciation (1) |
| FPA Capital (1) | CGM Capital Appreciation (3) |
| United Growth (1) | Monetta (1) |
| Merrill Lynch Retirement Equity (2) | Merrill Lynch Retirement Equity (2) |
| Fidelity Growth Company (2) | Axe-Houghton Growth (1) |
| Massachusetts Inv. Growth Stock (1) | Fidelity Growth Company (2) |
| CGM Capital Development (3) | MIM Stock Appreciation (1) |
| Harbor Growth (1) | Wescore MIDCO Growth (1) |
| Pasadena Growth (1) | Brandywine (2) |
| Plymouth Growth Opportunities Port. (1) | Eaton Vance Special Equities (1) |

| Five Years | Ten Years |
|---|---|
| Idex (1) | Fidelity Magellan (1) |
| Aim Weingarten (2) | CGM Capital Development (3) |
| Fidelity Contrafund (1) | Phoenix Growth (1) |
| IDS New Dimensions (2) | Sequoia (1) |
| Strong Opportunity (1) | Quest For Value (1) |
| IAI Regional (2) | Janus (1) |
| 20th. Century Growth (1) | IDS New Dimensions (2) |
| Associated Planners Stock (1) | IAI Regional (2) |
| Thomson Growth B (1) | AIM Weingarten (2) |
| Brandywine (2) | New York Venture (1) |

The numbers in parenthesis indicate the frequency of appearance in the table.

periods. After the name of each fund appears the number of times it appears on the table. A total of 32 different funds appear on the table. Of these 32 funds, 25 (78)% appear only once in a moment of glory. Just six funds (19%) appear twice and only one fund (3%) appears on three occasions. No fund appears on all four occasions. What does this tell us? It indicates that there is little consistency in very high performance and that just looking at such past performance won't tell you much.

Perhaps your curiosity is drawn to CGM Capital Development, being the only fund that appeared on three out of four occasions. Is this perhaps a hidden gem? Hardly. It had a recent alpha of -2.4%, a beta of 1.28 and a standard deviation of 8.56%. It was the most volatile of more than 250 growth funds examined. Although in some years it ranked at the top, in others it sunk to the bottom 4% of all growth funds.

So much for the conventional wisdom of just looking at the winners of past years. The odds favor the proposition that once there, they may never reappear.

A more sophisticated approach is not just to measure performance over a given time but to measure it separately over both bull and bear markets. This has been the basis of the venerable Forbes magazines's annual fund performance ratings. These have been published each year since 1956 and constitute one of the longest periods of continuous data on mutual funds. Other magazines have more recently followed their approach.

The Forbes survey is published in the early September issue of Forbes magazines each year and compares hundreds of equity funds and fixed income funds. The survey measures performance both in up and down markets over the past three market cycles and places the most consistently high performers during this period in their annual "honor roll" of about 20 funds. This should be the cream of the crop from which to choose. Is it?

We have examined the performance of all open-ended domestic funds in each year's honor roll over a ten-year period to determine whether this is a useful approach to fund selection. We need to know whether it really has any useful predictive value in selecting funds which will show superior performance in the future. Our study assumes the purchase of all the qualifying funds in the honor roll and replacing them one year later with the next year's honor roll, starting in July 1981 and finishing in June 1990. The results are then compared to a Forbes composite of all stock funds surveyed and to the Vanguard Index Trust 500 Portfolio fund, representing the S&P 500 index. In addition to the average of the honor roll performance, we also examined the highest and the lowest performing fund in the honor roll each year.

For each of these measurements, the results were compounded annually to produce a comparable average annual compound rate of total return. The results are shown in Table 31. Buying and holding an index fund of the S&P 500 would have produced an average compound return of 16.3% per year. The Forbes stock composite of several hundred funds produced only 15.0%, and this reflects the under performance of most funds in the 80's compared to the market index. The honor roll funds, on average, produced about the same return as the composite. Throwing a dart at the funds to select them would have produced about the same effect. Even the careful study of performance in up and down markets over many years achieved nothing. This certainly challenges conventional wisdom, but is based on a large number of observations over an extended period. The honor roll out-performed the S&P 500 only in 1981, 1983 and 1988. The honor roll and the Forbes composite tracked very close to each other in most years.

Looking a little deeper, we see that investing in the subsequently best performers each year produced very large gains of 32%, whereas the worst performers only returned

TABLE 31

**PERFORMANCE OF THE FORBES "HONOR ROLL" OVER A TEN YEAR PERIOD**

Performance of the open-ended domestic funds in the Honor Roll, 1981 through 1990. Represents the first year of performance after being nominated to the Honor Roll.

| | Average Annual Compound Total Return |
|---|---|
| S&P 500 Index Fund | 16.3% |
| Forbes Stock Fund Average | 15.0% |
| Honor Roll Average | 15.4% |
| Best Performer Each Year in Honor Roll | 32.0% |
| Worst Performer Each Year in Honor Roll | 1.4% |
| No-Load Funds Most Frequently Appearing in the Honor Roll: | |
| Nicholas (9) | 19.2% |
| Twentieth Century Select (7) | 20.3% |
| Acorn (5) | 16.1% |
| Janus (5) | 21.0% |
| Mutual Shares (5) | 17.8% |
| Average | 19.3% |

Numbers in parenthesis indicate frequency of appearance over a ten year period.

1.4%. This is a disturbing lack of consistency among the honor roll, if this is the cream of the crop.

We then went back and selected out the no-load funds in each year and calculated the frequency with which they had appeared. Would consistency of appearance in the honor roll indicate good performance? Many funds appear just once, but we isolated those that had appeared in five or more of the ten years studied. The results in Table 31 show that, indeed, consistency of appearance was associated with well above average performance. On average, these relatively consistent performers achieved 19.3% return, well above the average honor roll return of 15.4% and above both the stock market composite and the S&P 500 index fund.

This leads us to a general observation that among any list of past high performers, however arrived at, there is a majority of funds which are there due to chance or unusual market conditions and which may never be there again. There is also a minority of funds which are there because they belong there, as consistently high performers. However, even these consistently high performers will have good and bad periods, and they will appear in lists of high performers repeatedly but irregularly, and perhaps not much more than half the time.

This brings us to an important conclusion, that there are basically "good" funds that are reasonably consistent in producing superior returns. Having identified these funds, then we need to recognize that each will have its own cycle of performance. This means that first we have to identify a preferred list of "good " funds, such as the example of the five funds shown in Table 31, and then we should invest just in those that are performing well at the time. That is, ones that are in the rising part of their own particular cycle. We shall be developing this approach further.

An examination of the top performing no-load fund in each year's honor roll is instructive. In every year, the top performer had a good previous ten-year performance but that, of course, does not mean that every fund with a good ten-year performance is a consistent performer. In any year, the number of no-load honor roll funds that beat the S&P 500 was small; in fact none did so in 1988 or 1989. Of those that did, we again see the more consistent performers; Mutual Shares and Nicholas did so for three years while Twentieth Century Select, Evergreen and Acorn did so for two. No top no-load honor roll performer ever reached the top again the following year.

We next determined how the honor roll candidates performed over time. Since this is intended to be a means of selecting funds to hold for some significant period, how well did they perform in the years following their recommendation and did they hold on to any advantage? In the year in which they qualified for the honor roll, that is the year immediately before they were recommended, they performed significantly better than the average. In the year following nomination, that is their first year of being recommended, they performed slightly better than the average, and in each of the following two years they were within 1% of the performance of the average. Thus any advantage gained in the first year was small, and there was no advantage in subsequent years.

Since being an occasional top performer is less significant than being a fairly consistently good performer, we questioned whether the better and more consistent funds would remain in the top quartile or even the top half of a group of similar funds. We examined 50 no-load growth funds over each of 11 years, ranking each fund each year within a larger universe of over 250 load and no-load growth funds.

We then determined how many years of the 11-year period each fund was in the first, second, third and fourth quartile. No fund remained in the top quartile or even the top half throughout the period. There are no funds for all seasons. A modest target for consistency was to be in the top half for more than half the time and never to be in the bottom quartile. Out of 50 funds, only five met this modest challenge. They were Ivy Growth, Janus, Neuberger Manhattan, Neuberger Partner and the Nicholas fund.

Although consistency was largely elusive, it became even more apparent that every good fund has its "hot" periods. Once or twice, or occasionally three times in a decade, half of these funds rose to the top quartile for more than one year. In fact, of the 50 funds, there were 30 occasions when a fund stayed in the top quartile for two more years and seven occasions when one stayed there for three or more years. The most consistent high performer was Twentieth Century Select, which was in the top quartile for six of the eleven years, although at times it was in the bottom quartile. Had it been possible to move from one fund which was ending a hot period to another just beginning one, the results would have been spectacular and switches would have been quite infrequent.

It is not meaningful to present all the details of this study, but the selection of just a few funds will illustrate the point. Table 32 shows just five of the no-load funds which have been in the top quartile for one or more years in an extended 12-year period. Their percentile ranking is shown for each year. For example, in 1982 and 1983, Twentieth Century Select was in the top 13% of all monitored growth funds. Rankings in the top quartile for two or more years are underlined. These are all historically top rated funds, yet all have spent some time in the bottom quartile of performance rankings. They have also spent two or three consecutive years in the top quartile. If we had a means of measuring which funds are hot and when they start to cool off, we could, for example, have bought Twentieth Century Select, then switched to Janus, then back to Twentieth Century Select, then to Mutual Shares, then to Twentieth Century Select, then to Mutual Shares and finally back to Janus. This is using three funds and just six switches in 12

TABLE 32

**SELECTED NO-LOAD GROWTH FUNDS WHICH HAVE BEEN IN THE TOP QUARTILE PERFORMANCE OVER A TWELVE YEAR PERIOD**

Annual Percentile Rankings of Growth Funds in Each Year

| Fund | 1979 | 1980 | 1981 | 1982 | 1983 | 1984 | 1985 | 1986 | 1987 | 1988 | 1989 | 1990 | 1991 |
|---|---|---|---|---|---|---|---|---|---|---|---|---|---|
| Janus | 35 | 15 | 11 | 37 | 27 | 39 | 75 | 76 | 42 | 43 | 2 | 22 | 25 |
| Mutual Shares | 20 | 94 | 8 | 90 | 5 | 2 | 66 | 32 | 25 | 4 | 92 | 77 | 91 |
| Neuberger Manhattan | 39 | 47 | 76 | 43 | 23 | 14 | 9 | 32 | 65 | 35 | 38 | 70 | 61 |
| Stein Roe Special | 10 | 15 | 88 | 18 | 8 | 43 | 48 | 47 | 39 | 25 | 11 | 56 | 51 |
| 20th Century Select | 12 | 19 | 38 | 12 | 13 | 81 | 23 | 14 | 28 | 90 | 8 | 21 | 59 |

Rankings underlined are in the top quartile for two or more consecutive years.

Based on data from Morningstar Mutual Funds, May 1992.

years. In practice this could never be done precisely, but it gives us a type of model to aim at. Even an imperfect switching system would avoid living through some of the otherwise inevitable years in the bottom quartile.

This switchback or counter cyclical effect is clearly shown in Figure 14, which depicts the 12 month trailing total return for three funds, plotted monthly for 4 1/2 years. The values were smoothed somewhat by using a three-month moving average. The heavy solid line shows an S&P 500 index fund as representative of the overall market. Against this can be compared two funds, Mutual Shares and Twentieth Century Select, which during this time period showed counter cyclical movement. Generally, when one was in the first or second quartile, the other fund was in the third or fourth quartile. Quite clearly, neither performed outstandingly well throughout the entire period when compared to the index fund, but each was hot during its own particular cycle. An ability to make a timely switch from one to the other would have been very well rewarded. Just as there is no class of investment for all seasons, so there is no single fund for all seasons, but the better ones have their own periodic seasons. The way to maximize profits is simply to capture them when they are hot.

So what have we learned and what is the fallacy of past performance? We have learned that a fund having been in the top 10 or top 20 for any prior period means very little and may simply have been due to chance. Certainly the element of chance diminishes with a period of, say, ten years but so does the relevance of this experience in today's market. Some of the high fliers of 20 years ago have disappeared. Some funds reach, if not the top, at least the upper quartile (which is a better measure) not entirely due to chance. They are more likely to show positive alpha values, and they will appear repeatedly, although irregularly, in the upper quartile over the years. Past performance can really only benefit us by its consistency rather

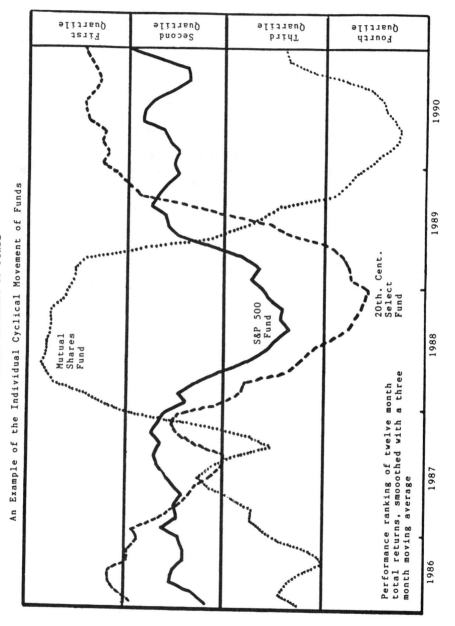

FIGURE 14

**THE COUNTER CYCLICAL MOVEMENT OF FUNDS**

An Example of the Individual Cyclical Movement of Funds

First Quartile

Second Quartile

Third Quartile

Fourth Quartile

Mutual Shares Fund

S&P 500 Fund

20th. Cent. Select Fund

Performance ranking of twelve month total returns, smoothed with a three month moving average

1986  1987  1988  1989  1990

than by its magnitude during a given period. Our study of the Forbes honor roll showed us that historically high performance was not at all predictive of future performance, but that knowing the frequency and consistency of past high performance might be of some value. The value of past performance, as such, is largely a fallacy. Consistent and repeated good (though not necessarily excellent) performance with the same management over many different time periods is what we should be seeking. We have shown, however, that even among the better funds, consistently good performance is very rare. To be in the top half for half of the time and never in the bottom quartile is a standard only achieved by about 10% of all growth funds.

## NOW COMPILE YOUR LIST OF WINNERS

We started this chapter looking for a growth fund. We have discussed in the first section the simple things to do to separate out the better funds of any type. This is the first and probably the most important screening process. The second screening process is the intelligent use of past performance, primarily to measure the consistency of acceptable performance. This second screen will remove the fund which chance has brought into the daylight and which is now being enthusiastically written about in the financial press. It will expose the gems which may never hit the top ten hit list and are rarely written about but which are the winners and are likely to make you the most money.

If you are prepared to spend the time and do the work, you can quite easily put together a list of basically good winning funds using this first and second screen. A visit to the library to consult a good fund tracking service will give you what you need. For example, Morningstar Mutual Funds will clearly show you the performance, each year for 15 years, of all the more than 250 growth funds that it tracks. Put together your own list of, maybe, 20 funds that meet the requirements that we have discussed and that you feel comfortable with. You will have to compromise on some of the criteria. The perfect fund does not exist. Only you can decide what are the most important features for you. You will find some gems. For example, look at the Brandywine fund if you want a slightly higher risk growth fund. It has been among the top performing growth funds for a recent one, three and five-year period. Look at the Twentieth Century funds if you want to be fully invested at all times, with no attempt at market timing by the fund. Look at the Vanguard funds if you want a wide selection of funds having very low expenses. Look at the Janus and Gabelli families. Go exploring.

If, on the other hand, you don't have the time or inclination to prepare your own list of superior funds, never fear — others have done it for you. The financial services industry provides every conceivable type of service. It is not as good as doing it yourself, because only you know your personal priorities, but it is better than not adopting a collection of winners. If you go this route, be selective and be skeptical. You are now relying on other people to make very important decisions for you. They don't have any magic knowledge that is not available to you. Examine several newsletters and mutual fund services that adopt a well founded set of criteria. Some of these are described in Chapter 14. One of the oldest mutual fund newsletters is Growth Fund Guide. Compare their selected list of funds to others. Check out the L/G No-Load Fund Analyst. It very carefully evaluates about 50 funds. If you are looking at Mutual Fund Values, examine their fund rating system. They apply a system of from one to five stars to the funds they rate, based mainly on a risk-adjusted historical return. If you use someone else's list of winners, check out their funds against your criteria.

Whether you do this yourself or rely on a publication in which you have confidence, you should now have a list of top quality funds with the characteristics that we have discussed in this chapter. You have dismissed all the "dogs" and collected the cream of the crop. However, remember that there is no fund for all seasons, so now we need to know when the good ones are hot and when they are not.

## HOW TO SPOT THE HOT FUNDS

Your first two screens have taken you from several hundred funds to a list of maybe 20 winners. Now we come to the third and final screen.

We have seen that even a good fund has a cycle of its own. This is not to be confused with the overall market cycle. We have been looking at rankings against similar types of funds, not absolute performance. The causes of a fund's own unique cycle are many. Most funds concentrate in certain areas of the market, with the expectation that they will soon rapidly grow in value. If the manager is right, the fund may take off ,and if he is smart enough to recognize value before the herd does, he may be sitting on rapidly appreciating assets. Sometimes, due to no action of the manager, his style of investing becomes fashionable. People suddenly want value investing or growth investing or whatever is the fashion of the time. And then there is the element of just blind luck; of being in the right place at the right time, by chance. Our job as investors is to manage our money by keeping it simple. It does not matter why a fund is hot, our only task is to be there at the right time and not to be there at the wrong time. This is not easy, and there are no guarantees of success. It is merely an alternative to buying and holding the same fund forever; you may choose which you wish.

First, we should clearly separate what we are considering from the frequent short-term trading of funds, which is a burden upon the industry and frequently upon the investor. We are considering moving out of a fund only when necessary, due to declining performance within its own cycle, which may last one or several years. Also, this is not "timing the market" which will be discussed later; this is optimal cyclical fund selection, assuming that you should be participating in the overall stock market.

Our objective should be to improve the odds in our favor by being in one of the better performing funds, not to achieve perfectly timed switches. However, a few percentage points of additional gain have a remarkable effect when compounded over time. There are several useful approaches to being in the best of your winning funds at any given time and we will now review them.

1. STAGES OF THE MARKET CYCLE

This is a simple guideline, whereby at different stages of the four-year market cycle, different types of fund are likely to be hot.

The early stages of a bull market are characterized by rapid growth when the more aggressive funds, and sometimes the smaller company funds, will excel. During the following stage of steady growth, the regular growth funds will perform well. Then, as the market cycle matures and growth slows down, the income component of the total return becomes more significant, so growth and income, and equity income funds tend to perform well compared to other types of funds. These more conservative funds are also very suitable to hold in the later stage of a market cycle. If you are invested during the subsequent inevitable decline, they will decline less than the higher beta funds.

## 2. HISTORICAL ALPHA VALUES

We have discussed the merit of examining alpha values under our list of simple things to do as part of your first screen. Funds having significantly positive alpha values may be expected to perform better than those having significantly negative values.

However, the alpha value of a fund does not change very rapidly, given consistent fund management. If it continues to remain high, the fund will inevitably perform better than expected in relation to its own beta value, at least for a while. Does this mean that the recent past alpha value of a fund can have predictive value in determining the future performance of the fund during the following months? Can we anticipate a period of future good performance? Theoretically this should be possible.

To investigate this approach, we selected 26 diversified domestic equity funds having positive alphas and an average beta of 1.0 over the prior three years and a similar group having negative alphas and also having an average beta of 1.0. The only apparent difference between the two groups was, therefore, their alpha values. We then measured the total return of each group over four consecutive and separate three-month periods. The results are shown in Table 33 and compared with the average performance of all domestic diversified equity funds.

During the first three-month period, the positive alpha group produced a total return of 20.6% compared to only 17.0% for the group having a negative alpha. This represented a 21.2% greater return (i.e. 20.6% versus 17.0%) for the positive alpha group. During the second three-month period, a rather similar advantage was seen.

TABLE 33

**THE INFLUENCE OF HISTORICAL ALPHA VALUES ON FUTURE FUND PERFORMANCE**

| Historical | | Fund Group | Subsequent Total Return | | | |
|---|---|---|---|---|---|---|
| Alpha | Beta | | First 3 Months | Second 3 Months | Third 3 Months | Fourth 3 Months |
| 6.0 | 1.0 | Group A – Positive Alphas | 20.6% | 13.0% | 6.7% | 6.8% |
| (6.6) | 1.0 | Group B – Negative Alphas | 17.0% | 11.1% | 4.4% | 4.5% |
| | | Domestic Diversified Equity Fund Average | 16.7% | 10.8% | 4.1% | 4.6% |

Each fund group contains twenty-six funds.
Period covers twelve months ending 10/91.

During the third and fourth separate three-month periods, the absolute rate of growth of the market was much less, but still the positive alpha group continued to out-perform the negative alpha group. The Domestic Diversified Equity Fund Average performed rather similarly to the negative alpha group throughout the entire period.

These results suggest that, on average, alpha values have some predictive value in anticipating fund performance, simply by the continuation for a period of an existing established trend. If you are looking for a hot fund among your list of winners, don't forget to check its alpha value over prior years.

3. PERFORMANCE RANKINGS

A great deal can be learned by studying the ranking of performance within a large group of mutual funds. It immediately removes performance related to the movement of the total market and limits it to a direct comparison with other mutual funds. Because individual funds have their own cycles, you can see many of the better funds periodically moving up the rankings, until they reach their zenith and then eventually start to decline.

Performance rankings can, of course, cover any chosen time period and the big question is - what period is best? This is hard to answer, but we know that one month performance is virtually a random event and does not normally indicate a meaningful trend. At the other end of the scale, anything over twelve months is of limited value as it measures history which is too old to be very useful for this purpose. The optimal period is probably between six and twelve months, depending upon the nature of the market. In a long steady climbing market we have found a

12 month performance ranking, smoothed with a three-month moving average, to be of value.  During the second half of the 80's, by using this measure it was possible to remain in one fund and be in the top quartile of a universe of funds for many months.   For example, Vanguard Trustees International Commingled fund remained in the top quartile for 28 months, Gabelli Growth for 25 months and Mutual Shares, Gabelli Asset, Stein Roe Special and several others for 15 months or more.  However, in the change from a bull to a bear market, a much shorter time period may be necessary to avoid false signals.

How you use performance rankings depends upon the frequency with which you are willing to switch funds.  We do not advocate frequent switching, but if you wish to, you may simply hold a fund until it ceases to be in, say, the top quartile or even the top 10% of a large group of funds, using a six or nine-month period for the rankings.

It usually takes a while for a fund to rise in its ranking towards the upper levels, and one that has previously risen high and is now again on a steady rise could be very suitable for purchase.  Conversely, why buy a good fund as it is cooling off and steadily slipping down the rankings?

Once again, you don't, of course, have to spend your time ranking funds.  A number of newsletters and mutual fund tracking services do so regularly for you.  One good source is Mutual Fund Trends.  This supplies each month, three, six and nine-month rankings for more than 200 funds and also a special intermediate term ranking, based on performance over the previous several months, with more weight given to the most recent performance.  Rankings during recent market rises and declines are provided monthly by

Mutual Fund Trends and Growth Fund Guide, two newsletters published by Growth Fund Research. Morningstar Mutual Funds also provides a very comprehensive ranking service.

4. MOMENTUM AND PERFORMANCE

Technical analysts have many ways of determining trends after they have occurred, but there are a couple of interesting techniques that we shall examine which may indicate a change of direction of a fund before the price trend so indicates.

One technique is to measure momentum or rate of change. Martin J. Pring, in his classic book "Technical Analysis Explained," likens this effect to throwing a ball in the air and measuring the speed at which it moves. It will gradually slow down in its ascent, until it ultimately stops and then rapidly falls. The market, or a single fund, often does the same. If you measure its deceleration, or rate of change, you will anticipate its inevitable ultimate descent. For example, if you take the current price of a fund and divide it by its price ten weeks ago, if the fund is rising, you will obtain a positive value.

If you do this weekly and plot the results, you will obtain a rate of change or momentum line which will, typically, gradually slow down before the price declines and then ultimately descends. A momentum line is one very simple way of anticipating a price decline before it occurs.

Using the same principle of momentum, we can also use a different approach. Instead of dividing the prior price into the current price, we can simply subtract it to produce the actual gain (or loss) during the period. We now have a direct measure of the change in value during a given period. The higher the change, of course, the greater the momentum.

We have earlier concluded that fund performance over the past month is, on its own, largely a random event. Three, six or twelve months may be useful in detecting an intermediate term cycle of a fund, but which time period is best depends largely upon the current volatility of the market. It will have a different momentum during each time period. Supposing we measure the total change in value for the previous one, three, six and twelve months and add these together, what would we have? It would be a weighted average with a bias toward the shorter term values, as these would occur more frequently. Yet it would not ignore the longer, twelve month performance. This provides a broader base for measuring performance than would the measurement of any one time period.

This approach helps to solve the difficult question of what length of time to use. If we use this composite performance index (one, three, six and twelve months total gain or loss) we may then rank the performance of two funds and periodically switch to the higher ranked fund. We calculated this effect using just Mutual Shares fund and Twentieth Century Select fund, from the end of 1982 through 1990. The results are shown in Table 34. Mutual Shares alone, if held throughout the period, averaged 16.3% annual return and Twentieth Century Select 14.8%. Since we could not have known which fund would perform better, we must assume that we placed equal amounts in each fund and averaged a return of 15.5% Using the composite performance ranking, we switched just four times in eight years and achieved an average return of 17.7% per year, or an increased return of 14% over the buy-and-hold

TABLE 34

**THE USE OF A COMPOSITE PERFORMANCE INDEX**

Switching Between Two Funds Using The Fund With The Greater Sum of its
One, Three, Six and Twelve Month Trailing Total Returns, (1982 - 1990).

| Fund | Mode | Number of Switches in Eight Years | Average Annual Compound Return |
|---|---|---|---|
| Mutual Shares | Buy & Hold | 0 | 16.3% |
| Twentieth Century Select | Buy & Hold | 0 | 14.8% |
| Average of Both Funds | Buy & Hold | 0 | 15.5% |
| Fund With Higher Composite Momentum | Switching | 4 | 17.7% |

Advantage of Switching over Buy & Hold = 17.7/15.5 = 14.2%

Switching delayed by one month to reduce whipsaws.
For simplicity, this example uses only two funds. The use of more funds
increases the chances for upgrading and greater incremental returns.

situation (i.e. 17.7% versus 15.5%). This is a significant but not particularly large improvement, but there are two considerations to add. First, if you keep on compounding this difference, it will gradually increase until after 15 years the switching strategy would have produced an additional gain of 33% over the buy-and-hold approach. The second fact is that this example is based just on a comparison of two funds. Suppose we used our entire list of funds, so that we could always be in the higher ranking funds of a larger group? This should provide even better opportunities.

This type of approach has been pioneered by Burton Berry, editor of the No-Load Fund-X newsletter. He ranks four different classes of funds, his preference being Class Three, covering high quality growth funds. The funds in each class are ranked monthly, based on performance. The top five funds are given two stars and the top ten are listed in bold type. The score of each fund is based on the average of its latest one, three, six and twelve months performance, with credit added for stars awarded in each of the four time periods. He then simply recommends holding the funds having the highest score. Berry wisely makes no performance predictions but simply calls his approach "upgrading." In a recent interview, he described it as follows:

*"There are always winners and losers among mutual funds and the rankings are continually changing. Upgrading is simply sticking with the winning funds until they are no longer winners, then selling and reinvesting the proceeds with the new leaders. It is not a hot-shot, beat-the-market system. Upgrading is horizontal exchanging within a given class of mutual funds (for example, high quality growth funds). Upgrading is not*

*market timing, nor is it vertical exchanging, which involves attempting to predict when you should switch your holdings from, say, equity to money funds. We also don't believe that a mutual fund's long-term performance is a guide to future performance."*

The results of Berry's system have been independently monitored by Mark Hulbert and reported in the fourth edition of The Hulbert Guide to Financial Newsletters. Hulbert's data show that Berry's system does not work very well for speculative funds, perhaps because of their extreme volatility, but for growth funds its performance has been impressive. It was the number one performer of all portfolios monitored for both the seven and ten-year periods ending in mid-1990, both on a total return basis and also on a risk-adjusted basis. During the three years ending mid-1990, its performance has slipped somewhat, but it is still in the top ten fund portfolios monitored.

There is a great advantage in a system which does not require frequent switching. The example shown in Table 34 only required switching on average every two years and Berry's method using a large group of funds only required, on average, switching every nine months over a ten-year period. Overall, it seems most improbable that over a ten-year period these outstanding results were due to chance.

It is, of course, quite practical to calculate these values yourself for a limited group of your winning funds, or else you may purchase a service that does the work for you. Whichever you choose, the use of a composite performance index to measure and rank recent performance clearly indicates which funds are hot and which are not.

## 5. SIMILAR MARKET MOVEMENTS

The market moves in a series of short-term oscillations within a general upward or downward longer term trend.

These short-term oscillations may last weeks or a few months, and they provide a valuable indication of how a fund is currently performing in both up and down markets. Unless it has a very high turnover ratio, a fund's relative performance in a given market situation does not change very rapidly. For this reason, the performance of a fund in a recent short, sharp, general market rally can provide a valuable insight as to how it may perform in an extended market advance. If the market is in a long term upward trend, then its recent performance under similar market conditions is highly indicative of its future performance. If it has recently been a winning fund, it is likely to be so again as soon as the same market conditions prevail.

This type of information can, of course, be generally deduced from a fund's historical alpha and beta or its standard deviation. These measures are normally established over a period of several years, whereas what we are now considering is a practical demonstration of quite recent performance.

This effect can be clearly shown if we examine an actual example. Figure 15 shows the S&P 500 index from July 1990 to February 1991. A significant decline started at point 'A' and the market declined 19.2% to point 'B'. It then had a minor rally from point 'B' to 'C', in which period we could judge the current hot funds in a market advance. The real advance of almost 30% occurred rapidly from point 'D' to point 'E'. If our assumption is correct, the best performing funds in the rise from 'B' to 'C' should also

FIGURE 15

**THE RECESSION OF 1990 – 1991**

The Value of the S&P 500 Index From July 1990 Through February 1991

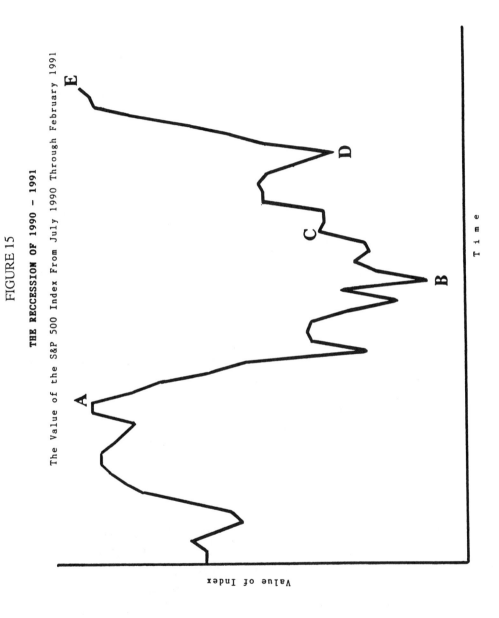

Value of Index

Time

perform well in the rise from 'D' to 'E', whereas those that held up well and did not fall significantly during the market decline from 'A' to 'B' would not perform as well during the subsequent rally.

The results are shown in Table 35. We tracked three defensive, low volatility funds and three aggressive funds, and compared their performance to the S&P 500 in the one down market period and the two up market periods. We also measured performance over the entire period from 'A' to 'E'. As expected, the more conservative defensive funds held up well in the down markets, losing only 3.1% in a 19.2% market decline. In fact, these funds were 'hot' because they performed better than almost all funds during this period. Period 'B' to 'C' gave us a preview of what would do well in a rising market, and our aggressive funds grew by 10.7% compared to 7.5% for the index and just 0.6% for the defensive funds. If we learned from this lesson, we were then ready to enjoy an average 29.8% rise from 'D' to 'E', while the market only rose 17.3%, and the defensive funds a mere 5.6%. The fact that these funds were hot in this market environment had already been demonstrated by their strong movement from 'B' to 'C'. The movement from 'D' to 'E' was simply following an existing trend, first demonstrated in the movement from 'B' to 'C'.

The period chosen for this example was one in which, overall, the market went nowhere. The last column showing 'A' to 'E' indicates that overall, neither the index nor either of the two groups of funds made any significant movement, but over this seven-month period we saw two groups of funds being both hot and cold. This suggests that it is possible to make profit in a market going nowhere,

TABLE 35

**FUND PERFORMANCE IN UP AND DOWN MARKETS**

Refers to Figure 15

| | Down Market | Up Market | Up Market | Total Period |
|---|---|---|---|---|
| Reference Letters on Figure 15 | A - B | B - C | D - E | A - E |
| Dates  From:  Through: | 7/19/90 10/11/90 | 10/11/90 11/15/90 | 1/9/91 2/28/91 | 7/19/90/ 2/28/91 |
| S&P 500 Index | 365 - 295 | 295 - 317 | 313 - 367 | 365 - 367 |
| Percentage Movement | (19.2%) | 7.5% | 17.3% | 0.5% |
| **Defensive Funds** | | | | |
| Mathers | (0.5%) | 1.7% | 2.4% | (0.9%) |
| Strong Investment | (3.0%) | 1.1% | 4.5% | 1.0% |
| Lindner Dividend | (5.8%) | (1.0%) | 9.8% | (2.0%) |
| Average | **(3.1%)** | **0.6%** | **5.6%** | **(0.6%)** |
| **Aggressive Funds** | | | | |
| T. R. Price Science and Technology | (33.1%) | 15.3% | 36.4% | 10.1% |
| 20th Cent. Vista | (35.1%) | 8.7% | 31.5% | (6.6%) |
| Neuberger Guardian | (20.8%) | 8.0% | 21.6% | 3.6% |
| Average | **(29.7%)** | **10.7%** | **29.8%** | **2.4%** |

Figures in parenthesis represent negative values.

provided that it is volatile (but short-term trading was not our purpose).

The movement of funds during similar recent prior periods of market performance is a useful way of anticipating what will be hot, because if it's going to be hot, it probably quite recently has been so.

6. RELATIVE STRENGTH
Since man is unable consistently to predict the future, he is well advised to study current trends, as these will continue into the future until circumstances change.

In the case of a mutual fund, we are concerned with the trend of price performance compared to other funds, and compared to the market as a whole, using an index such as the S&P 500. We are looking for those funds currently performing better than the market and outperforming most other funds having similar objectives. We need to be able to measure the relative strength of a fund and whether that strength is increasing or decreasing over time. Obviously, hot funds will have an increasing relative strength.

Relative strength is determined very simply by dividing the price of a fund by the price of an index, or better still, by the price of an index fund such as the classic Vanguard S&P 500 index fund. The single number of relative strength on its own is meaningless, but it becomes valuable when plotted over time to determine a trend.

If, for example, the index fund has a price of 30 and fund 'X' has a price of 35, then its relative strength is 35/30 = 1.17. If the following week or month the fund price is 38 and the index price is 32, the relative strength is 38/32 =

1.9 and the fund is beginning to show a rising relative strength. A hot fund will have a rising relative strength line, and there is a tendency for the relative strength line to weaken and decline before a change in price trend is evident. This is a very simple technique, but one which has stood the tests of time and verification.

Like all techniques, the use of relative strength has some limitations and should be used in combination with other indicators rather than as a single decision-making tool on its own. It is important to remember that it is measuring relative and not absolute strength. In a severe bear market there will still be funds with strong relative strength, because they will not be declining as fast as the market. The technique can be used in both rising and falling markets, but the work of Fosback and others shows that it works best in rising markets. If the fund under evaluation is not reasonably correlated with the S&P 500, you may need to use a different and more appropriate index as in the case, for example, of international or gold funds. You may always use a composite of the average value of many funds having the same broad objective. If you wish to compare just two funds, you may do so directly by dividing the price of one into the price of the other. You may also plot the relative strength lines on semi-logarithmic paper, in which case direct comparisons can be made among any funds.

To illustrate the use of relative strength lines, Figure 16 shows lines drawn for Fidelity Equity Income Fund and Gabelli Growth Fund during the period November 1988 through February 1991. Also shown as dotted lines are the six month moving averages of the relative strength lines. We shall be discussing later the use of moving averages, but briefly, each point on the moving average line represents

FIGURE 16

**RELATIVE STRENGTH LINES**

(November, 1988 through February, 1991)

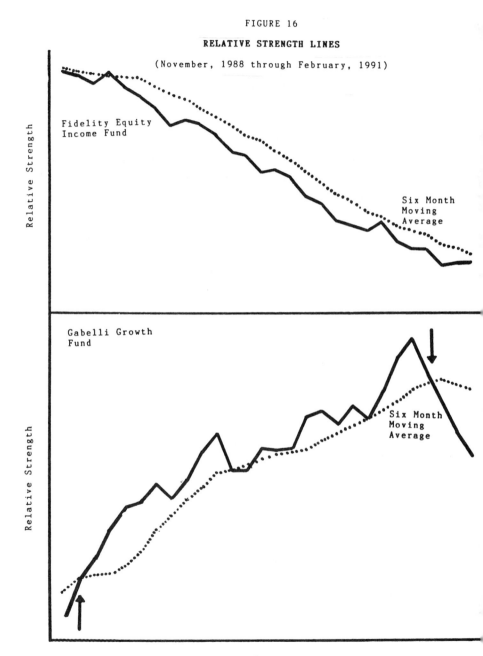

the average of each of the prior monthly values for six months. The use of a moving average line helps to smooth out the meaningless fluctuations of the relative strength lines and provides a historical base by which to judge the current trend. Basically, if the relative strength line is above its moving average, it is on an upswing and the fund is likely to be hot. When tracking below its moving average the reverse is true. Figure 16 shows that, in the case of Fidelity Equity Income, the fund has been losing relative strength throughout the period of observation. While in contrast, in the case of Gabelli Growth, the relative strength line crossed its moving average at the start of the period and remained on an upswing above its moving average until just before the end of the period, when it clearly descended through it. For almost two years the fund was hot, and the steep climb of its relative strength line attests to the fact that it consistently outperformed the index. In fact, for the first two years of this period, the price of Fidelity Equity Income declined by 11.5%, while Gabelli Growth grew by 33.4%.

The use of relative strength lines, particularly in combination with their moving averages, is one of the simplest and most effective ways of detecting when a fund is on a roll. It is quite simple to construct these yourself, but as always, there are good services to supply them, if you wish. Both Growth Fund Guide and Mutual Fund Trends, mentioned earlier, provide well laid out relative strength lines for many funds and Morningstar Mutual Funds does so for hundreds of funds. However, the moving average of relative strength lines is not often provided and this is one thing that you may have to provide for yourself.

We have now discussed six different ways of telling when a fund is hot — stage of the market cycle, historical alpha values, performance ranking, fund momentum, similar market movements and relative strength. Using several of these methods together will give you an excellent set of tools to select a mutual fund which is currently performing exceptionally well. This is the third and final screen you may use in selecting a specific mutual fund for purchase.

In the investment world there are no certainties, only an ability to increase probabilities. The use of each of our three levels of screens will significantly increase your probability of success; used together they constitute a thorough selection process.

The first screen lets us do the simple things and rightfully dismisses many of the funds for you. The second screen searches for consistency of performance, rather than an occasional outstanding performance which is perhaps due to chance. The third screen brought us to the here and now, to judge which from our list of winning funds was the best one to buy right now.

The third screen is really only necessary with equity funds, and it may be omitted if you decide upon a buy-and-hold approach with any or all of your portfolio. We shall discuss this alternative later, but even if you plan to buy-and-hold, you might as well select a fund which is currently hot, rather than one which is not.

We started this chapter with the formidable task of choosing the best funds from a selection of hundreds. We have since challenged some of the tenets of conventional thought and have seen what it really takes to select the best funds.

There is a series of simple, common sense steps that sort the wheat from the chaff and lead you to the best investments. Don't let it get any more complicated than that - there is no need. Fortunately, very few people know how to do it or have the determination to try!

CHAPTER 9

# INTERNATIONAL FUND INVESTING

Since time immemorial, those who have had the foresight and courage to seek their fortune in distant lands have been amply rewarded—if they knew what they were doing. It is now no longer necessary to sail around the world and face physical hardship to pursue international investments; you can stay home and just use your telephone, provided that you know what you are doing!

There was a time when what was good for General Motors was good for America, and what was good for America was good for the world, so why not just invest in General Motors. Times have changed and so must your investments. The United States is now the world's largest debtor nation; it no longer has the highest standard of living in the world and its stock market no longer represents the majority of the world market. New and sophisticated technologies are being developed in many countries and business opportunities abound. The world is rapidly becoming one vast and competitive single marketplace, with winners and losers emerging, irrespective of the national origins of the enterprise. Why limit your opportunities to those companies that happen to have head offices in the country where you are living? Just as you probably would not want to limit your investments to one state in the U.S.A., so you should not be limited to one country in the world economy, even if that one country is still the largest bastion of free enterprise.

In the simple words of Sir John Templeton, one of the world's most successful international investors and founder of the famed Templeton Growth Fund, *"If you search worldwide you will find more bargains and better bargains than by studying only one country, and will also gain the safety of diversification."*

In this chapter we will explore the international world of opportunities that is before you, highlight some of the unique risks of international investing, discuss the many types of international mutual funds available and show you how to take on the world and win.

## A WORLD OF OPPORTUNITIES

The invested wealth of the world has been estimated at over $20 trillion, of which somewhat over 40% is in bonds and a similar amount in stocks, with the balance mainly in real estate and cash. The international markets represent over 60% of the world's stock market and more than half of the world's bond market.

There are several important reasons why you should invest in these huge international markets:

1. With broad international investments, you will achieve greater diversification of your total portfolio than could be achieved with a portfolio limited to a single country, even the U.S.A.

2. With greater diversification, as we have seen earlier, you may achieve lower risk for the same returns or a greater return for the same level of risk.

3. With more markets in which to invest, the probability of finding good investment opportunities is greater than in any single country.

4. The United States has not been the best performing national stock market for any one of the past 30 years. It may be in the future, but it has not been in the past.

5. Excluding any gain or loss from currency exchange rates, a broad global stock investment has shown less risk, as measured by standard deviation, than a comparable investment limited to the United States. Similarly, most international bond markets have shown no more domestic risk than the United States bond market.

6. The timing of market cycles tends to differ between countries. At a time of a United States market decline, an international portfolio is likely to be in a somewhat different stage of the market cycle.

Most people are aware of the extraordinary long-term growth of the Japanese stock market, which is perhaps unequaled in any other country. At the end of 1949, the Tokyo stock price index stood at 22.85 and 40 years later it had reached the incredible level of 2,357. The subsequent sharp declines in 1990-1992 reduced this considerably, but the long-term record is still astounding. As stock prices have increased in Japan, the price/earnings ratio has risen into unheard of levels, and the dividend yield has dropped from double digits to less than 1%.

But what of other markets? Did you know, for example, that $100 invested in the Dutch stock market in 1981, with reinvested dividends, would be worth about $600 ten years later? This is an annual compound total return of 19.6%, surpassing both the Japanese and United States markets.

Germany, France and the United Kingdom all comfortably outperformed the United States market during this period.

Before you decide to invest in a particular one of these markets, you need to realize that just as there is no asset class for all seasons and no individual fund for all seasons, so there is no country for all seasons. Country market leadership rotates year-after-year, both for stocks and for bonds. The world market leaders for both stocks and bonds are shown in Table 36 for each year from 1979 through 1991. You can see that during the 80's, the stock market leadership was frequently seen in some of the smaller European countries. A similar picture appears if you examine the top five markets in each year. During the previous decades of the 60's and 70's, the most frequently appearing stock market leaders were Japan, the United Kingdom and Australia.

This patter of unpredictable rotation of market leadership is similar to what we saw when examining both asset classes and individual funds. It again leads to the conclusion that unless you are sufficiently gifted to know the future, you are well advised to invest broadly in funds that can, and do, spread their assets across many nations.

However, in this context, not all nations are equal. Remember that we are looking for diversification from a basically domestic portfolio. We should, therefore, be selecting investments particularly in those areas that historically have been poorly correlated with the United States market. For example, Canada is not a good country in which to invest if you are seeking a low correlation with the United States. On the other hand, some of the Asian and European markets have tended to show an attractive and rather weak correlation. The correlation coefficients of ten markets, compared to the United States over a five-year period, are shown in Table 37. A value of one (1) would indicate a perfect match with the United States, whereas a value of zero would indicate a total absence

TABLE 36

**WORLD MARKET LEADERSHIP BY COUNTRY**

| Year | Stocks | Bonds |
|------|--------|-------|
| 1979 | Norway | U.K. |
| 1980 | Italy | U.K. |
| 1981 | Sweden | Japan |
| 1982 | Sweden | U.S.A |
| 1983 | Mexico | Japan |
| 1984 | Hong Kong | U.S.A |
| 1985 | Austria | France |
| 1986 | Spain | Japan |
| 1987 | Japan | U.K. |
| 1988 | Belgium | Australia |
| 1989 | Austria | Canada |
| 1990 | U.K. | U.K. |
| 1991 | Hong Kong | Australia |

Excludes small emerging markets.

TABLE 37

**INTERNATIONAL STOCK MARKET CORRELATION COEFFICIENTS**

A value of one indicates complete correlation and a value of zero indicates no correlation.

| | |
|---|---|
| U.S.A. | 1.00 |
| Canada | 0.82 |
| Singapore | 0.73 |
| U.K. | 0.70 |
| Hong Kong | 0.66 |
| Switzerland | 0.61 |
| France | 0.53 |
| Australia | 0.51 |
| Germany | 0.42 |
| Italy | 0.34 |
| Japan | 0.32 |

Based on data from the Daiwa Institute of Research Ltd. 1992.

of correlation. The values shown are unlikely to be repeated exactly in the future, but they highlight the wide diversity of market character and give an indication of those regions that may provide a desirable low correlation with the United States.

How should the individual investor participate in the international markets? Without knowing it, you are probably doing so right now, to some extent. If you own directly or via a mutual fund some of the large United States multinational companies, you are participating in their international business. Well known companies such as Exxon, Dow Chemical, Colgate Palmolive, Gillette, Coca-Cola and IBM all typically have more than half their revenues derived internationally. However, studies have shown that the stock price of multinational companies tends to be closely correlated with the market of their home country, and so they are not the best way to achieve international diversification.

You can purchase, through a broker, American Depository Receipts (ADR's) which are negotiable receipts representing ownership of shares in a foreign corporation. The underlying certificates are usually held overseas by a bank. Only a limited number of stocks are available as ADR's, but if you wish to own individual foreign stocks directly, this is a reasonably convenient way to do so. If you are really determined, you can, in most but not all cases, purchase stocks through an overseas broker.

The hazards facing an investor owning individual foreign stocks are formidable unless you are very well versed in the language, customs, laws, economy, accounting practices and stock exchange of the country in question. If you are purchasing directly overseas, you have lost the protection of the SEC, which closely guards the domestic investor. Few countries have comparable organizations, although a few come close. You will be dealing through your broker with a foreign broker or bank, and the transaction may be both slow and expensive. Withholding taxes may be levied against you and commissions may be both high and negotiable. Information upon which to make good decisions may be difficult to obtain, even if you read the language. Accounting practices, including such items as the treatment of depreciation, vary from country to country. In some quite sophisticated markets there are no laws limiting insider trading and other practices with which you may not be familiar or comfortable. In many European countries, particularly in Germany, the banks are closely linked to the stock market, and it is through a bank that the individual must purchase stocks and bonds. However, things are changing and mutual funds, also known internationally as unit trusts, are rapidly growing in popularity, particularly in Japan, France and the United Kingdom. In Germany, almost 90% of the mutual funds bought are fixed income, whereas in the United Kingdom, ownership of equities through unit trusts is much more common.

For the United States investor, quite clearly the best way to diversify your portfolio internationally is by the use of diversified open ended no-load mutual funds. Here with no sales charge and usually a reasonable expense level, you are really getting expert management, broad diversification and amazing simplicity, to an extent which would otherwise be quite impossible.

Diversification, with its attendant benefits, is the prime purpose of international investing, but the long term record suggests that it may also be rewarded with higher returns over extended time periods.

The comparable returns from domestic and international stock and bond funds are shown in Table 38. Over 10-year periods ending September 1990 and also June 1992, the international funds outperformed the domestic funds. However, during the 5-year period ending June 1992, the international funds underperformed the domestic funds due to the collapse of the Japanese maket during 1990-1992. International bond funds have significantly out-performed domestic government taxable bond funds during both a recent five-year and ten-year period. However, it should be noted that during much of this period the United States dollar was declining against most foreign currencies, producing unusually high returns when measured in dollars.

International investing by individuals was slow to start but has gained tremendous momentum in the past decade. For several centuries in Europe it was the province only of the very rich individual and the major financial institutions. In the United States the domestic opportunities have historically been so great, and international investing so relatively com-

TABLE 38

**COMPARATIVE RETURNS FROM DOMESTIC AND INTERNATIONAL FUNDS**

| | Annualized Total Return in U.S. Dollars | |
|---|---|---|
| | 5 Years | 10 Years |
| **Stocks** | | |
| Period Ending 6/90 | | |
| International Equity Funds | 17.51% | 14.42% |
| Domestic Diversified Equity Funds | 10.19% | 11.30% |
| Period Ending 6/92 | | |
| International Equity Funds | 5.16%* | 16.43% |
| Domestic Diversified Equity Funds | 8.33% | 15.43% |
| **Bonds** | | |
| Period Ending 6/92 | | |
| International Bond Funds | 11.03% | 16.27% |
| Domestic Government Bond Funds | 9.00% | 11.64% |

\* Reflects the major decline of the Japanese market, 1990-1992.

Source: Morningstar Mutual Funds

plex, that there has been little incentive for the individual to undertake it.

The New York Stock Exchange was formed in 1817 and was off to a slow start, trading only 31 shares on March 16, 1830. However, it eventually grew rapidly, having its first million share day in 1886, its first 100 million share day in 1982 and reaching over 600 million shares on October 20, 1987. In spite of this rapid growth, it was not until 1968 that it transmitted its daily quotations overseas, and not until 1977 that foreign broker dealers were allowed membership. The first overseas office of the NYSE was not opened until 1988 when it established a presence in London. The Tokyo stock market admitted its first foreign members only in 1985, and the venerable London Stock Exchange, established in the 18th Century and known simply as "The Stock Exchange," finally changed its name in 1986 to become the "International Stock Exchange of the United Kingdom and the Republic of Ireland." Surely there could now be no doubt that international investing had arrived.

The United States mutual fund industry has been in the forefront of the recent globalization of world markets. In 1984, there was only one global bond fund and 13 international equity funds. Eight years later, these two groups accounted for over 100 funds. This trend will most likely continue and the individual investor will be offered increasingly attractive, efficient and convenient ways of investing in almost any aspect of the economy of the world in which we live. It has become, just in recent years, truly a world of opportunities.

## THE MATTER OF RISK

The various types of risk that were discussed in Chapter 6 apply to investments in all free market economies. However, international investing may create exposure to certain additional risks which we will now explore.

The salient factor overriding most types of risk is simply that if you are broadly invested in many different types of companies and many different countries, through one or more diversified mutual funds, then the specific company risks and even the individual country risks are substantially diversified away. While the concept of diversifying away the individual company risk in a fund has been discussed earlier, the concept of diversifying away individual country risk is perhaps new. It cannot, of course, apply to single country mutual funds or even regional funds, but rather to global and geographically diversified international funds. To take a specific example, let us consider the risk, as measured by annual standard deviation, of 17 country markets over a 14 year period. The measurement includes both local market risk and also exchange rate risk. The individual country risk values ranged from a low of 15.4% to a high of 40.0%. By comparison, the broad Morgan Stanley Europe, Asia and Far East Index (EAFE index) of more than 1,000 stocks covering many countries in Europe, Australia, New Zealand and the Far East, had a standard deviation of only 17.2%, and the World Index had a standard deviation of only 13.9%. This is lower than the very lowest individual country and certainly lower than the United States market, which has a historical standard deviation of approximately 21%.

Figure 17 shows a similar example with a shorter five-year period ending in 1990. The monthly standard deviation is plotted against the average national stock index return in U.S. dollars, for the United States and ten other countries. These together represented $7.8 trillion and covered most of the global market. As always, the objective is to achieve the highest return for a given level of risk. The Japanese market showed the highest return of 19.5%, but with high volatility. By contrast, the Canadian market showed low risk but a low

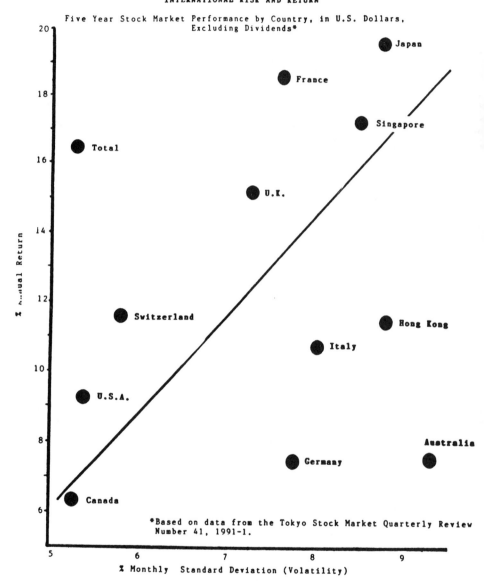

FIGURE 17

**INTERNATIONAL RISK AND RETURN**

Five Year Stock Market Performance by Country, in U.S. Dollars,
Excluding Dividends*

*Based on data from the Tokyo Stock Market Quarterly Review
Number 41, 1991-1.

average return of 6.3%. The least attractive market during this period was the Australian market, having both high risk and low returns. The best risk-adjusted return was clearly from a portfolio of all these countries (shown as "total"), which had the same low risk as the Canadian market but produced a far higher return of 16.5%, compared to only 6.3% for Canada. Such is the power of global diversification.

A year later a similar snapshot showed a higher U.S. and lower Japanese performance, but still no single country produced a risk-adjusted return better than the world total.

The risks unique to international investing are of three types:

1. Those resulting from adverse government, political or market events which would not or could not occur in the United States.
2. Those attributable to offshore funds not registered with the SEC or other comparable controlling agency.
3. Those resulting from the translation of foreign currency values into U.S. dollars, in the presence of a rising dollar value.

We will examine the nature of each of these areas of risk.


## GOVERNMENT, POLITICAL OR MARKET EVENTS

Many people contemplating international investing seem to assume that most countries have levels of prosperity, government reliability, economic strength and general market conduct well below that of the United States, and that overnight their assets may be confiscated, nationalized or otherwise ravished. While no doubt there are some countries where some of these things could occur, the larger companies, in which most funds invest, are usually based in more sophisticated, prosperous and fairly well-ordered nations.

The top 30 banks of the world are, with one exception, all foreign banks, many of whom have higher credit ratings than most of the largest United States banks. Similarly, of the top 30 public companies of the world, the majority are located overseas.

Many countries show a concentration of market capitalization into a small number of large corporations. In the United States, the top ten companies account for only 14% of the market, whereas in Holland, Spain, Belgium, Sweden, Switzerland and Italy, the top ten companies account for more than half of the total market capitalization. These companies are usually very well and securely established in their local markets. The economies of most major European countries are relatively stable, with an affluent local workforce, in many cases earning an hourly wage greater than that of the United States. In several European countries the major banks hold significant voting rights and exert other influences on companies, thus tending to provide a more conservative and longer term perspective than might otherwise exist.

To be sure, there are risks and uncertainties in international markets. The government may impose new taxes; they may freeze certain foreign assets; they may pass legislation which is detrimental to industry. All of these things have happened also in the United States. You need to differentiate what is specifically unique to foreign investments. It has been shown that, as in the United States, most of the movement of stock prices in a country is linked to local interest rates, local expectations of inflation and local economic conditions.

There may certainly be less market information available; the country markets may be small and some of the local stocks only thinly traded. These are mainly problems for your fund manager to handle. Some of the individual markets will be more volatile and, to the extent to which this is not diversified out by multiple country holdings, this may constitute additional risk.

offshore = in a foreign country.

Figure 17 showed us that stock market volatility or market risk of single international markets is frequently greater than in the United States, but the reverse has been true for a broad multi-country portfolio. The volatility of bond market prices in individual major markets has generally been no higher, on a local currency basis, than in the U.S.A.

As the choice of international mutual funds grows, the market is being segmented, and it is now possible to buy funds specializing in smaller companies and smaller, more volatile, less developed, emerging country markets. These may offer significant growth prospects over time, but they are also likely to be associated with above average risk.

## UNREGISTERED OFFSHORE FUNDS

If you are considering a fund which is not based in the United States, your first question must be whether it is registered with the SEC. If it is not, beware and ensure that it is adequately regulated by a government agency of comparable capability. For example, a well established unit trust managed by a major United Kingdom bank may be a perfectly good and safe investment, but an unregulated fund located in an emerging nation which is a tax haven may not be, and should be avoided. Hundreds of offshore funds are located in Guernsey, Jersey, Luxembourg, Bermuda and some of the Caribbean Islands. Many of these are run by major companies to provide genuine tax advantages to institutional investors, while others are not only of questionable origins but are highly speculative.

United States based investors have little reason to seek offshore funds unregistered in the United States unless they are attempting illegally to avoid United States taxes. This is one of the few financial risks which may lead to total loss in excess of your investment, combined with personal incarceration.

## CURRENCY EXCHANGE RISKS

When you invest in an international fund, in due course your money is converted into foreign currencies and forms part of the overseas invested assets of the fund. When dividends or interest on the foreign assets are paid, or the assets are sold, the proceeds will be converted back into U.S. dollars to provide your investment return. In the meantime, international rates of currency exchange will have altered, giving you either more or fewer dollars than would have been the case at the time of your original investment. This is a risk unique to international investing, although it is, of course, experienced by all U.S. multinational corporations.

In practice, the situation is far more complex. If your fund buys, say, a stock in a Japanese car manufacturer, part of the manufacturing process may be in Japan, the assembly might be in Korea, the inventory may be stored in Germany, the sale made in Austria and the dealer invoiced from an office in Switzerland. The exchange rate of each of these countries may affect the profit on the sale when it is all finally translated into Japanese Yen. The company's dividend will then be converted into U.S. dollars by the fund. This type of multi-country transaction is not uncommon in today's business world, and it has the effect of spreading exchange rate risk among several currencies, even within one company. In addition to this type of effect, the fund itself may hold sizable amounts of cash in U.S. dollars at certain times. It may also hedge against exchange rate risk by buying currency options. This is a commonly used technique which helps to provide some degree of insurance against losses due to adverse exchange rate movements.

Exchange rates, like most financial variables, tend to move in cycles, although there may also be very long term trends. For example, the weighted average value of the U.S. dollar against *parity = equality, as in amt, status, or character; equivalence or correspondence; similarity.*

a broad group of foreign currencies had an arbitrary value of 100 in March 1973. It was close to that value again in 1977, then rose 160 in early 1985, only to return to 100 in 1987, and again in late 1989 and then sink to a little above 80 in late 1990. In five years, the value of the dollar had almost halved. Put another way, the currencies against which it was measured had stengthened. However, over the ten-year period ending mid-1990, it finished just about where it started, completing a cycle.

Analysts in the United States attempting to forecast interest rates generally study in great depth the factors affecting the U.S. economy. There is a tendency to forget that this is only half the story. Exchange rates are comparative, not absolute, and the same degree of consideration needs to be given to both currencies in a simple comparison. A sudden change in interest rates in a foreign country may immediately affect the perceived strength of its currency and thus its relationship to other world currencies.

In the case of stock mutual funds, currency risk over time is typically much less than market risk and worldwide it accounts for about 15% of the total stock market risk. In the case of bonds this is not so, and currency risk may be the principal risk experienced.

The dollar yield on international bonds is particularly affected by the economic theory of purchasing power parity, which postulates that the expected rate of price inflation in a country will, in time, be offset by an equal and opposite movement in exchange rates. In this way depreciation of the currency by inflation is matched by depreciation against other currencies, and the cost of goods and services to foreigners remains the same. An increase in expected inflation is usually accompanied by an increase in bond yields, but this is lost by the offsetting currency loss. Experience shows that the theory of purchasing power parity, if correct, has many exceptions and applies only over long time periods. To the extent that it does apply, high coupon foreign bonds may not provide comparable dollar yields, as the high yields (based on local inflation expectations) will be offset by compensating currency depreciation.

What can be done to benefit from the diversification of international investing and the possibly higher returns, while minimizing the currency exchange risk? Basically, three things:

1. Invest internationally with the longest term money you have. In order to minimize exchange effects, the duration of the investment period should be greater than for domestic funds. A ten-year period will reduce the exchange effects which may be seen in a shorter period.

2. Invest in funds that cover many different countries. The risk of a world stock index expressed in U.S. dollars may slightly greater than for the same index in local currency values. On the other hand, the exchange risk of a single country investment may be much higher and has accounted for around 50% of the total risk.

3. Some funds hedge part or all of their foreign currency exposure, providing a degree of insurance against significant exchange losses. This is a specialized game best left to the judgment of a successful international money manager. You may, of course, choose to limit your exposure to international investments during long periods of a strengthening dollar, such as occurred from 1981 through 1984. Don't try to forecast short-term changes in exchange rates. The expert can't and neither can you.

## THE CHOICE OF INTERNATIONAL FUNDS

Running an international operation is a very different game from running a domestic operation, be it a mutual fund or any other type of business. The strategic decisions in a single country business can be complex and perhaps likened to a game of chess, but a truly international operation is better likened to a game of three dimensional chess. There are many more variables to assess and frequently less information with which to do it. International business is more complex, sometimes more risky and frequently more rewarding. A successful manager of a domestic business does not necessarily make a successful international manager. It is a game best left to the real experts having a proven international track record.

When choosing an international fund you should, therefore, look carefully at how it is managed. Some fund families, such as Fidelity and Templeton, have their own staff based overseas visiting local companies and assessing the local investment opportunities. If someone is investing your money in, say, South East Asia, it is better that he or she live there, mix with the local business community and absorb the subtleties of local politics, economics and business trends. By the time they have been doing this perceptively for several years, and perhaps reading the Asian Wall Street Journal, The Far Eastern Economic Review and the Economist, rather than just the United States press, they should be better qualified to participate in the management of your money.

Some fund families approach this problem by associating with long established and successful international money managers. For example, T. Rowe Price has a joint venture with the Fleming group, a London based investment organization with more than a century of international investment experience and with offices in Tokyo, Hong Kong, Frankfurt, Zurich and other major investment centers around the world. Similarly, the International Growth Portfolio of the Vanguard World Fund is managed by Schroder Capital Management International Inc., a subsidiary of the Schroder Group based in London and having offices in 17 countries.

Other fund families have built up in-house international expertise over several decades and manage their own funds. An example is the Scudder Group, which has been investing internationally for more than 30 years. Many of the more successful funds operating in this way have European managers or managers who have had direct overseas experience. Examples of this are Harbor International, International Equity fund, Ivy International, the GT international funds, Scudder International and SoGen International fund.

There are other funds which rely solely on computer analysis of data available in the United States to pick the best international stocks. This may be quite successful, but there is more to international business than the analysis of historical numbers. If there was not, managers could be replaced by computers.

Another question to consider when selecting a fund is whether the fund uses a top down or bottom up approach to stock selection. A top down approach typically starts with a macro-economic picture of the world and narrows it down by region and country and industry, finally selecting a stock which is expected to be in the right place at the right time and benefit from a major trend. An example is Vanguard World Fund - International Growth Portfolio. A bottom up approach starts by the selection of stocks according to the chosen criteria and is more concerned with the micro-economics of the company rather than the broader approach. An example is the Vanguard Trustees Commingled Fund - International Portfolio. Both these funds have a good long-term track record, and their performance has been rather similar, in spite of their very different management styles.

The selection of an international fund should be based on the general criteria discussed in previous chapters. The unique considerations for international funds further emphasize the importance of selecting open-ended, no-load (or low load), well geographically diversified funds having a good and consistent track record, expert international management, a positive alpha and a relatively low standard deviation. Your anticipated holding period should be longer than that of your domestic funds and ideally, at least ten years.

The choice before you is extensive and rapidly growing. Let's take a look.

## EQUITY FUNDS

Global Funds

If you are purchasing an international fund to diversify an existing domestic portfolio, a global fund may not be right for you. If, however, you are building a broadly diversified portfolio, a global fund may be very attractive. The global funds give the manager the freedom to invest in those countries he considers to be the most attractive, including the United States. If the particular fund is widely diversified, you are then truly investing in the world. It also permits the manager to identify industries and new technologies of promise, and then isolate those companies that may benefit most from them, irrespective of their location. He can view the world as one economy, without national restrictions.

One example of a global fund is the Scudder Global Fund; a no-load, well diversified growth fund with a good but fairly short track record. The fund may hold bonds and deal in options. Another example is Dreyfus Strategic World Investing, but this is a low load fund with a 3% initial sales charge. Established in 1987, its short record has been outstanding, providing good value-added at low risk.

International Funds

To balance a domestic portfolio, there is an excellent selection of broadly diversified, no-load, international funds with good performance records. They generally invest only outside the United States economy. Those with some of the best and longest track records include Scudder International, SoGen International and T. Rowe Price International Stock Fund, each having good long-term records. A somewhat newer fund, with an excellent record on a risk-adjusted basis, is Harbor International. For funds having good historical performance with low expense levels, you may consider Vanguard Trustees Commingled Fund - International Portfolio, or the Vanguard World Fund - International Growth Portfolio. An example of a fairly conservative, value-oriented fund is Ivy International, which invests very broadly and may also own United States equities for defensive purposes, if necessary. It has the same manager as Harbor International.

Regional Funds

If your objective is to invest only in one particular area, such as Europe or Asia, you may choose a regional fund which is limited to investment in that area. Also, if you wish to make a fixed allocation of assets to each area, rather than leave it to the judgement of an international fund manager, you may purchase an appropriate ratio of a European and an Asian fund. A regional fund has somewhat reduced diversification and increased risk. Examples of such funds are Financial Strategic European Portfolio or Financial Strategic Pacific Basin Portfolio, which are no-load growth funds, or Fidelity Europe which is a low load fund.

Emerging Market Funds

The assets of most international funds are invested in the stocks of about 20 major markets, which represents much of the developed world. These are generally considered to be basically efficient markets, widely studied by investment analysts and offering few, if any, real bargains. There are another 30 or more smaller markets, representing perhaps 5% of the world market, which may be less efficient and offer exciting possibilities to the more adventurous investor who can accept higher risk. These markets cover a wide diversity of countries which could include some of the smaller European countries, some Latin American countries and many of the countries of Asia excluding Japan. Countries such as Greece, Portugal and Turkey may show great growth in this decade, as they become part of a European market. Smaller Asian markets such as Thailand, Malaysia, and Indonesia may follow the path of Korea and Taiwan and enjoy a decade of rapid growth. Hong Kong and Singapore have shown what can be achieved. It has been estimated that over the past decade, the economies of the developing nations have grown 55% faster than their industrialized counterparts.

Quite recently, a new class of fund has developed with the objective of investing in this type of market. Time will tell what performance they achieve, but if selected carefully, they might comprise a small portion of a well-diversified international portfolio. An example of this type of fund is the T. Rowe Price International Discovery Fund, formed in 1988. This is a no-load fund which typically owns at least 100 stocks in ten countries, although this may include investment in smaller companies in developed countries. It is a rather volatile fund for the long-term investor and has adopted a 2% redemption fee paid to the fund to deter short-term traders. A newer and interesting fund, launched in 1992, is the Montgomery Emerging Markets Fund, a no-load fund run by two experienced international managers. This is likely to be a highly volatile fund with the potential for significant long-term growth.

## Single Country Funds

Single country funds suffer several disadvantages. They lack the broad market diversification of a general international fund; they lack any diversification of exchange rate risk; they tend to be highly volatile and most of them are closed-end load funds whose price may fluctuate very widely, irrespective of the value of the underlying assets. For example, during 1990, some single country closed-end funds were selling at three times the value of their underlying assets. Later the same year, they were selling below the value of their assets, which in turn had dropped sharply. You do not need to take such risks.

However, if you want to accept the risks of a single country fund and if you have the enviable foresight to know just which markets will prosper, and when, then there are a few open-ended funds available. The choice is limited, but examples are the Japan fund, a no-load growth fund distributed by Scudder and the Canada Fund, a low load fund distributed by Fidelity.

## Index Funds

The performance of the international stock market is normally measured by the EAFE index. This is a capitalization weighted index of the various national markets and containing over 1,000 stocks. Most fund managers have been unable consistently to match the performance of this index over time. If, however, you want to match it within perhaps one percentage point, you may simply buy a passively managed index fund. You will not match the better funds in those years when they exceed the performance of the index, but you will not join them in those years when they underperform it. An index fund has the advantage of very low operating expenses and very low fund transaction expenses. The classical example is the Vanguard International Equity Index fund, which is divided into two portfolios, one covering Europe and the other covering Asia. You may purchase either separately, or combine the two in a proportion to match the EAFE index. This will produce a very heavy allocation to Japan and to the United Kingdom, due to their size compared to other international markets. You will also be fully invested at all times, irrespective of market conditions. Expenses should be at least one percentage point less than with other international funds, which over time becomes significant. Index funds are discussed in further detail in the next chapter.

## Sector Funds

International or global sector funds have hardly yet appeared as a class but inevitably will. A few years ago international investing was itself looked upon somewhat as a sector. Now, the international market itself is being divided into sectors. An interesting example is the Evergreen Global Real Estate Equity Fund, a no-load fund specializing in companies that own real estate or are engaged in the real estate industry anywhere in the world.

The choice of international equity funds is steadily increasing, and before long, the market will be divided into as many different segments as the domestic market. Already the international choices include large company funds, small company funds, growth and income funds, index funds and specialized sector funds. Some funds, such as Fidelity's International Growth and Income Fund, combine equities with international bonds, aiming at a significant income component within the total return.

## FIXED INCOME

### Bond Funds

When considering international diversification in bonds, it is necessary to balance the undoubted value of diversification against the currency risks involved. Although the bonds of most major countries have had volatility somewhat similar to United States bonds in local currency terms, the significance of currency exchange risk is greater for bonds than for stocks. Approximately half of the total risk in foreign bonds is due to exchange risk, a much higher level than generally experienced with stocks. Nevertheless, studies have shown that the best risk-adjusted return had been achieved with a portfolio of 70% United States bonds and 30% foreign bonds.

When examining the literature on global or international bond funds, you may learn of the much higher yields of, say, foreign government bonds compared to U.S. Government bonds. However, this is only part of the story. For United States investors, bonds can only be compared on a total return basis (not just on yield) expressed in U.S. dollars (not in local currency). When the dollar is weakening, total returns may be much greater in U.S. dollars than in local currency, but the reverse is also true. Nevertheless, spectacular profits have been made in international bonds. In 1990, for example, an investment in British government bonds produced a total return in local currency of over 10%, which became 31% when translated into U.S. dollars. Most international bond funds have not yet existed through a long period of a strengthening dollar, and it remains to be seen how well they will manage potential exchange losses over a period of several years. Nevertheless, their ten-year historical average annual return of around 15% suggests that they may be excellent for the long-term investor who can ride out exchange rate fluctuations.

There are currently over 30 global and international bond funds available, but many of them are unfortunately load funds. However, there are several good no-load funds having relatively reasonable expense levels. The Scudder International Bond Fund is a pure no-load fund investing mainly in the bonds of governments in North America, Europe, Japan and Australia. All bonds are in the top three credit ratings and the portfolio is actively managed to optimize currency, interest rate and maturity exposure. Since its inception in 1988, the fund has performed well in a generally favorable market environment. The Fidelity Global Bond Fund is a no-load global bond fund with a short maturity of around five years and significant dollar holdings, both aimed at limiting volatility. More recently, Scudder has introduced their Short Term Global Income Fund, which is a no-load bond fund holding bonds with maturities not exceeding three years.

Money Markets

There are two distinct types of international money market funds available: those denominated in U.S. dollars, thus having no currency exchange risk, and those denominated in foreign currencies, which are managed in an attempt to benefit from the constant fluctuation of exchange rates.

The first type is exemplified by the Dreyfus Worldwide Dollar Money Market Fund, which invests only in dollar denominated very short-term obligations, mainly the debt obligations of the world's top banks. Since in the United States there is now only one AAA rated bank (for long-term debt), the fund can obtain better credit rated investments and frequently higher yields overseas. This makes sense and has led the fund to safe, highly competitive yields.

The second type of money market fund denominated in foreign currencies presents a totally different and much higher level of risk. This should be used only by individuals willing to accept the possibility of severe short-term exchange loss in the hope of achieving some exchange gains. In an extended period of rising dollar strength, these funds may have great difficulty in achieving their objective. Such funds tend to be high risk, high expense load funds.

## HOW TO TAKE ON THE WORLD AND WIN

First, you need to apply the principles outlined in the previous chapters, most of which apply equally to international investing.  Chapter 6 on managing risk and Chapter 8 on picking the best funds are particularly relevant.

Beyond that, follow these guidelines:

1. Invest internationally with your most patient money. That means the money that can be tied up for the longest period of time, preferably at least ten years.

2. Invest only in open-ended geographically diversified no-load (or if essential, low load) global or international funds.  Be slightly cautious of regional funds and view single country funds as speculative.  If appropriate to your portfolio, favor global funds.

3. Invest in more than one fund and balance off different international fund objectives and management styles. For example, some may move defensively into dollars or hedge currency risks, while others may remain fully invested at all times in local currencies.  Some will favor larger, or smaller, companies and some will favor different sizes and types of country market.

4. Favor funds that are managed by well experienced international managements, having a good track record and first hand experience with international investing.

5. If you wish to be proportionately represented in all the major international markets, invest a part of your international funds in a low expense international stock index fund.

6. If you wish to increase potential returns (and risk), add to your portfolio a small amount of a fund specializing in small company and emerging market opportunities.

7. Be cautious about investing heavily in international bond funds until they have a longer track record and

have performed acceptably during extended periods of adverse exchange rate conditions. Most of them practice defensive hedging techniques to minimize currency risks, but these have not yet been adequately tested in prolonged adversity. A small exposure to bond funds, to add diversity, may be appropriate with your most patient international fixed income money. Avoid money market funds denominated in foreign currencies.

8. Over extended time periods, with a globally diversified portfolio, exchange rate risk, at least for stock funds, is likely to account for a small proportion of total risk. Nevertheless, during extended periods of a generally strengthening dollar, it may be wise to reduce the commitment of new money to your international portfolio, or else to be in global funds where the fund manager can do this for you.

9. Don't be influenced by short-term market movements; don't try to forecast interest rates or exchange rates; don't try to forecast the future of any one country market, and do leave your investments to compound as long as possible.

CHAPTER 10

# THE CASE FOR INDEX FUNDS

Professor William F. Sharpe, of Stanford University, Nobel prize winner in economics, author of classical investment textbooks, inventor of the Sharpe Ratio of risk-adjusted returns and father of the famous Capital Asset Pricing Model, advises institutions and large pension funds on their investments. Where does he put his own personal investments? He puts them into index funds.

John Bogle, Chairman of the Vanguard group of mutual funds, has an academic background at Princeton University studying investment companies and has spent a distinguished career in the industry. His company offers about 50 different mutual funds. Where does he put his own IRA money? He puts it into index funds.

These two very knowledgeable investors are simply doing what many large financial institutions have been doing for many years. Institutions now have more than $250 billion invested in indexed portfolios. Why is this not also right for you?

In this chapter we shall address both the concepts and practical use of index funds so that you can decide what place they may have in your portfolio. They have many advantages, but they also have limitations which you should understand. Further information on many of the indexes referred to in this chapter may be found in Appendix D.

## THE S&P 500 INDEX FUNDS

If you believe, as many financial academics do, that the stock market is basically efficient, that is, by definition all stocks are fairly priced based on the sum of all publicly available information, then there is no such thing as a bargain and specific stock selection to maximize returns becomes non-sense. Certainly, the larger domestic stocks, which account for most of the value of the market, are all followed closely by innumerable investment analysts and traded by hundreds of well informed professional money managers who, together, virtually are the market. Those who believe in the efficient market ascribe successful mutual fund management basically to luck. The fact that few, if any, funds excel consistently over many years supports this view. The element of luck or chance in fund management is frequently grossly underestimated.

If the market if efficient, then the prime investment objectives must be to achieve broad diversification conveniently and at minimal cost. These objectives can best be achieved by a passively managed low cost index fund, which buys and holds all the individual stocks comprising an index, or at least a large and representative sample thereof.

Many investors collect several funds over time, which together more or less represent the market. In doing this they have in fact virtually acquired a portfolio which moves with the entire market and is functioning as an index fund. It has an $R^2$

close to 100. They are paying for active management, which they do not need, and paying for high fund transaction costs, which they do not want. In this case they would be better off in an index fund, unless they believe that their fund managers will successfully time the market for them and thereby reduce volatility. The track record of funds successfully timing the market is not good, partially due to the practical difficulties experienced by the larger funds if they want to move to cash in a hurry.

If we assume a typical gross fund return of 10%, the average net return after management expenses and transaction costs will be about 8%. The investor has immediately lost 20% of his gross return. The exact numbers will vary, but with an average turnover ratio, fund transaction costs may cost 0.5% and typical equity fund operating expenses are close to 1.5% of assets. Compare this with a good low cost index fund, which may have transaction costs of less than 0.1% and operating expenses of 0.25%. In this case, with a gross return of 10%, the net return will be greater than 9.6%, so the investor is losing less than 4% of the gross return, compared to around 20% in the typical fund.

However, not all index funds have low expenses and a few charge more than ten times the level cited here. There can be no justification for paying more than 0.5% total annual expenses in any type of passively managed domestic fund, and the best ones usually charge considerably less.

Apart from the matter of expenses, there is a difference in the proportion of assets invested. Most funds accumulate cash if they think the current investment climate is unfavorable. Their judgment has not proved very good, and since historically the market is rising for longer periods than it is falling, holding cash randomly will, over time, reduce the investment returns. You are also paying a high fee in an equity fund for a manager simply to be sitting on cash. Index funds, by comparison, are virtually fully invested at all times. They need cash for redemptions, but this is minimized in some cases by discouraging frequent trading. They may do this by limiting the number of switches to perhaps two per year, or by applying a redemption fee for a few months after purchase, which will effectively stop short-term trading. A further advantage of index funds is that their very low turnover ratio reduces current tax liability.

It soon becomes apparent when you consider the advantages of index funds that if you think the market is basically efficient, then they are the inevitable route to follow, but if you don't, then they still have some attractive features worth considering.

The only meaningful test of the concept of S&P 500 index funds is by examining their record. One of the earliest S&P 500 index funds, and still the industry standard, is the Vanguard Index Trust 500 Portfolio, established in 1976. Its record has been consistently respectable, and in each of the last ten years it was never in the bottom quartile ranking of equity funds monitored by Morningstar Inc. Over a three, five and ten-year period it was in the top quartile of all funds — an achievement reached by few other funds. As expected, of course, its alpha was close to zero, its beta was one and its $R^2$ was 100. The standard deviation was just over four. Over a ten-year period it surpassed more than three-quarters of all equity funds and produced cumulatively almost a 25% greater return than the average fund. If these consistent performance results had been achieved in an actively managed fund, the manager would have been hailed as an outstanding money manager! Its performance has attracted over $3 billion of assets and more than 100,000 shareholders.

Nothing, of course, is all good in the investment world and this is no exception. The risk level is very similar to the average growth fund and a little higher than the typical growth and income fund. Index funds have very small cash reserves to cushion the impact of bear markets and may decline more than funds which have accurately anticipated such a decline and increased their cash holdings. On the other hand, they will be fully invested to benefit from market rises.

Perhaps the greatest concern is that the S&P 500 index is heavily weighted towards large capitalization stocks and that at a time when smaller capitalization stocks are popular the S&P 500 index will be out-performed. Throughout most of the 80's the major stocks in the S&P 500 out-performed the total market, and it has been postulated that index funds became so popular that just being in the S&P 500 index elevated the price of a stock. In other words, the expected superior performance of the index became a self-fulfilling prophesy. Most fund managers prefer to buy the smaller stocks, hoping that market will be less efficient and because over very long time periods, such stocks have provided greater returns. At a time when small capitalization stocks excel, the typical funds are likely to out-perform the S&P 500 index. From 1983 to 1990, the index has beaten the average stock fund, but small capitalization stocks have been weak during this period. The record over the past 30 years shows that almost the only time that the average fund beats the S&P 500 index is when small stocks perform better than the larger stocks. When they do, the average fund is very likely to out-perform the S&P 500.

The future performance and popularity of the S&P 500 index funds seems directly linked to the future of small capitalization stocks. If we are now entering a prolonged period of many years of small stock superiority, then the S&P 500 index funds may no longer beat the average fund. However, they will still hold their own as a very cost effective and reliable way of participating in the growth and income sector of the equity market, which is what they really represent.

Several different S&P 500 index funds are available, but

our examples will be limited to selected no-load funds which are freely available to the public with initial investment requirements of less than $10,000 (and usually much less). This eliminates several funds aimed at institutions and several expensive load funds.

The Vanguard Index Trust 500 Portfolio is the only fund of its type with a significant track record and the only one with such low overall inherent expenses. It is clearly the fund of choice at the present time. Both Fidelity and Dreyfus offer similar funds. Dreyfus has been temporarily absorbing expenses in order to compete with Vanguard, but without this their expenses are higher. The Dreyfus fund charges a 1% redemption fee, and the Fidelity fund charges 0.5% for redemptions within six months of purchase.

Vanguard also offers a modified S&P 500 index fund known as the Vanguard Quantitative Portfolio, which slightly cherry picks the chosen stocks, with the objective of modestly exceeding the return of the S&P 500 index. Since the fund started in 1986, this objective has scarcely been achieved. The minor degree of discretionary stock selection is based on factors such as earnings momentum, relative valuation and future cash flow projections. The fund has an interesting, although not unique, feature whereby the management company receives a sliding performance fee for exceeding the index by 1% or more and a similar penalty for underperforming it. The effective fee may range form a low of 0.1% to a maximum of 0.5%. Based on a limited track record, this fund seems likely to perform similarly to the best S&P 500 index funds.

More recently, the Benham Group has introduced two no-load funds based on the same principle of quantitative management. The Benham Growth Fund and the Benham Income and Growth Fund have the objective of fairly closely following the performance of the S&P 500 index without being strictly index funds.

Other modified S&P 500 index funds attempt to enhance returns or reduce risk by hedging the stocks in the portfolio, or else hedging the index itself. An example is the Analytical Optioned Equity Fund, which sells covered call options and secured put options in an attempt to reduce volatility. It has achieved a low beta of about half that of the market, but has failed to match the performance of the index over the past ten years.

## OTHER TYPES OF INDEX FUNDS

Based on the success of the S&P 500 index funds, the concept of indexing has been applied to many other areas. You may now use an index fund to invest, for example, in the stocks of very large, medium sized or small companies. They may also be used to invest in foreign stocks, foreign small company stocks, bonds, precious metals, natural gas or just a group of five states. Some examples of the range of no-load index funds are shown in Table 39. Many of these funds are fairly new and have not yet acquired an adequate track record for evaluation. The fact that a fund has an objective of tracking a particular index does not mean that it will necessarily succeed in doing so. You should be sure that it has actually done what it says it will do before you invest.

In 1991, Standard and Poor's Corporation created the S&P MidCap 400 Index, which is composed of medium-sized companies having market capitalizations from $200 million to $5 billion. Dreyfus was quick to introduce the People's S&P MidCap Index Fund in an attempt to track this new index.

Several index funds have been based on the S&P 100 index. This consists of generally very large stocks for which options are listed on the Chicago Board Options Exchange. Options on the complete index are listed on the same exchange. An example is the Gateway Index Plus Fund, which

TABLE 39

**SELECTED NO-LOAD INDEX FUNDS**

| Fund | Index | Year of Inception |
|---|---|---|
| Analytical Optioned Equity Fund | S&P 500 | 1978 |
| DFA U.S. Large Company Portfolio | S&P 500 | 1991 |
| Dreyfus Peoples Index Fund | S&P 500 | 1990 |
| Fidelity Market Index Fund | S&P 500 | 1990 |
| Portico Equity Index Fund | S&P 500 | 1989 |
| United Services All American Equity Fund | S&P 500 | 1990 |
| Vanguard Index Trust, 500 Portfolio | S&P 500 | 1976 |
| Vanguard Quantitative Portfolios | S&P 500 | 1986 |
| Dreyfus Peoples S&P 400 MidCap Index Fund | S&P 400 | 1991 |
| Gateway Index Plus Fund | S&P 100 | 1977 |
| Rushmore Stock Market Index Plus | S&P 100 | 1985 |
| DFA U.S. 9-10 Small Company Portfolio | Smallest Quintile of NYSE | 1981 |
| Rushmore OTC Index Plus | NASDAQ 100 | 1985 |
| Schwab 1000 Fund | Largest 1000 U.S. Corporations | 1991 |
| Vanguard Index Trust, Extended Market | Wilshire 4500 | 1987 |
| Vanguard Index Trust Total Stock Market Portfolio | Wilshire 5000 | 1992 |
| Vanguard Small Capitalization Stock Fund | Russell 2000 | 1989 |
| DFA Continental Small Company Portfolio | Financial Times Actuaries World Index (Cont. Europe smallest 20%) | 1988 |
| DFA Large Cap International Portfolio | Financial Times Actuaries World Index (Top Half) | 1991 |
| DFA Japanese Small Company Portfolio | Tokyo Stock Exch. First Sec. (smaller half) | 1986 |
| DFA U.K. Small Company Portfolio | Fin. Times Actuaries All Shares Index (smaller half) | 1986 |
| United Services European Equity Fund | MSCI Europe* | 1990 |
| Vanguard International Equity Index Fund | | |
|     European Portfolio | MSCI Europe | 1990 |
|     Pacific Portfolio | MSCI Pacific* | 1990 |
| Portico Bond Immdex | Shearson Govt./Corp.Bond | 1989 |
| Vanguard Bond Market Fund | Salomon Bros. Inv. Grade Bonds | 1986 |
| Benham Gold Equities Index Fund | North American Gold Producers | 1988 |
| Rushmore Precious Metal Index Plus Portfolio | North American Precious Metal Producers | 1989 |
| Rushmore American Gas Index Fund | Members of American Gas Assoc. | 1989 |

*Morgan Stanley Capital International (MSCI) European and Pacific **Indexes** together represent the MSCI Europe, Australia, Far East (EAFE) **Index.**

Notes: Expense levels of no-load index funds vary widely from 0.2% to **more** than 2%. Generally, total expenses should be no more than 0.5%. Not all index funds succeed in tracking their chosen index. DFA index funds have a $50,000 initial minimum investment and are sold only through financial adviso attempts to match the S&P 100 index and reduce volatility by hedging with options on the index. It has produced a very low beta, a positive alpha and a good risk-adjusted return. A somewhat similar fund is the Rushmore Stock Market Index Plus Portfolio which has shown a rather lower risk-adjusted return.

At the other end of the market, several fund families have developed funds based on various indexes representing small company stocks. The S&P 500 index represents about 75% of the value of domestic investment grade stocks but tends to exclude many smaller capitalization stocks. Companies with market value greater than $300 million comprise about 90% of the total market value, but an additional 8% to 9% of the market is accounted for by companies with market values of from $20 million to $300 million. This small capitalization market segment is represented by the Russell 2000 Index. Studies have shown that whereas most funds have under-performed the S&P 500 index from 1983 through 1990, the average small capitalization fund has out-performed the Russell 2000 Index during this period. It is known that small company stocks behave differently in several ways, and their market may be much less efficient. Fewer analysts follow the smaller stocks and fund managers seem to perform better with this type of stock. The case for small capitalization index funds, therefore, appears somewhat weaker than it is for the S&P 500 index funds. Nevertheless, many of the general advantages that were discussed earlier apply equally.

Vanguard offers their Small Capitalization Stock Fund, which has the objective of paralleling the performance of the Russell 2000 Index. It has the usual low expenses, but charges an initial 1% transaction fee, which is paid into the fund and not to the fund management. This is intended to defray the cost of brokerage fees and the bid-ask spread in the over-the-counter market for small stocks. The fund was converted to an index fund in late 1989, and its relatively short performance record to date has been unspectacular. Further time is required to develop a track record.

A somewhat similar fund is the Vanguard Index Trust Extended Market Portfolio. This, however, is a little broader in scope and tracks the Wilshire 4500 Index, which represents all stocks except those included in the S&P 500 index. Although the S&P 500 covers about three-quarters of the total market value, it covers less than 10% of the number of companies traded. The Wilshire 4500 index covers the remaining companies, which include a large number of medium and small sized companies.

The Vanguard Index Trust Extended Market Portfolio is a sister portfolio of the Vanguard Index Trust 500 Portfolio. The entire domestic market may conveniently be purchased with a combination of these two portfolios within the same fund. The ratio necessary to match the total market may vary, but is currently 70% to 75% of the 500 Portfolio and 25% to 30% of the Extended Market Portfolio. If you just want to buy virtually the entire domestic stock market inexpensively and very conveniently, this is the one way to do it. The shares of the Extended Market Portfolio are subject to a 1% portfolio transaction fee, paid into the assets of the fund. If you believe that small capitalization stock funds are likely to perform well during the 90's, you may choose to increase the proportion accordingly.

However, if you just want to own the entire domestic stock market, without weighting it towards larger or smaller sized companies, there is now an even simpler way of doing so. In 1992, Vanguard introduced the Vanguard Index Trust Total Stock Market Portfolio fund, which is designed to track the Wilshire 5000 index. This represents the ultimate one-stop-shopping for virtually the entire market.

One of the newer innovations in index funds has been the

introduction of international funds as referred to in the previous chapter. Vanguard pioneered this effort for the individual investor and offers two portfolios, a European Portfolio and a Pacific Portfolio, both within the Vanguard International Equity Index Fund. With an appropriate ratio of the two portfolios you may cover the total international market. A 1% transaction fee, paid into the fund, is charged upon purchase.

The European portfolio tracks the Morgan Stanley Capital International (MSCI) Europe index covering 600 European companies, and the Pacific portfolio tracks the Pacific index covering some 400 stocks in Japan, Australia, New Zealand, Hong Kong and Singapore. The two indexes together comprise the widely recognized and broadly diversified Europe, Australia, Far East (EAFE) free index. The world "free" sometimes seen in the index name means that it excludes those stocks which the foreign investor is not allowed to buy. This represents certain stocks in Finland, Norway, Sweden and Switzerland.

The European index is dominated by the United Kingdom, Germany and France, which together account for more than two-thirds of the index. The Pacific index is dominated by Japan, which accounts for about 90% of the index. This is a direct reflection of the size of these markets in relation to the other international markets. The United Kingdom market contains a high proportion of foreign stocks and is therefore much larger than suggested by the size of the local economy. To some extent it alone provides exposure to the stocks of many countries.

If you can successfully index equity investments, can you index fixed income investments? Yes . . . both Vanguard and Portico have done it with their bond index funds which are included in Table 39. The Vanguard Bond Market fund attempts to track the Salomon Brothers Broad Investment-Grade Bond Index of high quality bonds. A recent composition was 54% United States Treasury obligations, 28% United States Government guaranteed mortgage backed issues and 18% investment grade corporate bonds. During the 80's, less than 30% of professional money mangers were able to beat this index. Vanguard's track record is still fairly short, but it has typically achieved at least 95% correlation with the index performance, with very low expenses and turnover ratio. This seems an efficient way to achieve broad diversification in high quality taxable bonds. The Portico Bond IMMDEX Fund simulates the return on the Lehman Brothers Government/ Corporate Bond Index. Its objective is to produce a return within half of 1% of the index, but it has too short a history to make meaningful judgements about its ability to achieve this objective.

Other types of index funds have quite recently appeared, and some of these are shown in Table 39. No doubt more will appear as the concept of indexing continues to gain favor. You may now index the precious metals using, for example, the Benham Gold Equities Index Fund, which attempts to match the performance of an index comprising the stocks of a group of North American gold producing companies.

Alternatively, you may choose the Rushmore Precious Metals Index Plus Portfolio which follows a similar index and which may purchase or sell options and futures contracts.

If you have a burning desire to invest in the natural gas industry, you may purchase the Rushmore American Gas Index Fund, which follows an index comprising the publicly traded common stock of the member companies of the American Gas Association.

You no longer have to pick a particular stock within an industry, or even a sector fund which may select certain stocks within an industry; you can just buy the industry. In this way, of course, you are guaranteed to own both the very best and the very worst performers. Likewise, rather than buying an industry, you may wish to buy a region. For example, you may buy the Composite Northwest 50 Fund, which tracks an index based on the stocks of companies based in, or doing business in, the states of Alaska, Idaho, Montana, Oregon and Washington. However, this particular fund is a load fund, which unnecessarily weights the odds against you.

The case for index funds is strong if you carefully pick the best funds and use them as a part of a core holding in a long-term investment program. Some of the great minds of the investment world have concluded that this is a smart thing to do. Others have decried it as the pursuit of mediocrity. You should listen to such critics carefully, provided that they have personally succeeded in beating a chosen index consistently for the past five or ten years with a comparable level of risk.

## HOW TO PICK AN INDEX FUND

1. Give careful thought to just what index you really want. Do you want to buy an index of larger stocks, smaller stocks or the entire market? Internationally, do you want Europe, Asia or the total international market? Would you like to track an index of high quality government and corporate bonds?

2. For ultimate simplicity, you can buy the world stock market by buying just two funds; the Vanguard Index Trust Total Stock Market Portfolio (representing the domestic market) and the Vanguard International Equity Index Fund (representing the international markets). The latter fund comprises two portfolios, one covering Europe and the other Asia.

3. Remember that indexing can be a simple, elegant and inexpensive way of owning a market. Be cautious of complicated index funds.

4. Ensure that a particular index fund has actually succeeded over several years in matching, or nearly matching, the performance of its index. Achieving this is more difficult than having it as an objective.

5. Avoid load funds; you don't need them. Also avoid index funds that have high expense ratios. The extra expense does nothing for you. Do not pay more than 0.5% total expenses for any passively managed domestic index fund.

6. Avoid funds that have high turnover ratios. This usually indicates frequent trading by short-term market timers, which is not in the interests of the remaining shareholders.

7. Don't expect to beat the market with an index fund. It is the market that you will own.

**PART THREE**

**PROTECTING YOUR INVESTMENTS**

## CHAPTER 11

# UNDERSTANDING MARKET CYCLES

Perhaps the most dangerous statement periodically heard on Wall Street is "Ah, but it's different this time." This naively optimistic phrase is usually uttered towards the end of a bull market cycle, in an attempt to deny the inevitability of decline following ascent.

In addition to death and taxes, you may also rely on cycles occurring widely in many physical, biological and economic systems. These are as certain as the cyclical rising and setting of the sun, although unfortunately not usually so predictable.

Stock market cycles are a fact of life and can be a problem or an opportunity, depending upon your reaction to them. The majority of investors, both individuals and professional money managers, react emotionally rather than objectively to market cycles and suffer accordingly.

In this chapter we will stand back and take a longer term look at market cycles, study their dangers and opportunities, and begin to see how we may turn a potential problem into a manageable opportunity.

## A GLIMPSE AT HISTORY

In 1926, Nicolai Kondratieff, an obscure 34-year-old Russian economist, observed that wholesale prices in the United States moved in long cycles of 50 to 54 years, with a rising period of around 20 years, a plateau of around ten years and a declining period of about 20 years. The cycles started with very depressed economic and business conditions. Frequently, a war was the catalyst to stir up the economy and to increase employment, plant utilization and investment. This lead to economic prosperity, adoption of new technology and ultimately to economic excesses, industrial inefficiencies, rising prices and interest rates and, after a while, to a downward movement of prices and economic activity. This cleaned out the system, returned it to a lean, efficient economy and prepared it for a subsequent rise. Kondratieff also identified similar cycles of interest rates in the French and English economies, and he postulated that capitalism was thus self-perpetuating. This dangerous thought lead him to a life of exile and death in Siberia. Since that time, scholars in England have traced similar 50 to 52-year cycles right back to the 13th Century.

So where are we today on the Kondratieff long wave? According to the pattern established from the early 18th Century, the down leg of the cycle should have started in the mid-80's and lasted through the end of this century. However, for more than 50 years the United States economy has been in an unprecedented period of continually rising prices due to uncontrolled government borrowing and spending. This may have distorted the short-term picture, but it is very probable that sooner or later the very long-term trend line will prevail.

Remember, though, that this is based on wholesale prices, not the stock market. During previous down legs of the Kondratieff cycle stock market growth has still occurred, but bear markets have been longer and more severe than normal, and it becomes even more important to manage market cycles.

In addition to the very long 50-year cycles, several other long cycles have been identified, which together produce a situation of cycles within cycles. An 18-year cycle has been occurring for almost the last 200 years, not only in the stock market but also in real estate and financial markets. Similarly, a nine-year stock market cycle has existed for at least 150 years and has been validated by the Foundation For The Study Of Cycles.

An understanding of these several longer term cycles, and many others that have been reported, helps us to understand why the commonly studied four-year stock market cycle is rather unpredictable. It is occurring within the broader context of longer term market trends. If the longer term trends are favorable, a normal bull market may be longer and steeper than average and the bear market may be milder. The converse is also true. Certainly it will be "different this time;" it always is, but ultimately the cyclical nature of the market is inevitable.

## THE STAGES OF THE CYCLE

The most commonly followed market cycle is the so-called four-year cycle, which occurs not only in stocks, but also in interest rates, wholesale prices and commodities. It is known to have occurred for more than 100 years, and it has been observed both in the United States and United Kingdom markets.

There have been over 20 such economic cycles in the United States this century; on average they have lasted about 47 months. The recessional phase has averaged about 15 months, and during this time the stock market typically declined for about the first ten months and then began to pick up before the recession bottom was reached. The economic recovery lasted for an average of 32 months. The Dow Jones Industrial Average typically declined around 35%, increased by almost the same amount during the latter stages of the recession and then proceeded to increase throughout the recovery phase until it had approximately doubled in value from its low, 32 months earlier.

The length of each part of the cycle may vary widely. When a particularly long expansion or recovery phase occurs, it may be interrupted by short periods of little or no market growth. This occurred several times within the long bull market from 1982 through 1990.

Within this overall stock market cycle, there will be leading market segments which are likely to be the first to decline, such as the more speculative stocks and perhaps the high technology stocks, while other classes of stock, such as the more basic industries, may follow later.

An economic cycle consists of various stages which occur approximately in consecutive order. An understanding of this can prove helpful for objective evaluation of where you are now. It can put into perspective the multitude of conflicting forecasts and dramatic possibilities which tend to preoccupy the financial news media. The market is said to climb a wall of worry; only by knowing where you are in the market cycle can you hope to know whether today's well publicized worry is likely to be of any lasting significance.

Figure 18 is a simple schematic summary of an economic cycle. There will inevitably be variations in the sequence of events shown. The cycle starts with a slowing economy gradually coming to a halt. The stock market usually anticipates the economic cycle by three to six months, so at this stage the market is falling, the investor is pessimistic and interest rates, which have been creeping up steadily for about the last year, finally peak. The high cost of money finally chokes off

FIGURE 18

THE MARKET CYCLE

economic growth and leads to a decline in economic activity. This leads to a recession, which cannot be confirmed at the time. But assuming it to be imminent, the stock market declines further. No one wants to buy stocks, the demand for credit subsides, the Federal Reserve has eased interest rates. The investor is paralyzed with fear, having lost a lot, but still contemplates selling to stop any further losses. This, of course, is the prime time to buy. The press is now filled with tales of woe and similarities with historical great depressions. Magazine covers pronounce the end of the stock market as a viable investment medium for the individual.

When there are no more sellers left, the first person to buy finds a shortage of stock. Suddenly, in the midst of gloom and despondency, the market rises very rapidly for several months. By the time the recession is over, the stock market has regained most of the value that it lost, interest rates have come right down, money is cheap and investment in productive capacity increases. Unemployment drops, consumer spending picks up and fuels economic growth. Stock market sentiment at this stage is cautious, wondering if this is simply a bear market rally. Recent losses reduce self confidence. The economy now enters a long expansionary phase, and the stock market enters a period of steady growth after its initial rapid rise. Confidence slowly returns to the market, but both interest rates and inflation have bottomed out and are starting to climb. Investors slowly become fully invested, convinced that at last the market is really safe and rising. Greed replaces reason and people now borrow money to invest in stocks. Meanwhile, stock market growth is starting to slow due to high interest rates and market saturation. The economy now starts another cycle. Those that have entered the market towards the end of the expansionary phase once again lose their money.

For the past 50 years, most of the market rise has occurred very early in each bull market. If the total duration of the rise is divided into four equal periods, more than half the total rise has occurred in the first quarter and more than three-quarters during the first half. This has important implications for your portfolio management.

## WHAT SHOULD YOU DO
## ABOUT MARKET CYCLES?

Since economic expansion and contraction occurs repeatedly, it might be assumed that expert economists could recognize each stage of a cycle and accurately predict its future course. In fact, government economists rarely publicly predict a recession, while private economists tend to predict far more than actually occur.

You may think, when looking at Figure 18, that investor sentiment cannot be so wrong as to repeatedly misjudge the stages of the market cycle. Unfortunately it can. Investors become too closely involved with day-to-day fluctuations and become victims of herd opinion, as presented in the news media.

A useful measure of the timing of individual investor's purchases is the level of sale of equity mutual funds. Throughout the 80's, those periods when mutual fund sales were at their peak were always followed by periods of poor market performance. The typical investor, buying at the peak of fund sales and selling at times of minimum sales (and high redemptions), would have been in the market for only about 3 1/2 years of the decade and would have made a total profit of only 16%. A simple buy-and-hold strategy would have produced a gain of about 400%. Several other indicators show that the individual investor is usually at the wrong place at the right time.

Should the investor perhaps rely on the expert advisors who provide newsletters and other advisory services? Their advice should be both objective and expert. Regrettably no, they should not rely on these experts. While there are some successful advisors, as a group they are quite consistently wrong at major market turning points (although they may frequently be right during long sustained market trends). In aggregate, advisory services follow the trend of stock prices, becoming strongly bullish close to market tops and strongly bearish around market bottoms. They represent the majority opinion which is traditionally wrong. Historically it would have been more profitable to have taken a position contrary to their advice than to have followed it. In fact, over the past 25 years an investor would have been well advised to sell every time the consensus advisory sentiment was bullish and buy every time it became bearish. On this basis the signals would have been quite good seven times out of eight. The greatest buying opportunity in decades occurred in the middle of 1982. This was the low point prior to the longest bull market this century and surely the chance in a lifetime. Throughout much of this time, aggregate advisory service sentiment was classified as extremely pessimistic. This does not, of course, mean that all advisors were wrong, simply that most of them were.

But what of our mutual fund managers? Surely they know when to invest the fund's cash and when to just sit on it. It is only a question of understanding market cycles isn't it? Unfortunately, here too, the answer is surprising and disappointing. When the stock mutual fund cash position reaches a high level, it should be because the market is close to a peak and no significant rise is likely. In reality, it is just the opposite. With one exception, every peak in mutual fund cash for the past 25 years would have been a good buying opportunity. From 1965 through 1988, there were only two occasions when their average cash position exceeded 11%. One was just before the great market rise starting in 1974, and the other was just before the great buying opportunity in 1982. These are exactly the times when they should have been fully invested, rather than holding cash. However, to put this in the right perspective, there are two mitigating reasons. First, when stock prices decline prior to an ideal buying opportunity, this automatically increases the ratio of cash to invested assets. Second, funds may need to increase their cash reserves at market bottoms in anticipation of many shareholders wanting to sell. Nevertheless, it is not in the stockholder's interests for funds to be high in cash at a critical buying opportunity. It strongly suggests that, on average, they do not recognize an outstanding buying opportunity caused by the stage of the market cycle. Some fund families, such as Twentieth Century Investors Inc. and all index funds, bypass this issue by remaining fully invested at all times, but these are the exceptions.

All of these examples demonstrate that most investors, whether individual investors or professionals, cannot achieve the degree of objectivity necessary to recognize a given stage in the market cycle, or if they do, they fail to take the appropriate action. They are swayed by the majority opinion and act like sheep.

Instead of being a sheep, we should try to follow the advice of Sir John Templeton. When he started his investment advisory business in 1940, on the front page of his descriptive booklet were written these simple words *"To buy when others are despondently selling and to sell when others are avidly buying requires the greatest fortitude and pays the greatest rewards."*

There are two obvious reasons why market cycles are of importance to the investor. First, because the loss sustained during a serious bear market constitutes a major risk and may take years to recover from. Second, purchases made somewhere close to a market bottom will be far more profitable and present much less risk. The prime rule of investing is - do not unavoidably lose money. Understanding market cycles can take you far toward that goal.

How great is the risk? Very considerable. To take an extreme example, the Dow Jones Industrial Average dropped more than 22% in one day on October 19, 1987. Table 40 shows the major bear markets during this century. The average decline was 40%. There were other smaller recessions which, if included, would bring the average decline to about 25%. Remember that a 50% drop requires a 100% gain to get back where you were. Similarly, a 40% drop requires a 67% gain. Quite clearly, if you could avoid even half of this periodic loss, it would make your portfolio much less volatile and also greatly increase the returns over time. Is this feasible?

## DOES MARKET TIMING HAVE A PLACE?

This brings us to the major question of whether the investor should attempt to time the market; that is, buy at times when a market price increase is expected and sell in anticipation of a market price decline. This is a question which has been hotly debated for many years, with both sides producing convincing evidence in their support.

The individual investor basically has four alternatives:

1.  Buy an investment and hold it indefinitely until the assets are required, or until the performance of the fund, when compared to other funds having similar objectives, is inferior over an extended time period.

    This is the classic buy-and-hold strategy which ignores the volatility of market cycles. It is the alternative preferred by most academics and many experienced investors. It has the great advantage that the typical rapid rise at the beginning of a bull market is fully exploited. It also permits tax deferred compounding of unrealized fund capital gains.

TABLE 40

**THE MAJOR BEAR MARKETS OF THE TWENTIETH CENTURY**

| Year | Duration (months) | Decline of Dow Jones Industrial Average |
|------|------|------|
| 1900 | 12 | 32% |
| 1903 | 12 | 38% |
| 1907 | 10 | 45% |
| 1912 | 26 | 24% |
| 1917 | 13 | 40% |
| 1919 | 21 | 46% |
| 1929 | 34 | 90% |
| 1937 | 56 | 52% |
| 1946 | 37 | 25% |
| 1966 | 8 | 27% |
| 1968 | 18 | 37% |
| 1973 | 24 | 47% |
| 1977 | 15 | 26% |
| 1981 | 16 | 25% |
| 1987 | 2 | 41% |

Note: Smaller bear markets have occurred in addition to those cited, for example a 20% decline in 1990.

It has the obvious disadvantage that the next bear market may be one of the very severe ones, which take many years to recover from. To this extent, it requires a very long time horizon. It may not be the safest alternative. For example, during the bear market of 1973-74, the S&P 500 index dropped by 37%. However, many well known funds such as Fidelity Magellan, Nicholas, and Vanguard Explorer lost more than half their value. Others, such as Scudder Development and Pennsylvania Mutual, dropped in value by more than 70%. After years of hard work and saving, you would have just lost the money game!

2. Invest on a regular basis with a fixed amount, say every month, irrespective of the stage of the market cycle. This is known as dollar cost averaging and presents several advantages. When prices are high, fewer shares will be purchased and when prices are low, more shares will be purchased. Due to an arithmetic quirk this results in an average cost slightly below the average price, and it smoothes out the effect of fluctuating market prices. When practiced routinely over many years, this can be a very effective way of accumulating wealth. There is usually an assumption that the investor will stay with the same investment throughout the period, but this is not necessarily so. The dollar cost averaging method is favored by many advisors and financial planners.

3. Buy and sell according to short-term market movements, measured typically in weeks, or perhaps a month or two. This is what many people mean by market timing and is a principal reason why the practice may have acquired a bad reputation. Short-term stock or bond market movements are random events and no consistently reliable trends can be established over such short periods. This short-term

market timing is most unlikely to be profitable over extended periods, although purely due to chance it will appear to work on some occasions. Short-term market timing is not recommended for the long term investor.

4. Buy close to primary cyclical market lows when stocks are unpopular and historically inexpensive and hold, usually for several years, until close to market highs when stocks are over-priced, everyone is optimistically buying and the downside risk is substantially greater than the upside opportunity. This is cyclical market timing, practiced mainly for defensive reasons.

It ignores the short and medium-term secondary movements of the market and follows well established, longer term primary movements, based on the typical four-year cycle. It results in a minimum number of transactions and is strategically unrelated to the market timing of short-term trading. This approach is a reasonable alternative to the buy-and-hold technique and may be both safer and more rewarding if executed correctly. One of the secrets of success for this approach is to re-enter the market sooner than appears warranted, so as not to miss the typical initial very rapid market rise. The merit of this approach would be questioned by many buy-and-hold investors whose arguments can be supported by formidable evidence. However, many, if not most, investors are in practice not prepared to passively await the next recession, which may perhaps reduce their carefully accumulated wealth by half.

While these comments apply principally to stock funds, essentially the same considerations apply to fixed income funds. Interest rates, and therefore bond prices, follow a similar cyclical pattern as shown in Figure 18. There is no need to buy a bond fund when interest rates are at their cyclical lowest, causing bond prices to be at a peak. Similar cyclical patterns are seen in real estate, precious metals and most other classes of assets, although the cycles may not be in unison with the stock market cycle.

Whether you choose a buy-and-hold approach or a cyclical market timing strategy is a personal decision. Some of the advocates for the buy-and-hold strategy claim that there are really no patterns of market cycles but merely rises and falls in market value purely due to chance. This observation does not seem to be supported by historical fact.

In any consideration of cyclical market timing versus a buy-and-hold approach, there are three important facts to consider:

1.  The risk of the buy-and-hold approach is that the losses incurred in a severe bear market may take many years to recover from.

2.  The rewards of the stock market occur in a few short dramatic periods. Over a 62-year period, the entire return of the S&P 500 index was confined to only 50 months, or 6.7% of the time. If you had missed these key months, you would have achieved zero return throughout the period. Returns above the level of Treasury Bills occurred in only 3.5% of the time. Many of these explosive periods occur during the early stages of a cycle. To time the market successfully, you must be invested during these few key periods. Always re-enter the market "too early."

3.  The great majority of professional investors and advisors cannot successfully and consistently time the market.

Professor W. F. Sharpe studied this subject in some detail

*Predicate = to connote ; to imply ; to base on .*

and concluded that a predictive accuracy of over 70% would be necessary to justify market timing, and he doubted whether such a level was achievable.  Separate studies, using 26 different market timing techniques, confirm that this level of consistent accuracy is unachievable.  Other investigators in the United States and Canada have confirmed that a similar high level of accuracy would be necessary for profitable timing.  This is partially because of the risk of being out of the market during the few short periods that account for most of the market movement and which occur most frequently at the beginning of a bull market.  For this reason, they found it more important to correctly predict bull markets than bear markets.

The high levels of required predictive accuracy were predicated upon investments in larger stocks, paying transaction costs of 2% and adjusting portfolios only once a year.  No-load mutual fund investors, of course, are not directly affected by transaction costs and more frequent portfolio adjustments have been shown to reduce the necessary predictive accuracy. The question of timing with large versus small stocks raises an interesting question, since their performance has been shown to be different in several ways.  This question was addressed by George Kester and reported in the Financial Analysts Journal for September/October 1990.  Kester found that timing with smaller company stocks required slightly less predictive accuracy.  With transaction costs of 0.25%, only a 58% predictive accuracy was required, using where necessary, monthly portfolio revisions. The required accuracy would, of course, be even less using no-load mutual funds.

These various studies highlight the fact that broad generalizations about the merits or demerits of market timing are dangerous, and that results will depend upon the circumstances and the timing system used.  Certainly, the no-load mutual fund investor has a great advantage due to the absence of direct transaction costs.

A practical way of assessing the value of market timing has been introduced by Mark Hulbert, who analyzes the leading advisory newsletters. He analyzed 30 newsletters over a six-year period and isolated the results of the market timing actions from those of fund selection. The results showed a wide range of performance levels, but he concluded that in the majority of cases, market timing succeeded in reducing market risk, on average about 25%. However, most active timers missed some important market rallies, and the market timer who was willing to tolerate larger losses, and ride through the smaller market corrections, made more money in the end. It is significant that the major benefit that he identified was risk reduction rather than performance enhancement.

In his book "The Hulbert Guide to Financial Newsletters," fourth edition, 1991, Hulbert finds that over a three, five, seven and ten-year period, about one-third of the newsletters beat a buy-and-hold approach. Over the ten-year period, the average number of switches recommended by those who beat a buy-and-hold strategy was about one per year, whereas those that failed to beat a buy-and-hold strategy used more than twice as many switches. One of the successful timers only made one move in the ten-year period but still beat the buy-and-hold return.

The period studied was predominantly a period of rising market values, but the successful timers nevertheless, on average, produced about a 21% greater return than the buy-and-hold approach. The unsuccessful timers, on average, reduced returns by 47%.

Hulbert's studies and those of others, as well as our own research, help us to take the view that:

1.  Timing the market effectively is likely to reduce risk and possibly avoid a devastating loss of principal. With many recent years of generally rising prices, it is easy to underestimate the downside risk of the stock market.

2. The system used should produce the minimum necessary interference with market movements, should focus only on major cyclical moves and should be as infrequent as possible. More is not better.

3. It does not matter if the investor moves out of the market a little early. The latter part of a market cycle tends to have a poor risk/reward ratio.

4. The investor should attempt to be in the market during the middle to latter part of a recession in order to take advantage of the normal sharp stock market rise which occurs before the recession is over. This means investing before fund prices have started to rise. It is essential not to miss the few key months of explosive growth that make investing in stocks profitable.

5. The average newsletter editor and professional money manager has not timed the market successfully. Market timing is not a proven way of consistently increasing returns. Poor timing can seriously reduce returns. It should be used primarily as a defensive strategy to reduce market risk.

6. The prime objective in a market timing system should be to identify periods of great market risk, and the secondary objective to identify periods of outstanding opportunity. All periods in between should be largely ignored.

These principles will serve to guide us in actually managing stock market cycles, which will be discussed in the next chapter.

The timing of bond fund investments is a different matter and is, of course, dependent upon determining the direction of interest rates. This is a subject upon which most investment managers and advisors will feel firmly confident. There are several well accepted techniques for this, and bond timing services frequently claim consistently effective performance records.  However, Hulbert's independent examination of many newsletters, over three and five-year periods, shows that over a three-year period only one beat the Shearson Lehman Hutton All Maturities Treasury Index.  Over a five-year period, none did.  This index represents all United States Treasury securities with maturities over one year.  Perhaps what is even more surprising is that only about half beat a simple portfolio of Treasury Bills.

When the record is examined objectively in this way, the assumption that it is relatively simple to forecast interest rates, and therefore bond prices, seems to be a case where hope prevails over reality.  Market timing of bond funds is not recommended.  Both the record of achievement and the downside risk are less with bond funds than with most stock funds.

## JUST WHAT DO INDICATORS INDICATE?

An indicator, in this context, is a measurement of some type, which purports to be useful in determining the present condition of the market or its future course of events.  The Encyclopedia of Technical Market Indicators cites over 100 different indicators, all of which are used with varying frequency by market analysts.  Unfortunately, they rarely, if ever, all point in the same direction.  Most of them attempt to characterize the current market cycle, although some focus on the very short-term while others relate to the entire cycle.

It is not our purpose here to describe all of these indicators, but rather to indicate their general scope and usefulness so that you may better understand how market cycles are analyzed.  If you follow a newsletter or other advisory service, it will most likely follow a few selected indicators (perhaps slightly modified and called proprietary) and will claim virtually foolproof results from using them. Be skeptical and seek independent confirmation. Any set of indicators will work periodically, simply due to chance. What is their performance over multiple time periods, when compared to other systems and to a simple buy-and-hold approach? The perfect system does not exist.

Any assessment of future performance is based either upon forecasting the economic future, or studying existing trends. This distinction cannot be complete, as there are many gray areas, but it provides at least a framework for classification.

Forecasting the economic future is the task of economists who, as a group, have not historically proved particularly adept at it. Their broad macroeconomic approach and sophisticated econometric computer models have not generally proved a useful means of determining major turning points in the economy. Much of their input data has been from government statistics, which are often not timely and frequently subject to subsequent revision.

Following existing trends at least has the advantage of being based on current reality. Existing trends are here right now. They will not last forever, but they will last until the circumstances change which affect the trend. The longer established and more consistent the trend, the more reliable it may be considered. Classical trend following indicators are:

- fund price patterns
- moving averages
- rate of change indicators - such as momentum indexes and oscillators, and
- the trend of interest rates

Moving averages help to smooth out the random market fluctuations and reveal true trends and changes in trends. Rate of change indicators highlight just how much speed and force exists behind market movements.

Many indicators are based on movements of interest rates as these profoundly affect the entire economy and specifically the stock and bond markets. Popular indicators include changes in the Federal Fund rate, which is the interest rate charged between banks for short-term loans. For example, when the Federal Fund rate drops below its level of a year ago, this is considered bullish. Another popular indicator is changes in the discount rate, which is the rate of interest charged by the Federal Reserve Board to its member banks.

History shows that whenever the Federal Reserve reduces the discount rate (or bank reserve requirement or stock margin requirement) twice in succession, conditions favor a long-term stock market advance. Conversely, an increase in these rates three times in succession favors a long-term decline. Other indicators compare short and long-term interest rates and growth in the money supply.

If you simply wish to forecast the interest rate on Treasury Bills for the following year, you may either follow the consensus advice of about 50 top economists, or you may simply look up in the newspaper the yield on 90-day Treasury Bills at year-end and naively assume that this will be the average for the year. Over a ten-year period comprising the 80's, the latter simple approach would have been more accurate than the consensus view of the nation's top economists. Remember to keep it simple!

One of the areas where indicators can help you understand the market cycle is by measurement of market value. Market value may be measured by comparing the value of stocks to the underlying book value or asset value of the company, or by comparing stock price to either earnings or dividends. History shows us that when stocks become seriously overvalued by historical norms, they are likely to decline to within the range of normality or below, and when they become seriously undervalued they are likely to rise in price accordingly. This is why the price/earnings ratio is so widely followed. Different analysts have their own criteria for assessing over and under-valuation.

The structure of the market can be measured not only by price movements over time, but also by the volume of trading and the breadth or diversity of stocks that are being traded. A large trading volume of stocks representing the entire market is considered more significant than a price movement based solely on a thinly traded narrow range of stocks. For this reason, the advance/decline ratio is widely followed as a fairly short-term indicator. It indicates the ratio of actively traded stocks that are increasing and decreasing in value.

Since at the end of the day the market is driven by perception rather than reality, and by assumptions about the future rather than today's reality, it follows that indicators which measure investor sentiment will be widely followed. Most of these operate on the assumption that the majority opinion is usually wrong and, therefore, one should do the opposite. These contrary indicators include the odd lot sales volume, which is typified by the small investor who does not buy a round lot of, say, 100 shares but a smaller odd lot. Since the small investor is usually wrong, it follows that a high level of odd lot sales is a bullish sign. On a similar basis, the put/call ratio is an established contrary indicator, as it measures the sentiment of option traders, who are usually wrong. Likewise, the non-member short sales ratio measures short sales by the public, which is usually wrong. We have previously mentioned advisory service sentiment as a contrary indicator and mutual fund cash position as being high when it should be low at good buying opportunities.

So what do all these numerous indicators really mean? Are they helpful? Should one use them? Do they help you to understand where you are in the market cycle?

These are difficult questions, but we can arrive at some guidelines as follows:

1. No single market indicator is sufficiently reliable to use in isolation.

2.  A small number of very carefully selected indicators, each measuring substantially different aspects of the market, may be used together with good effect, but they are still fallible.
3.  Trend-following indicators are generally to be preferred; at least they are based on current reality.
4.  Within reason, the simpler a system of indicators is, the better it is likely to work. To quote Martin J. Pring in his classic book, Technical Analysis Explained, *"most things done well are also done simply. Because the market operates on common sense, the best approaches to it are basically very simple. If one must resort to complex computer programming and model building, the chances are that the basic techniques have not been mastered and, therefore, an analytical crutch is required."*
5.  Don't be deafened by the sound of a hundred somewhat conflicting indicators. They vary from arcane beliefs originating in the mists of time to simple observations validated by years of testing. Stick to just a few well proven and complementary indicators. We will show you which are the best to use. If you ask a man with ten watches to tell you the time, he probably can't. A man with one watch knows the time.

In this chapter we have stood back to look at market cycles in a broad context. We have considered some typical market cycles and have identified the various stages of the average four-year cycle and how to recognize just where you are within it. We have discussed what you should do about market cycles and have reviewed the pros and cons of market timing. We have outlined guidelines to follow in the management of cycles and discussed how best to use the many types of market indicators that are available.

With a better general understanding of market cycles and

broad guidelines to follow, we now can proceed to consider very specifically how we should actually manage them.

CHAPTER 12

# MANAGING MARKET CYCLES

In the previous chapter, we studied market cycles and arrived at guidelines on such difficult subjects as market timing and the use of market indicators. We will now build on this framework and describe specific techniques for managing market cycles, using these guidelines.

We shall select just three measures of market performance, each one quite separate and addressing different aspects of the market. When used together, they are complementary and will provide you with a valuable tool for reducing the risk of serious bear markets. They will also greatly increase your chances of buying near the bottom of the market.

There are many other indicators which could be used, some followed by the better newsletters. In the interest of simplicity we have selected just these three approaches, which are among the most reliable and well validated of the many indicators available.

Our primary objective is to reduce cyclical market risk. We are concerned with primary market moves within the four-year cycle, not the intermediate or short-term fluctuations. We are not attempting to sell at the very top or buy at the very bottom — that is impossible on a consistent basis. Rather, we seek to emulate the fabulously successful and wealthy Rothschild family of 19th Century Europe, whose habit was to leave 20% at the top, 20% at the bottom, and "only" take the middle 60%. Greed is not a characteristic of the successful investor.

## MARKET VALUE - PRICE/DIVIDEND RATIO

Most people, when they buy a new automobile, will take considerable care to ensure that they do not pay more than it is worth. They will have a good sense of its value and buy at a time and place where they can get a good price. They certainly would not pay 10% or 20% more than the established market price.

The same person, when buying an investment, particularly a stock or stock fund, will be concerned with how much it may increase in value in the future (which is an unknown), but will pay little attention to whether they are paying a fair price for it now (which is a known). Stocks and bonds, like anything else, can be overpriced, fairly priced or underpriced, based on established norms. Whether it may increase in value in the future depends to a large extent upon the price you paid for it in the first place.

Perhaps people think that it is not easy to fairly value, say, the price of stocks, but this is not so. Remember that investing is a simple matter and should be kept simple. It is not easy, but it is simple. All you have to do in this case is to compare the price of the market with its historical price range to determine whether the price is fair. When buying diversified mutual funds, it is appropriate to use a suitable market index, most frequently the S&P 500 index as it represents the majority of the market.

There are several accepted ways of measuring market value. The most commonly used measures are the price/book value ratio, price/earnings ratio and price/dividend ratio. The historic high, low and average value for each of these measures is shown in Table 41. These are your yardsticks for measuring value.

TABLE 41

**MEASURES OF MARKET VALUE**

| Ratio | Average Value | Historic High | Historic Low |
|---|---|---|---|
| Price to Book Value (Assets minus liabilities per share outstanding) | 1.6 | 4.2 (1929) | 0.5 (1932) |
| Price to Earnings (Price divided by earnings per share outstanding) | 14.1 | 28.0 (1935) | 6.0 (1979) |
| Price to Dividends (Price divided by dividend per share outstanding) | 22.6 | 38.4 (1987) | 6.0 (1932) |

Based on the Dow Jones Industrial Average. Numbers in parenthesis indicate years of occurrence.

PRICE/BOOK VALUE RATIO

Book value, for a single company, is the value of the assets less the liabilities, divided by the number of shares issued. The price of a share is then compared to its book value and that ratio compared to its historical values. Shares have historically averaged a price to book value ratio of about 1.6, but have varied from an undervalued level of 0.5 to an overvalued level of 4.2.

The weakness of this measure is that the valuation may be somewhat arbitrary. You can really only tell what something is worth by selling it, not by valuing it. Company management may feel overconfident about the value of the assets of the company. Nevertheless, for a fund or group of funds, it provides a useful measure of relative valuation. For example, sector funds investing in the high priced health stocks recently had a price to book value ratio of about six, whereas utility stock funds averaged less than two.

PRICE/EARNINGS RATIO

Another widely used method of valuation is the price/earnings ratio or P/E ratio. This is obtained by dividing the current market price by the latest 12 months earnings per share. It indicates how many dollars are required to buy $1 of earnings per year, based on the recent rate of earnings. If future earnings are expected to increase rapidly, then the stock price will increase and produce a higher price/earnings ratio, because this is normally based on recent past earnings. The price/earnings ratio is thus based on current price and recent earnings, but its level reflects market expectations of future earnings.

The historical average price/earnings ratio of the market is about 14.1, but it has ranged from an undervalued level of 6.0

to an overvalued level as high as 28.0. The ratio for individual stocks will depend on the general level for the total market and the earnings expectations for the individual stock. The average ratio for various types of equity mutual funds will tend to be lowest in the more conservative types of fund, such as equity income, and highest in the more aggressive types of fund, such as aggressive growth.

Although superficially useful, the value of the price/earnings ratio is limited by the reliability and consistency of the earnings component. If we are looking for longer term indicators, we should remember that earnings can fluctuate widely from period to period in the real world. Company managements can quite easily adjust reported earnings to meet market expectations and to optimize tax liability. There may also be one-time credits and debits to earnings which are unlikely to be repeated. It has rightly been said that financial statements are like fine perfume; to be sniffed but not swallowed. Among the smaller companies, substantially all the earnings may be reinvested in the business, and in this case, the price/earnings ratio is not measuring current return to the investor at all, but at best an implied promise of future dividends if the company survives and grows.

The problem of using reported earnings, rather than actual cash distributions, for valuation goes back to the year 1661. The governor of the East India Company, an organization chartered by Queen Elizabeth I of England, decided that rather than continuing to divide up the spoils at the end of each spice trading voyage to Asia, and giving a cash payment or dividend to each owner, it would retain its profits and pay them out at a later time, after provisions had been made for repairing the ships and maintaining company assets. That was the start of accrual accounting, which led to a separation of reported, (and sometimes "massaged"), earnings from the hard cash of dividend payouts, which are the investor's real and irrevocable rewards.

## PRICE/DIVIDEND RATIO

The preferred means of measuring market value is the price/dividend ratio, also known as the P/D ratio and more commonly expressed as the dividend yield. This has a number of advantages over the P/E ratio. It is a real measure of cash actually paid to the stockholder. While earnings may fluctuate widely, dividends are more constant. The Board of Directors will take a good hard realistic look at probable future earnings before fixing a dividend level. Companies hate to reduce dividend distributions, and they may be more conservatively arrived at than stated earnings. As a shareholder, you can't spend a company's earnings; you can spend its dividends.

The price/dividend ratio is particularly useful because of the relative stability of dividends. It means that over a shorter term period much of the change in the ratio is due to price movements. Occasionally, the ratio is calculated on 12 months projected dividend instead of the actual 12 months past dividend. It is obviously less reliable, unless the company has already committed to a future dividend level.

Criticism of the price/dividend ratio may be based on the fact that it cannot correctly be used for companies paying little or no dividend, but that fact alone is significant. It also is mainly considered a longer term indicator, suggesting market behavior perhaps several years in advance. The price/dividend ratio of the overall market is usually based on the S&P 500 Index. However, there may be market segments to which it does not readily apply, such as international stocks and perhaps company stocks. It can, of course, be constructed using any market index, but our comments relate to the use of the S&P 500.

As a practical matter, we should distinguish between price/dividend ratio and dividend yield. They both measure the same thing, with one number simply the reciprocal of the other. The price/dividend ratio is the current price divided by the recent

12 months dividend. Thus, if the price is 100 and the dividend is 3, the P/D ratio is 100/3 = 33.33. The dividend yield is the same measure expressed the other way around, namely 3/100 = 0.03 or 3%. In financial publications such as Barrons, it is often quoted as dividend yield, but you can rapidly convert it to P/D ratio by dividing it into 100. Thus, dividend yield of 3% is a P/D ratio of 33.33; 4% is 25.0%; 5% is 20.0 and 6% is 16.66. Expressing it as a P/D ratio has the advantage that it is calculated the same way as the P/E ratio, and it represents the number of dollars an investor is being asked to pay for $1 of annual dividend income.

The single value of P/D ratio incorporates the market's assessment of many things; future dividend distributions, expected interest rates and inflation rates, risk levels and even, to some extent, exchange rates. As a long-term market indicator it is very simple and hard to beat.

Although the price of a stock index varies widely over time and is on a long-term upward trend, the amount of money that investors in general are prepared to pay for $1 of dividend fluctuates only within fairly well defined limits, which have been in existence throughout this century. The record shows that investors will usually buy stocks when the cost of $1 of dividend is around $15, but that investors in general will be reluctant to buy them when the price is above $33 to $35. The highest price ever paid was, not surprisingly, just before the crash of 1987, when stocks were grossly overvalued at $38 per $1 of dividend. Conversely, at the beginning of the major bull market which started in 1982, stocks were clearly undervalued at a P/D ratio of only 16. The average value for the century is around 23. Whenever it has sunk to about 15 it has always risen up to 25 and usually to 30 or above, reflecting a major bull market.

We, therefore, have a simple tool to measure whether the market is overvalued, fairly valued or undervalued. The P/D ratio slowly swings back and forth over the years like a pendulum, between the extremes of investor tolerance. When it has reached one extreme, you may be sure that it will inexorably start to move toward the other extreme; but we don't know, of course, how long it will take, or how directly it will move there. It is, nevertheless, a long-term indicator of great value.

Many technical analysts have studied this subject, but in recent years the work of Growth Fund Research Inc., the Publisher of Growth Fund Guide and Mutual Fund Trends, has been particularly enlightening. The results of their research are drawn upon freely in the following discussion.

Table 42 shows the proportion of the time throughout this century that the P/D ratio has been at varying levels. For about 90% of the time it has been moving back and forth between $15 and $34. For more than 75% of the time it has been between $15 and $30. Figure 19 shows the relationship between the extreme values of the P/D ratio and the extreme values of the S&P 500 index. The lower part of Figure 19 shows the P/D ratio throughout this century, with its periodic excesses in either direction. The upper part of Figure 19 shows the value of the S&P 500 index. Whenever the P/D ratio declined to around $15 it was an excellent time to buy for the long term, and whenever it rose into the $33 to $35 area was an excellent time to sell. At these levels the market becomes dangerous with more downside risk than upside potential. Since wise investing is essentially a question of carefully assessing probabilities, these indications of a highly probable decline at a very high P/D ratio and a highly probable rise at a very low P/D ratio are extremely valuable.

Growth Fund Research Inc., has used these historical data to calculate the probability of market rises and declines at varying P/D ratios. Table 43 shows both the probability of gains and losses and their average magnitude during the 12-month period after the P/D ratio reached various levels. For

TABLE 42

**FREQUENCY OF VARIOUS PRICE/DIVIDEND RATIOS OF THE S&P 500**

(The historical average value is 23)

| Price/Dividend Ratio | Percentage of Total Time during the Twentieth century |
|---|---|
| 7.0 - 14.99 | 7% |
| 15.0 - 19.99 | 27% |
| 20.0 - 22.99 | 20% |
| 23.0 - 29.99 | 30% |
| 30.0 - 33.99 | 13% |
| 34.0 + | 3% |

Based on data from Growth Fund Research, Inc.

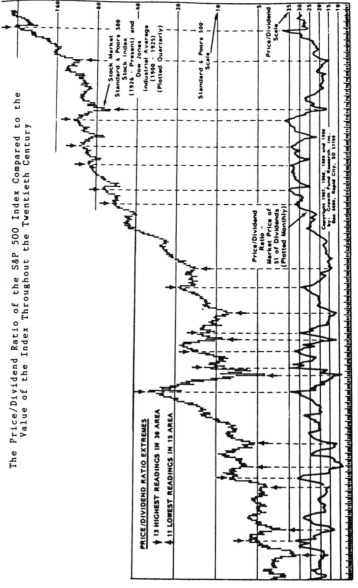

FIGURE 19

NINETY YEARS OF PRICE/DIVIDEND RATIOS

The Price/Dividend Ratio of the S&P 500 Index Compared to the
Value of the Index Throughout the Twentieth Century

Reproduced by permission of Growth Fund Research, Inc.

TABLE 43

## THE PROBABLE CONSEQUENCES OF VARIOUS PRICE/DIVIDEND RATIOS

The Probability and Magnitude of Gains and Losses in the Twelve Months Following Various Price/Dividend Ratios, 1871 Through 1990.

| Price/Dividend Ratio | Rising Market | | Declining Market | |
|---|---|---|---|---|
| | Chance of Gain | Average Gain | Chance of Loss | Average Loss |
| 8.0 - 11.99 | 76% | 41% | 24% | (13%) |
| 12.0 - 15.99 | 69% | 21% | 31% | (14%) |
| 16.0 - 19.99 | 63% | 19% | 38% | (11%) |
| 20.0 - 23.99 | 62% | 21% | 38% | (15%) |
| 24.0 - 27.99 | 57% | 18% | 43% | (21%) |
| 28.0 - 31.99 | 55% | 15% | 45% | (17%) |
| 32.0 - 35.99 | 40% | 8% | 60% | (12%) |
| 36.0 - 39.99 | 0% | 0% | 100% | (17%) |

Numbers in parenthesis indicate negative values.
Based on data from Growth Fund Research, Inc.

example, if the P/D ratio is within the range of $8 to $11.99, there was a 76% chance of a market price gain during the ensuing 12 months, and the average gain was 41%. Similarly, there was only a 24% chance of a decline, and the loss in that event would have averaged 13%. These are perhaps the best odds that the stock market is likely to offer, but the situation only occurs rarely, as seen in Figure 19. As the P/D ratio increases, the probability of gain becomes progressively less. Once the P/D ratio exceeds about $32, the chances of decline are significantly greater than the chances of an advance, and the most probable upside reward becomes much smaller than the downside risk. Once the P/D ratio exceeds 36, the chances of gain during the following 12 months have been zero and the average loss has been 17%. Further studies have shown that over a 24-month period, there is a 75% chance of loss following a P/D ratio of 36 or higher and the average loss has been 39%. This would require a subsequent gain of 64% to recover your losses. There is no need to be exposed to such hazards, and you would be much better off sheltered tempo-rarily in a money market fund, until the odds return to your favor.

This is a most revealing table and a good item to refer to before making any major buy or sell decision. It is a simple but excellent way of measuring current market value and invest-ment prospects over the longer term.

No two market cycles are exactly the same, but by studying all the significant recessions over a 90-year period, it is possible to establish at least the average market performance. Typi-cally, at the beginning of a market cycle the P/D ratio is close to its historical average level of $23. As a recession gets underway, it steadily sinks to around $17. The market normally begins to recover before the economy does, and at the end of the recession, it has risen to $21; during the ensuing bull market it rises to an average peak of $30.

During recent decades, the P/D ratio has been a little more volatile. For example, from 1920 to 1991, the cyclical low averaged $16.40 and the high $34.70. During the rising period the market gained, on average, 198% and during the declining phase it lost 36%.

It is useful to examine the performance of the P/D ratio in 1987, as this was the time when it reached its all-time high. At the beginning of the year it stood at around $30. The market was somewhat, but not severely, overvalued. It had historically only spent 20% of the time at or above this level. It was well above its historical average of $23. By early March it had risen to $34, and this was clearly the signal to get out of the market. It continued to rise to $35 in late March, $36 in early August and almost $38 in late August. No rational and knowledgeable investor would have stayed in this market, as it was now grossly overvalued and had been for some months. There was very adequate time to leave the market — but very few did. The market finally, and quite predictably, crashed in late October, losing more than 22% in a single day. The drop was too sudden to have been anticipated by moving average trends, and this is a good example of the need to use several proven and complementary indicators.

When P/D ratios are very low, the chances of gain are high and so is the magnitude of the future price increases. At this phase of the cycle, with very little downside risk and large upside potential, it is the time to be very fully invested in fairly aggressive funds with high betas, which will, by definition, rise more than the market. As the cycle matures, the potential gains are less and the downside risk steadily increases. It makes more sense now to be less aggressively positioned with lower beta funds. This is the time for the less aggressive growth funds and the growth and income funds. As the market rises into somewhat overvalued areas, it is wise to be in conservative funds, such as equity income funds. As the market rises to a

P/D ratio significantly above $30, it is time to start reducing your exposure to stocks, and by the time it reaches $34-$35, you should be completely out of the market.

To summarize, market value can best be measured by the price/dividend ratio or dividend yield. This will slowly swing between extremes, the lows being in the teens and the highs in the thirties. The first area indicates an excellent buying opportunity and the second a necessary selling situation. Between these two extremes, it is possible to estimate the probability of upside and downside market movements and the size of such movements. The P/D ratio or the dividend yield of the S&P 500 may be found in Barron's, or in Section C of Monday's Wall Street Journal.

The use of this market value indicator should help to avoid being invested during serious bear markets, and it should also identify magnificent buying opportunities. You may, if you wish, adjust the overall risk level of your portfolio in line with the current risk level of the market.


## MARKET PRICE TRENDS - MOVING AVERAGES

Mutual fund prices move in trends and as long as circumstances remain constant a given trend will continue to exist. The longer the existence of a trend, the greater its significance and the more it takes to change it.

If it is possible to determine the trend of a fund price, it will indicate whether the general direction is up, down or sideways. If the trend is a long-term one, it is likely to continue and then change only gradually, so that riding the long-term up trend and then avoiding the long-term down trend becomes a possibility. This approaches the timeless dream of investors to buy near the bottom, at the beginnings of a downward trend. More importantly, it may reduce risk by avoiding at least a significant part of a major long-term price decline.

If you plot the price of a market index, such as the S&P 500, over time, it will produce widely fluctuating points, reflecting short-term random movements. Over a longer period, a general price direction may appear, but this will be confused by the random fluctuations. A moving average is a simple means of smoothing out the short-term fluctuations, to reveal a true trend. It is extremely simple to do.

Suppose that you plot the index price weekly. In addition to this, now add up the last ten weekly values and divide the total by ten to get the average. You now plot this first ten-week average. Next week add the latest weekly value to the previous total and remove the oldest value, so that you still have ten values. The average of this revised number provides the ten-week average for the second week. Continue this each week and join the average values together on the chart. It will produce a line which is much smoother than the line representing the single weekly index values. You have now plotted a ten-week moving average of the market index.

However, this ten-week moving average has several limitations. First, it only detects short-term trends rather than the primary longer term trends of the four-year cycle. Second, it is not up to date because it is the average of ten past weeks, and the oldest value has as much influence on the average as does the current week's value. There are ways of at least reducing this problem. One is to use what is called an exponential moving average, which assigns an arbitrary factor to the most recent price to enhance its influence and then declining values to the remainder. An alternative and perhaps the simplest approach is to use several moving averages, each covering a different duration and reflecting different lengths of the prior period.

Technical analysts debate the ideal length of moving averages to detect primary market trends. Studies have shown a 40-week moving average to be superior to 20 or 30-week moving averages when compared over a 70-year period.

Perhaps it is this which has caused 40 weeks to be so widely used. However, other studies have compared moving average durations ranging from 2 to 24 months over a 22-year period. The most profitable period to use was 12 months in relation to the S&P 500 index. Shorter periods can usefully be used together with a 40 or 52-week moving average to obtain an earlier tentative indication of a trend reversal. The simultaneous use of a ten-week, 25-week and 50-week moving average provides an excellent combination and an ability to evaluate both intermediate-term and long-term price trends.

The interpretation of moving averages is achieved in several ways:

1. The first sign of a trend reversal is given when an index, such as the S&P 500, crosses its moving average when the moving average is flat or heading in the same direction as the index.

2. A later and more definitive indication is given when the moving average itself changes in the same direction, if it was flat or moving in the opposite direction when initially crossed by the index.

3. When two or more moving averages are used, a signal can be generated when one moving average crosses another one.

Each of these indications requires an explanation, which can best be achieved by considering an example. Figure 20 shows the S&P 500 plotted weekly for a ten-year period, from 1982 through 1991. The index is represented by the light solid line which shows typical random week-to-week fluctuations and changes in direction. The dotted line represents the 25-week moving average, and the heavy solid line the 50-week moving average. Looking at this 50-week moving average it is easy to see, in retrospect, the long-term trend of the market. It started to rise in late 1982 and, apart from a very slight decline in 1984, continued to rise until October 1987. Just

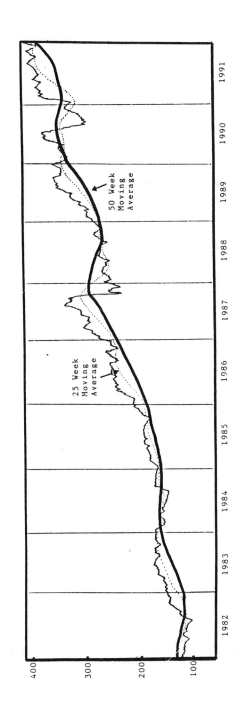

FIGURE 20

**TEN YEARS OF MOVING AVERAGES**

The S&P 500 Index Plotted Weekly, Together with its Twenty Five and Fifty Week Moving Averages

watching the index during this time would have led to many
occasions when it looked as if the long-term bull market was
over, but a glance at the 50-week moving average would have
shown that it was not. The decline of 1987 was one of the
largest and most sudden in history and would have been
difficult to have anticipated from these charts. However, as we
saw earlier, the price/dividend ratio had been steadily rising to
unsustainable levels well before the October crash and reached
an all-time high of $38.

If we refer to our original data, which contains more detail
than can be depicted in Figure 20, it is possible to make a few
interesting observations about the 1987 decline. In its precipi-
tous and rapid drop, the index first crossed its ten-week moving
average, then its 25-week and finally its 50-week moving
average line. This is a typical pattern and normally provides
progressive warnings of a weakening market, but in this case
it all occurred within one week. A prompt sale then, had it been
possible, would have avoided about half of the total decline. In
addition to moving averages, we also routinely plot a ten-week
momentum index of the S&P 500. This is simply the value of
the index divided by its value ten weeks earlier. It is sometimes
a useful early warning of a change in market direction, and the
crash of 1987 was no exception. Momentum started to decline
during the week ending September 11, and continued to
decline each week from the week ending September 26
through the crash in mid-October. This indicator, together
with the P/D ratio, loudly warned all who would listen to get
out of the market.

Figure 20 shows that thereafter, in 1988, the index first
crossed its 25-week moving average, heading upwards, and
later in the year, its 50-week moving average. This led to
another period in which it rode comfortably above both the 25
and 50-week moving averages throughout the whole of 1989,
while the index, on a total return basis, rose more than 30%.

The market became very fully valued at year-end with a P/D ratio of over $30.

The period of 1990 and early 1991 is particularly interesting and is shown in more detail in Figure 21, which also includes a ten-week moving average. Following this period on a month-to-month basis serves to illustrate a number of principles in the use of moving averages.

In January 1990, the index, shown in the figure as the thin solid line, dropped down through its 10, 25 and 50-week moving average lines. However, the 50-week moving average was moving up, and this does not usually indicate a cyclical trend reversal. If the 50-week moving average had been flat or heading downwards it would have indicated a clear change of trend. Just occasionally, even this will give a false signal or whipsaw. For this reason some experts suggest that the index must penetrate the moving average line by 3% or more. Although January did not produce a major trend reversal, it did produce penetration of the 25-week moving average while it was flat, indiating the likelihood of at least a short-term trend reversal.

In February, March and April of 1990, the index crossed the 50-week moving average twice in both directions, but the trend of the market was determined by the steadily rising 50-week moving average.

In July and August, after a rapid rise, the index first fell through the ten-week moving average, which was of little significance, then the 25-week moving average, which was of more significance, and finally it crossed the 50-week moving average when it was flat. This indicated a clear trend reversal and a sell signal. Subsequently, both the 10 and 25-week moving averages crossed the 50-week moving average. The bear market proved to be both shallow and short, but this cannot be determined at the time — it could have been the beginning of a major decline.

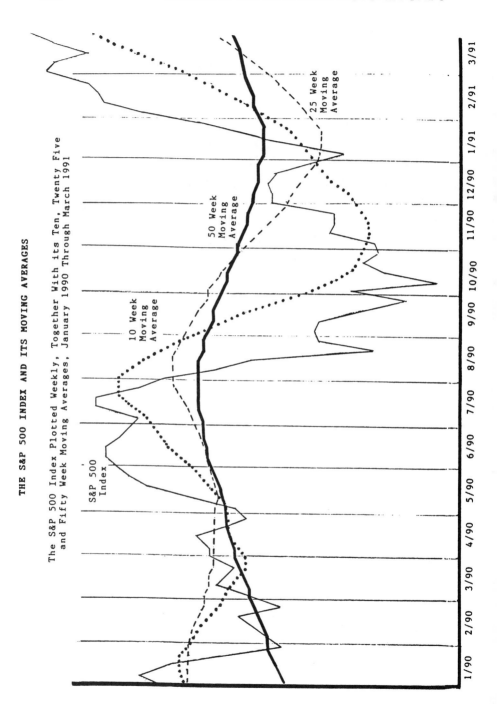

FIGURE 21

THE S&P 500 INDEX AND ITS MOVING AVERAGES

The S&P 500 Index Plotted Weekly, Together With its Ten, Twenty Five and Fifty Week Moving Averages, January 1990 Through March 1991

By November, the ten-week moving average turned up-wards and by January, the index rose through the 50-week moving average while it was flat. This marked a trend reversal and triggered a buy signal. This again was shortly followed by the 10-week and the 25-week moving averages crossing the 50-week moving average.

It would have been appropriate to have started cautiously re-entering the market in November and December and to have been fully invested by late January.

What did this exercise achieve? We sold and bought back at virtually the same level of the index. We had the slight advantage of a higher yield in a money market fund than the dividend yield on the equity market during this period, but this was a minor benefit. The real benefit was risk reduction. If this had been a recession with a 40% to 50% price drop in the market, much of that loss would have been avoided. The sell and formal buy signals were late, but they were reliable. Using shorter moving averages would have produced signals sooner, but they would have been less reliable. Most people who use moving averages tend to use shorter time periods and fre-quently only one moving average. For these reasons, the use of moving averages is sometimes considered to be of limited value, which is to be expected. Since our purpose is primarily to reduce risk, rather than to catch every market move, we can afford to use longer time periods. This, together with the use of multiple moving averages, provides an unusually reliable system. The particular illustration that we have examined in some detail provides an example of the principles stated earlier. With a little practice their application is quite simple.

It is suggested that you use a 50-week moving average, preferably also with a 25 and 10-week moving average. If you wish to also use a 10-week momentum index, it is easy and quick to calculate and can be very useful as an early indicator. Weekly plotting is ideal. As we have seen, major trend reversals occur when the 50-week moving average is penetrated by the index, provided that the moving average is flat or heading in the same direction as the index. If the index is moving in the opposite direction, subsequent confirmation occurs when it becomes flat or starts to trend in the same direction as the index. Signals are also given when moving averages cross each other significantly, both heading in the same direction, but this will often occur later than the crossing of the 50-week moving average by the index.

Moving averages may easily be constructed using any index with which the fund or group of funds are closely correlated. Convention assumes that the S&P 500 represents the market, but on some occasions it may be preferable to use, for example, either the Wilshire 5000 index which really does represent the domestic stock market, a small company index such as the Wilshire 4500 index or the Russell 2000 index, or in the case of international equities, the EAFE index. For broadly diversified bond funds it may be desirable to use a bond index. Details of the more commonly used market indexes are given in Appendix D.

Plotting the moving average of an individual fund is more difficult than plotting an index, because profits are accumulated in the fund until the periodic distributions are made. At this time the price of the fund naturally declines, due to the loss of the assets paid out to shareholders. Compensating for this price drop involves adjusting prior values, which can be a tiresome task unless you are using a suitable computer program. Many newsletters provide the moving averages for individual funds, and this is probably the simplest way of obtaining them.

There is a broader question as to whether you should maintain any moving averages yourself or rely entirely on outside sources. We have so far encouraged the investor to act as the general manager of his portfolio and to delegate much of the detailed work to carefully chosen managers. You may decide to do the same with moving averages, but there are, in this particular case, advantages to doing some of it yourself. It only takes a few minutes per week, once you have set up the system; virtually any index can be found in Barron's, and the commoner ones in the Wall Street Journal or Investor's Business Daily. It obliges you to adopt the discipline of checking the market on a weekly basis, and it provides you with a permanent record using the particular index and the particular moving averages that you want.

For example, if you choose to plot the 10, 25 and 50-week moving averages of a suitable index, it would not be easy to find a suitable source of this information. The same may be true if you choose any but the most frequently used indexes. If you just want, perhaps, the 13 or 39-week moving average of the S&P 500, it is available from various newsletters. But perhaps the greatest advantage of doing this yourself is the opportunity to plot the results and judge the market situation yourself, and then see in time whether your interpretations of the trend was correct. This provides a learning experience which is hard to get from reading someone else's results later on. It provides an involvement and feeling for the market which is hard to get secondhand. It is the difference between reading about something and actually doing it.

What does the record show about moving averages? Of course, many market timing services claim consistently outstanding results and provide charts to "prove" it. As always, be skeptical. It is true that a few advisors have a good track record, but by no means do all of them. Many are using short-term market timing in an attempt to increase profits, rather than to reduce long-term risk. This approach is, at best, questionable. We earlier reviewed the use of market timing generally - of which the use of moving averages is usually an important part - and concluded that its main advantage was the reduction of market risk. This applied significantly to the majority of timers and resulted on average in 25% less volatility. The results of just the use of moving averages alone are harder to measure. One newsletter, The Telephone Switch Newsletter, uses just a 39-week moving average to generate buy and sell signals. Mark Hulbert has calculated the return due to the switching, separating out the individual fund selection and assuming simply that one was buying the market. Over a period from mid-1980 to the end of 1989, this simple system modestly beat a buy-and-hold approach. Apart from the atypical crash of 1987, this was a period of generally rising prices with rather few and mild market declines.

It is interesting to note that the editor of the newsletter, Dick Fabian, has been reported to say that the use of a 52-week moving average would produce superior results compared to his currently used 39-week moving average; but that relatively few of his subscribers would be willing to remain fully invested during the market corrections that would be tolerated by a 52-week moving average timing system.

Other studies have compared 25 different timing models over 19 years and measured comparative total profits. The various models represented many different types of indicators, including those based on market volume, relative strength and moving averages. A 50-week moving average was not included, but a 45-week one was, and it was among the top four models tested. It comfortably beat both a buy-and-hold approach and a 40-week moving average. The top four models all used extended time periods ranging from 39 to 66 weeks duration. Short-term market timing is not recommended.

It is probable that next time the market declines by 40% or more, as it has in the past, those following a proven longer term moving average timing system will be well protected, especially if used in conjunction with the few other indicators that we suggest. Unfortunately, memories are short, and because this type of decline has not occurred in recent years, people tend to forget that sooner or later it will happen again - it is only a matter of when. In the meantime, there is a very good chance of reducing risk and a reasonable chance of increasing profits by using appropriate moving averages as part of a timing system. No one indicator alone should be relied upon totally, and this includes moving averages. They are not infallible and should be used in combination with just a few other well chosen complementary indicators.

One simple way of adding further validity to moving average signals is by using them in conjunction with measures of price momentum, as previously mentioned briefly. These are simple to calculate and are usually recorded on the bottom of the same charts that are used for moving averages. They measure the rate of change of prices over a given period and reflect the sentiment of the market. You may liken the effect to a ball attached to a long length of elastic; if it moves too far and too fast in one direction, it will inevitably swing back in the other direction rapidly. So it is with price momentum. The further and faster a price moves in one direction, whether up or down, the more likely it is to swing back and experience a price correction.

Short-term momentum can be seen using a ten-week momentum oscillator. To calculate this, simply divide today's price by that of ten weeks ago and plot the answer as a percentage gain or loss. Over time, the value will oscillate back and forth each side of the zero line. This will give some feel for the short-term market behavior, which can be useful at danger points, such as in September and October 1987. It serves to give a close-up or magnification of your standard long-term trend indicators.

For longer term price momentum, a 12-month momentum oscillator is most useful. History shows that when this oscillator drops to about -25%, and then starts to rise, a good buying opportunity exists, and that when it rises to +30% and then falls back down below 30%, it is usually time to get out of the market. These signals do not occur very often but when they do they are most useful and confirm moving average indicators.

Newsletters that cover mutual fund moving averages include Mutual Fund Trends, Growth Fund Guide, The Telephone Switch Newsletter and The Chartist Mutual Fund Timer.

## THE COST OF MONEY - INTEREST RATES

Money is a commodity whose price fluctuates, depending upon current supply, demand and competition. The consumer, industry and government all use debt to an extraordinary extent, and the cost of borrowing money becomes a major element in the cost of operating the nation.

Most companies use debt, and the cost of borrowing directly affects their operating costs, their profits and, therefore, their stock price. It also affects the customer's willingness to buy. The sale of an automobile or a new house, for example, represents a product manufactured largely using debt and purchased on credit or mortgage, once again using debt. Debt is paid off with income after paying taxes; a steadily increasing portion of which is used to service federal and local government debt. Cheap money acts as a lubricant throughout the economy, and expensive money does just the opposite. The purchase of stock may be made on margin or credit, and when the interest debt burden becomes too great, stocks have to be sold to meet current obligations. When interest rates are high, the rapid and positive compounding of assets is equally matched by the negative and disastrous compounding of debt.

The cost of money is a basic and fundamental element of

the economy, and its behavior will drive the money markets, stocks, bonds and real estate. Furthermore, there is constant competition between these classes of assets for investor's money. If, say, stocks rise to a level whereby the dividend yield plus expected appreciation can no longer match the yield on bonds, then stock prices will decline, at least until they can.

There are several widely used market indicators based on interest rates. These can be generally classified as being based on short-term rates, long-term rates or the relationship between the two.

Long-term rates reflect the consensus of the market outlook for future inflation and economic activity, while short-term rates reflect more the market forces determining the price of money today - supply, demand and competition. Supply is controlled largely by the Federal Government, demand is provided by the Federal Government, industry and private debt and competition is provided mainly by domestic users and by the cost of foreign debt. The dollar is not the only financial commodity in the world marketplace.

Short-term rates are measured by Treasury Bill rates or more frequently by the federal funds rate. This is the rate at which banks which are members of the Federal Reserve Banking System borrow from each other overnight. This rate fluctuates daily.

A perhaps more attractive rate to use is the discount rate, which is the rate which the Federal Reserve charges member banks for loans. The central bank is reluctant to frequently change the discount rate, as it is seen by the markets as an expression of policy to influence the price of money. It is normally only changed about twice a year. Several successive increases or decreases in the discount rate are unlikely to be reversed rapidly, and, therefore, assume an aura of relative permanence and stability not otherwise found in most constantly fluctuating interest rates. Just as the company dividend is seen to be a statement of corporate health and having some stability, so the discount rate is seen as a statement of monetary health having some stability. So, just as we selected the P/D ratio over the P/E ratio as a more stable indicator, we now select the discount rate over the federal funds rate as a major interest rate indicator.

There are three principal ways in which the Federal Reserve Board can influence interest rates; using the discount rate, as just described, requiring banks to increase their reserves, and requiring brokers to increase the down payment for stocks bought on credit. Of these three alternatives, by far the most common means used is adjustment of the discount rate. The Federal Reserve tends to tighten money supply, and, therefore, increase interest rates before stock market peaks are reached and reduce rates before market bottoms are reached.

Experience shows that whenever the Federal Reserve eases money by reducing one of these requirements (usually by lowering the discount rate) twice in succession, a long-term stock market rise is likely to occur. This simple but significant observation was made by Fosback in 1973 and has since been supported by additional experience. It must now be rated as one of the most reliable market indicators known. While no signal is perfect, long-term studies with both the Dow Jones Industrial Average and the S&P 500 index have shown unusually consistent results. Over a period of 67 years, the S&P 500 index showed a median maximum gain of 31% during the year following this signal and only a 3% median maximum loss. Over a 70-year period, the Dow Jones Industrial Average showed a market decline averaging only 36 days, followed by gains over a period of almost three years and averaging over 120%. The signal was given 18 times over this period, and the only time it was not followed by some gain during the following 12 months was during the great depression of 1929. Then even this stimulus of a reduction of interest rates could not prevent a further decline.

The average gains in the Dow Jones Industrial Average (DJIA) in the periods prior to and following a Federal Reserve signal, are shown in Figure 22. During the six months prior to the signal, the DJIA declined 2.2%. During the three months before and the month after the signal, it was almost flat, and then it typically took off — rising 14% in the first three months and 30% in the first 12 months following the signal.

If changes in the discount rate can be used to detect market bottoms, can they also be used to detect market tops? The answer is yes, but not with the same high level of historical reliability. The rule here is slightly different. It requires that the discount rate be raised three times in succession, following an earlier series of declines. This usually causes the stock market to come to a standstill and then decline.

As a means of confirming signals arising from changes in the discount rate, the federal funds rate may be examined, but this mainly tends to give signals of shorter term significance as it is a more volatile measure. Some analysts track the trend of the federal funds rate using moving averages and momentum indexes, just as we discussed for stock index price movements. Others have studied the relationship between the federal funds rate and the discount rate. They have concluded that, whereas the federal funds rate has normally been lower than the discount rate, periods when it remains above the discount rate portend a very tight money situation and a poor outlook for the stock market. Basically, it means that the banks are charging each other more for money than the rate available from the Federal Reserve, which indicates that money is in short supply.

A simple way of examining the trend of the federal funds rate is to construct a 12-month momentum oscillator which shows the percentage change compared to a year ago. If the value is negative, that is rates have declined over the year, it is considered bullish for stocks. If they are more than 15% higher, and have thus significantly increased, it is considered bearish. This has given quite good signals in the past, but

FIGURE 2·2

**STOCK PRICES AND FEDERAL RESERVE ACTION**

Changes in the Dow Jones Industrial Average before and after
the Federal Reserve Board eases monetary policy on two consecutive
occassions. Most signals result from two consecutive reductions
in the discount rate. Values are averages, 1914 – 1991.

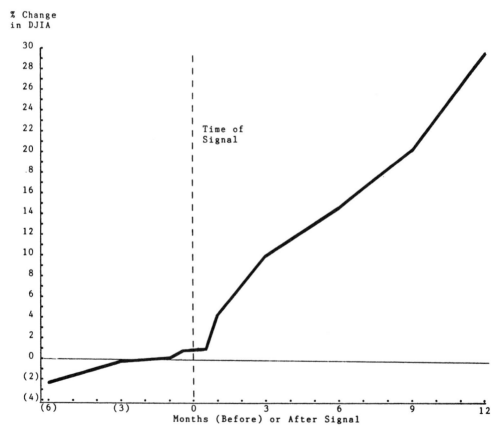

Based on data from Growth Fund Research, inc.

should only be used as a confirming signal, together with changes in the discount rate.

Another very simple and handy confirmatory check using interest rates is just to compare the yield on three-month Treasury Bills with the dividend yield on the S&P 500. When the yield on Treasury bills is twice, or more than twice, the yield on stocks it suggests a highly priced and therefore weak stock market. When it falls to 1 1/2 times the yield on stocks, it suggests the opposite.

## IDENTIFYING BULL AND BEAR MARKETS

In the real world, even well established indicators may contradict each other and investment decisions are rarely totally objective. Nevertheless, if you can separate yourself from the current emotions of the majority, which are driven alternatively by greed and fear and can coolly read what the market is telling you about the long-term trend, you can be right much of the time.

To conclude this chapter on managing market cycles, we will summarize two scenarios: one typical of the very early stages of a bull market and the other typical of the very early stages of a bear market. We are not attempting to identify exact market tops or bottoms but rather to identify those times when it is better to be buying than selling and vice versa. The identification of market tops is more difficult than identifying market bottoms, but at those times when the market is dangerously overvalued, it is important to recognize this and reduce your exposure to it.

## IDENTIFYING THE BULL

You are about to witness a bull market when:

1.  You wish you had allocated less of your assets to the stock market, and as soon as you can get out of the market you will. You have lost a lot of money, and there seems to be no end in sight.

2.  Your friends are no longer boasting of their successes. Your broker, if you find the need to have one, is tactfully silent or unavailable and the press is loudly concluding that the stock market is no place for the small investor and never will be again because this time it is different and the rules have changed.

3.  The television news and your favorite news magazine is likening this to the previous great recessions and depressions. They may even be showing pictures of the old soup kitchen and unemployment lines of the 1929 to 1932 depression. The government should do something!

4.  Financial newsletters are forecasting further declines, mutual funds are accumulating cash in spite of heavy redemptions, and many professional money managers are, in fact, paralyzed with fear. They are following the herd for safety. Some of the younger ones have never experienced such markets — they have only excelled in bull markets.

5.  The compulsive traders are selling short, that is, promising to deliver shares at today's price sometime in the future; convinced that at that time they will be able to buy them at a lower price and make a profit.

6.  Unemployment is still high and rising, interest rates and inflation are rather low and falling, bankruptcies and defaults are increasing, and the general economy has been in recession now for some months, maybe a year or a little longer.

7. Raw material surpluses exist, commodity prices are depressed and manufacturing capacity is under-utilized. People want your business.

8. There was a presidential election just over two years ago, but after an initial short spurt, the economy seemed to start falling apart. It may well be either the 5th or 8th year of the decade.

9. The price/dividend ratio of the S&P 500 has dropped from the 30's down into the teens. The dividend yield is now between 5% and 6%.

10. The market has rebounded from its last major low point, dropped back to that low point once or twice and has now advanced off it. Volume has been low.

11. Your S&P 500 moving average chart shows that the index has dropped through the 50, 25 and 10-week moving average lines. The downward slope of at least the ten-week moving average is not as steep as it was; it is levelling out, or may already be flat. The ten-week momentum oscillator is certainly less negative than it was and may even have recently turned up into a positive area. The 12-month momentum oscillator has been down around -25 but has picked up a bit.

12. Interest rates have been declining, the Federal Reserve Board has lowered the discount rate twice since it last raised it. The last time it was lowered was about a month ago. The federal funds rate is moving below the discount rate, short-term rates are lower than long-term rates, and the yield on Treasury Bills is no more than 1 1/2 times that of the S&P 500 index.

13. When the overall market has been declining recently, the proportion of individual stocks that are increasing in price is greater than it has been previously.

   During the random short periods of rising prices, the market breadth is wide. That is, many different stocks are traded and there are far more advances than declines. During these short periods of advance, it is mainly the smaller, more aggressive mutual funds that move up the most.

When many of these circumstances are recognizable, the bull is snorting to be let out, but most people will still mistake it for the growl of a bear.

This is likely to mark the very early stages of a new long-term price trend. However, it may be no more than a rally in a bear market. Bull markets frequently start suddenly, as soon as a few buyers appear after most of the selling is over. This often forms a price pattern in a V shape rather than the flatter inverted U shape more typical of an early bear market.

If it is a true bull market, soon the momentum indicators will move up and the index will rapidly move up to penetrate its moving averages. The ten-week moving average will turn up, and somewhat later the 25-week will become flat and then move up. By this time you should be buying, if you have not already done so. During this time, market volume, breadth and price will all increase sharply, led by the more aggressive higher beta issues. Finally, the 50-week moving average will be flat and then move upward.

The bull has finally broken out, but many will still not recognize it. You should now be very full invested. Remember that the entire market gain occurs in only 6.7% of the time and much of that is in the early stages of a bull market. Be there! If the market has already suffered a severe drop, buy too early rather than too late.

## IDENTIFYING THE BEAR

The bear will appear growling when:
1.    Times are good, and at last the stock market looks both safe and rewarding. Nearly everyone is agreed on this and they can't all be wrong, can they?

2.  For the past two years the stock market has been the place to be, leaving bonds and money markets far behind. In any case, it's not difficult to make money in the stock market, so why do the old timers keep talking about risk? If ever there was a time for aggressive investing this must be it. Everyone is doing it, and you just can't afford to be left out of it. Surely the way to make money is to buy on margin?

3.  The newspapers are filled with advertisements for mutual funds which you should buy because of their outstanding recent performance. Editorial opinion tacitly supports these advertisers. Advisory services are bullish, convinced that the market has more yet to offer, and in any case, they will tell you in plenty of time when and if to get out, they say.

4.  Most mutual funds are receiving a lot of new cash from investors, and they are investing it all. Mutual fund cash positions are very low. The individual investor is buying avidly, but insider purchases are low and market specialist short selling is high.

5.  This year and last year have seen low unemployment and a high level of business activity which has reduced the level of service to consumers. The economy has been on a roll for a while; college graduates with useful skills are sought out by employers, and life has become a little fat and happy. Many organizations are overstaffed. We had a presidential election just last year and now everyone feels much happier about the economy.

6.  All the same, inflation has been accelerating and interest rates have been rising for a while. The Federal Reserve Board has increased the discount rate three times running, to try to control inflation, but it doesn't seem to trouble anyone. Some raw materials seem to be in temporary short supply.

7.   Short term interest rates are now much higher than longer term interest rates. The federal funds rate is now more than 15% higher than it was a year ago. Three month Treasury Bills are yielding more than twice the yield of the S&P 500 index, but who needs Treasury Bills when the stock market is so strong?

8.   The price/dividend ratio of the S&P 500 has been edging up. It has been above $30 for quite a while and now it is edging up to between $33 and $34 and is rising steadily. Both prices and dividends are increasing, but company profits seem to be slowing down. A big part of their rise is due to an increasing level of inflation, which is a little troublesome. Although the markets generally are rising, on many days more stocks are declining than rising.

9.   Economic news contains some serious negative signs, but the market seems rather unconcerned. The experts explain to us that the market has already discounted all this bad news and will shortly be continuing its upward path. A few of the advisors and money managers with the best documented track record turn bearish. They are generally ignored by the profit-hungry pack.

10.  The moving average charts show that the index has been bounding around a bit lately, dropping from its previous highs a couple of times and then recovering. Both the short and long-term momentum oscillators are heading down and the short-term one may be negative. Clearly, the rate of growth has slowed down. The moving averages and the index are much closer together than they were this time last year, and the ten-week moving average is no longer going up. The 25-week and 50-week moving averages at this time are leveling off.

When much of all this seems familiar, the good times may be over, and it is certainly no time to put new money into the market. The cautious investor should get out of the market at this stage. It is likely that soon the index will rapidly penetrate its moving averages on the way down, both momentum oscillators will be declining and negative, and the ten-week moving average will head down, if it has not already done so. The 25-week moving average will later decline, and by this time a significant market drop may have occurred. The bear market will finally be confirmed when the 50-week moving average declines. At this time you should certainly be totally out of the market, but you may not want to wait for this final signal.

The very late stages of a bull market have a poor risk/reward ratio, and there is little harm in leaving for the safety of a money market before the game is over. Perhaps you should leave something for the person who wants to buy your fund at this stage of the cycle!

You will never see these two scenarios exactly as described, because market cycles never repeat themselves exactly. However, they should help you to gain an objective view of the current stage of the market cycle — a thing that few individual or professional investors can consistently do.

You may have noticed that throughout this chapter on managing market cycles, we have not included speculation on the future state of the economy, likely political actions, what the Federal Reserve Board may or may not do in the future, or other futuristic prognostications. We have included no economic indicators to predict the growth of G.N.P. or any other measure. We have not predicated our management of market cycles on the forecasting ability of economists. This removes a vast amount of generally conflicting and unreliable data.

In the words of the world famous economist, John Kenneth Galbraith *"the safe rule for the citizen on economic predictions is to ignore them."*

We have simply observed where we are now, what has already actually happened and what trends have been established. Following trends means that you may not be on the very cutting edge of change, but cutting edges can be sharp and dangerous. We are managing the cycle by carefully following established trends and existing market patterns. We are using just an understanding of market value, market price movements and interest rate changes. For each of these areas we have chosen one principal indicator — the P/D ratio, moving averages and changes in the discount rate. For each indicator we have provided confirmatory signals, if needed. The intelligent use of just these three indicators will greatly help you to protect your assets and win the money game.

CHAPTER 13

# HOW TO MANAGE YOUR PORTFOLIO

In previous chapters we have discussed why you need to invest effectively; how you can construct an ideal portfolio for your particular needs; how to select the best funds; and how to manage both risk and market cycles. We have advocated investing for the long-term, using broad diversification, and avoiding unnecessary risk. Remain skeptical and questioning and don't mindlessly follow the crowd. We have encouraged you to act as the manager of your own financial destiny, emphasizing patience, discipline and a rare commodity — just plain common sense.

Successful investing should not be complicated. By following these simple ideas, you will, over time, amass considerable wealth. This cannot be left to grow wild. It needs monitoring and careful management but not frequent tinkering. Just how it should be managed will depend on your investment time horizon, your risk tolerance and the time and effort that you wish to devote to building wealth. You alone can determine that.

In this chapter, we will present some of the more attractive alternatives that you may choose for managing your portfolio. Some of these techniques can be combined to suit your own particular needs. Many of the ideas have been discussed in previous chapters and will be referred to only briefly here. This chapter should not be read until you have studied the previous chapters. On its own it may not be self-explanatory. It is, to some extent, a synthesis of previous discussions applied to the practical matter of managing your assets.

From this chapter you will be able to select a specific management style that suits your needs and your temperament. Having chosen it, you should stick with it.

## THE EQUITY PORTFOLIO

## THE BUY-AND-HOLD APPROACH

If your time horizon is very long, if you can suffer serious bear market losses with equanimity and if you have very little time or inclination to manage your financial affairs, you may be well advised to follow a buy-and-hold approach. It is certainly better than the average attempt at market timing.

If, on the other hand, you may need to liquidate your assets within, say, five to ten years, or if, say, a 30% to 40% drop in value of your equities during a severe bear market will give you sleepless nights, this may not be the best approach for you.

A buy-and-hold approach worked well throughout most of the 80's and very early 90's, when the market was on an unusually long general up-trend. Remember though, that since 1926 there have been six different periods which produced losses in common stocks bought and held for five years. There were only two separate ten-year periods that produced a loss (1929-1938 and 1930-1939), which covered the great depression. No 20-year period has produced a loss.

The concept of buy-and-hold should not be interpreted as necessarily buying one or more fund and locking them away and forgetting them. That is an unwarranted risk. By definition, it means being fully invested in the market at all times but switching between funds as necessary.

You should now decide whether a buy-and-hold approach is right for you in regard to either all or a part of your assets.

## WHEN TO BUY

Whether you decide to buy and remain fully invested forever, or whether you intend to move to cash when the market becomes too risky, the question still arises as to when to buy. If you have a lump sum to invest, this may not be an easy decision. If you park it in a money market fund until a propitious time arises, you may miss a sudden and significant bull market rise. If, on the other hand, you invest when the market is seriously overvalued, it may take years to regain your original investment. You should not rely on how the market is perceived but upon what it actually does. There is nearly always bad news on the horizon, and today's trying times become tomorrow's "good old days." One of Wall Street's truest sayings is that the market climbs a wall of worry. If there is nothing to worry about, the market is most likely overvalued and heading for a correction. Also, you will never have all the facts. The person who insists on seeing with perfect clarity before deciding never decides. Rather, you should use objective measures of the market, such as those we have discussed. Then decisions will be automatic.

For example, you could well decide not to invest when the market is overvalued, as judged by the price/dividend ratio. Certainly, it would seem unwise to make major new investments when the P/D ratio is much above $30 and positively foolish to do so when it is over $34. You can look this up in Barron's, where it appears as the dividend yield in the section entitled "Market Laboratory" under the heading "Indexes P/Es and Yields." As we have shown previously, it is necessary to divide the dividend yield into 100 to get the P/D ratio. You may also find the dividend yield for the S&P 500 index in Monday's Wall Street Journal in Section C, in a block within the chart of the DJIA.

You may also use the moving averages of the relevant stock index, for example the S&P 500, to judge market condition. You could well decide to wait until the index is below its long-term moving average and moving up before investing, but this would take some time, depending upon the stage of the cycle.

You can confirm these two approaches by checking interest rates, particularly the discount rate. Has the discount rate recently risen three consecutive times or been reduced on two consecutive occasions? The discount rate, together with the federal funds rate and the Treasury Bill yields, can be found in Barron's in the section entitled "Market Laboratory/Economic Indicators" under the heading of "Money Rates." They may also be found in the Wall Street Journal under the heading "Money Rates."

Finally, if by checking these three complementary indicators you think that the market may be near a major turning point, check the scenarios identifying bulls and bears in the previous chapter.

If you are still undecided, invest a portion of your lump sum now and decide what specific event will need to occur in relation to the above indicators before you will invest the remainder. Then, when that signal is given - just do it. You have to get wet before you can swim.

## DOLLAR COST AVERAGING

If instead of investing a lump sum, you are investing out of income, you have the interesting possibility of what is commonly called "dollar cost averaging." This implies that you undertake to invest a fixed amount every period, such as each month, for many years. This fixed amount is regularly placed in a chosen fund, quite irrespective of the state of the market cycle. The success of the method is dependent upon first selecting good funds, and then continuing to invest at regular periods, even at extremes of bull and bear markets. If strictly practiced, this will reduce the average cost of shares bought, because more will be purchased with a given sum when the price is depressed and fewer will be purchased when the price is higher. Psychologically, the investor has the comfort of knowing that when prices decline it will be possible to purchase more shares than previously. However, if you do not have a time horizon of at least one market cycle, or you do not have the resolve to invest automatically every month, whatever the state of the market and the state of your finances, then this is not for you.

To understand the benefits, it is helpful to take an example. Table 44 shows an example in which $300 is invested each period, of perhaps one month or one-quarter. The share price fluctuates from period to period, and this determines the number of shares purchased each period. At the end of ten periods, $3,000 has been invested, 363.4 shares have been purchased and the average price during the period was $9.40. The actual cost to the dollar cost averaging investor was only $8.26, calculated by dividing the sum invested ($3,000) by the number of shares acquired (363.4). The investor is, in effect, buying below the average market price. In addition to this example, which used fluctuating market prices, it can be shown that comparable benefits are obtained in only rising or declining markets.

Various attempts have been made to modify the dollar cost averaging approach in order to enhance returns, but caution is indicated as the benefit can easily be lost. It is essential to

TABLE 44

**THE ADVANTAGE OF DOLLAR COST AVERAGING**

$300 Invested Per Period For Ten Periods

| Investment Per Period ($) | Share Price ($) | Shares Acquired # |
|---|---|---|
| 300 | 10 | 30.0 |
| 300 | 9 | 33.3 |
| 300 | 7 | 42.9 |
| 300 | 5 | 60.0 |
| 300 | 5 | 60.0 |
| 300 | 8 | 37.5 |
| 300 | 9 | 33.3 |
| 300 | 12 | 25.0 |
| 300 | 14 | 21.4 |
| 300 | 15 | 20.0 |
| Total: 3,000 | Average: 9.4 | Total: 363.4 |

Average Price Per Share = $9.40
Average Price Actually Paid = $8.26  ($3,000/363.4)

continue investing throughout a bear market, but a case could be made for putting the regular monthly sum into a money market fund when the market becomes severely overvalued, say if the P/D ratio rises over $34. However, for most people it is probably better to adopt a strict routine of dollar cost averaging into their chosen funds, rather than trying to modify the system. Their management efforts can then be focused entirely on fund selection. As with the buy-and-hold approach, dollar cost averaging simply implies being fully invested at all times; it does not preclude switching between funds as appropriate.

## CYCLICAL MARKET TIMING

We recommend that you never attempt to use market timing to switch between asset classes, such as stocks and bonds. It generally does not work and can be dangerous to your overall wealth if you consistently get it wrong. Within your equity portfolio, short-term market timing is unlikely to be consistently successful, due to the random short-term movements of the market. Longer term market timing, based on the primary movements of a complete four-year cycle, is more likely to be successful, particularly if achieved by following existing trends and using a few well proven complementary indicators, such as were described in the previous chapter. The study of market value, moving averages of price, and interest rate movements provides a powerful management tool.

The objective in this case is not primarily to increase investment returns, although this is likely to result; it is to reduce market risk. This position on market timing will satisfy neither the supporters of the efficient market theory, who claim timing to be futile, nor most of the market timing services and newsletters who generally claim dramatic results using their individual brand of usually shorter term market timing. In reality, the shorter term the indicators used, the more often they will be wrong, and the longer term the indicators used, the later the signals will be, missing some of the market movement.

Most investors who are prepared to make the effort would be well advised to practice cyclical market timing as previously described, at least with their more volatile funds. That is, unless they have an investment time horizon of several decades, in which case it becomes less important. As a practical matter, few people can observe with equanimity the loss of up to half their stock assets, which can readily occur in a major recession. A decline of 40% in the total market will typically produce a loss of 50% or more in the higher beta funds.

It is important to remember that the entire market rise of the S&P 500 index has occurred in only 50 months of a 62-year period, or 6.7% of the time. In the case of small company stocks, it occurred in only 4.0% of the time. These rare periods occur most frequently in the early stages of a bull market. If a timing system misses a significant part of this early rise, it is unlikely to be satisfactory. Therefore, you should tend to re-enter the market "too soon." You don't have to wait for the absolute bottom. Once the market has dropped 20% or 30%, the downside risk is likely to be much smaller than the upside potential. Conversely, late in a market rise the total returns will probably decrease to a level where the risk/reward ratio becomes poor. It is better to move into a money market fund sooner rather than later. Towards the end of a bull market the downside risk is likely to be far greater than the upside potential. Only about 10% of the total rise occurs in the last quarter of the cycle's duration.

The use of cyclical market timing means that for perhaps 1/3 of the time, the equity portfolio will be placed in a money market fund awaiting a re-investment opportunity. This has certain advantages. It means that for 1/3 of the time, the portfolio is experiencing zero market risk. The total returns are also likely to be greater during this period. For example, from the market peak of 1987 until the end of the first quarter of 1991, the returns from a money market fund would have comfortably exceeded the total return on a group of high quality growth funds. It also means that during a period of market decline, not only is the decline avoided, but additional funds are accumulated for subsequent re-investment at a lower share price. This can be quite significant. For example, if you are out of the stock market for 12 months, and earning 6% in a money market fund while the stock market declines 30%, you may subsequently buy 51% more shares than you would otherwise have owned (i.e. 1.06/0.70 = 1.51 or 51% more). If the decline is only 15%, you can still obtain almost 1/4 more shares (i.e. 1.06/0.85 = 1.24 or 24% more).

We can examine the practical use of our three major timing indicators during the period August 1982 through March 1991, and see how market value indicators, price moving averages and interest rate indicators each make a useful contribution.

A buy signal was given in August 1982, which can now be seen as the beginning of a very long market rise. The indicator was the S&P 500 crossing its 50-week moving average, which was flat. A sell signal occurred in February 1984, due to the same indicator, but this proved only to be a minor decline and a 50-week moving average buy signal was given six months later in August 1984. This was further confirmed in December 1984, when the Federal Reserve Board had lowered the discount rate twice. The market then rose sharply for more than three years, becoming grossly overvalued in 1987. The P/D ratio reached $34 in March 1987, triggering a sell signal. The next buy signal did not occur until November 1988, well after the rise had begun. It was produced by the index crossing its 12-month moving average. The market continued to rise until the next 50-week moving average sell signal in August

1990; a similar buy signal followed in early February 1991, soon confirmed in mid-February by changes in the discount rate. The market continued to rise until the end of the observation period.

During this period of almost a decade, the system produced just three sell signals - in 1984, 1987 and 1990. Most signals were initially given by moving averages, but the P/D ratio gave a very valuable signal in 1987, thus avoiding a big decline. The Federal Reserve action on the discount rate provided useful later confirmation of buy signals in 1984 and again in 1991. Each type of signal clearly has its place. When used together, they have provided the desired reduction of volatility.

It was a period of generally rising prices during which market timing is hard to justify. Furthermore, we used the most conservative 50-week moving average signals on most occasions. However, during this period, while the S&P 500 index rose from 119 to 380, producing a gain of 219%, the timing model, as described, produced a gain of 281%, assuming a money market yield of 7% when not invested in stocks. This was appropriate for the period. This increased gain produced 28% more cash at the end of the period than a buy-and-hold approach. Greatly reduced risk, together with increased profits, were adequate rewards for the long-term timing.

We have indicated sources of information for the indicators recommended if you wish to prepare charts yourself. The dividend yield and the discount rate are quite simple to look up in the newspaper. Maintaining moving averages is a simple matter once you have set your record system. For example, for a 50-week moving average, you initially need to obtain from your library past data for each of the last 50 weeks. You simply total them and divide by 50, adding one new value and subtracting the oldest value each week. Twenty-five and ten-week moving averages may be similarly prepared. Some people prefer to do this on a computer, but it is not necessary.

If you wish to add refinements when plotting the data, you should use semi-logarithmic paper. This will ensure that the slope of any part of the chart may be directly compared with any other part. Otherwise, the slope will inevitably become steeper over time in a generally rising market.

If you prefer to have the work done for you, a number of useful newsletters provide comprehensive information. These will be reviewed in the next chapter.

## SWITCHING BETWEEN FUNDS

Whether you practice a buy-and-hold approach, use dollar cost averaging or cyclical market timing, you will need to ensure that you remain in the better performing funds within a given group. There is no fund for all seasons. Fund managements change, market segments come and go in popularity, and even investment styles have their own periods of fashion. It does not matter what is "right," only what people are buying or are about to buy. Market segments and styles may be out of fashion for many years; there is no point in investing in those out of fashion merely to wait for several years for their merit to be realized. This does not mean that it is wise to hop frequently from one fund to another, it is not. It does mean that funds should be selected on their known perfor- mance trends and not on speculation about their future.

In Chapter 8 we discussed in detail how to pick the best funds for your purpose, within any type of fund. This applies not only to your initial selection of funds but equally to the ongoing management of the portfolio. Sooner or later, you will need to sell the funds that you have so carefully selected. You may do this for the following reasons:

1. Your timing indicators may tell you to get out of the market and move to cash, if you are practicing cyclical market timing.

2.  The long-term moving average of the individual fund is clearly crossed by the fund price moving down and the moving average also moving down. For this purpose, a 39 or 40-week moving average is most commonly used by advisory newsletters.

3.  The relative strength line is below its moving average or is trending sharply down over a period of at least three to six months. Since certain types of fund will typically over or under-perform the market at different stages of the cycle, it is helpful to compare the slope of the relative strength line with other funds having similar objectives.

4.  The performance ranking of the fund, based on the average of several prior periods, is significantly declining. This approach was discussed in Chapter 8, and its practical use over a decade has produced generally good results. You may choose to upgrade to a better performing fund when the monthly ranking of your present fund is steadily declining and ceases to be, for example, in the top quartile of comparable funds. More or less switching can be achieved simply by changing the performance requirement. You could choose either the top 10% if you wish to upgrade frequently or the top half if you do not. Whatever criterion you select should then be adopted consistently.

5.  You wish to adjust your portfolio for the stage of the market cycle. The early stages of a bull market favor high beta funds, and the later stages tend to favor lower beta funds having a higher dividend yield. It may make sense part way through the market rise to switch to a balance containing more growth and income funds and equity income funds and less aggressive growth and aggressive sector funds.

6.  The fund management changes and the new manager

has inadequate proven and relevant experience or if the objectives or operation of the fund change adversely. An example would be if a fund implemented a significant 12b-1 plan or otherwise unreasonably reduced its efficiency. Beware of funds that are temporarily absorbing management expenses to induce you to invest. They will ultimately charge you a fee which should be examined carefully.

7. Your long-term investment objectives change.

In addition to these specific reasons to sell a fund, it is instructive periodically to examine your portfolio and ask yourself the question - would I buy these funds today if I were setting up a new portfolio? Carefully review the criteria described in Chapter 8. If the answer is no, then why do you hold them?

When initially investing in a fund you should determine how to sell it when the time comes. In some fund families, redemption can be achieved by telephone if prior arrangements are made. In many cases it is convenient to open a money market account within the same fund family, using just a nominal investment. Frequently a switch can be made by telephone from an equity fund to an existing money market fund account. Quite often the money market fund will offer check writing privileges, so that you can write a check to purchase your new fund.

Some investors find it worth the convenience to open an account with a discount broker who handles many no-load mutual funds, such as Charles Schwab. For a small fee they will arrange the transaction for you and provide a consolidated statement of your account. This may be convenient if you own a large number of funds or want to invest less than the normal minimum sum. Some fund families, perhaps to frustrate short-term market traders, require a written request to sell with a guaranteed signature, and then seem to complete the transaction with a sense of leisure. Most of the large families of funds, and many of the smaller ones, offer a high level of good service.

## THE CONCEPT OF A CORE HOLDING

A practical question facing investors is how to put together the various useful management techniques and actually manage a portfolio of funds on an ongoing basis.

First of all, it is necessary to decide how many different funds should be managed. In the interests of effective diversification, no more than 10% of total invested assets, equity and fixed income, should be assigned to a single mutual fund. The only exceptions are money market funds and index funds representing a major market segment, if such funds have shown the ability to approximately match their index. Holding a number of equity funds permits diversification across fund objectives, management styles, risk level and company size. It also permits some global diversification. Most of these considerations apply also to fixed income funds.

There are, however, two other dimensions to consider: 1) whether to assign a part or all of the portfolio to a particular investment method, such as buy-and-hold, dollar cost averaging or cyclical market timing, and 2) whether to use more frequent or just occasional fund switching.

Experience shows that no one approach is consistently perfect, and a very important consideration is the comfort level of the individual investor. It is likely that if the method chosen is temperamentally compatible, and not particularly worrisome, then objective decisions rather than emotional reactions are more likely to prevail.

One approach which has proved useful to many experienced investors is to assign part of the equity portfolio, let us say one-half, and consider that as a steady, conservative core holding which will tend to track the total market and compound nicely over many years. Broad based index funds are an ideal choice for at least a part of such a holding. The better ones do track the markets they represent and permit broad diversification very inexpensively. In this way, even a fairly small core holding can represent virtually the entire world stock market. If you plan to use a buy-and-hold approach for any part of your portfolio, this is the place to do so. Even here though, if the market becomes grossly over valued, as it did in 1987, you may still decide to move into a money market fund, but this would be rather rare.

When in an index fund, there is no longer any reason to periodically switch between funds, provided that the fund is achieving its objective. Using this approach of index funds in a core holding, you may have perhaps half your portfolio very effectively diversified and passively managed very inexpensively.

An example of how such a core holding could be structured is shown in Table 45. First you need to decide what proportion of domestic and international markets you wish to own. The example shown reflects 75% domestic and 25% international, but you may adjust this as you wish. Within the domestic market, the S&P 500 index contains mainly large and medium sized companies and represents around 73% of the total domestic capitalization. This proportion will vary a little over time, but the exact proportion is unimportant. Smaller companies, represented by the Wilshire 4500 index, constitute the remaining approximately 27% of the market. If you choose the total domestic market to be 75% of the core holding, then 55% (75 x 0.73) should be placed in an index fund representing the S&P 500 and 20% (75 x 0.27) in an index fund representing the Wilshire 4500 index. A simpler method is to use the Vanguard Index Trust Total Market Portfolio fund, which attempts to track the Wilshire 5000

TABLE 45

**AN EXAMPLE OF A GLOBAL CORE HOLDING USING INDEX FUNDS**

| Global Distribution | Market Segment | Proportion of Total | Suitable Index Fund |
|---|---|---|---|
| Total Domestic Market (75%) | Virtually the entire U.S. Stock Market as Represented by the Wilshire 5000 Index | 75% | Vanguard Index Trust Total Market Portfolio |
| Total International Market (25%) | Pacific Area, as Represented by the MSCI-Pacific Index (47% of international allocation) | 12% | Vanguard International Equity Index Fund, Pacific Portfolio |
| | Europe, as Represented by the MSCI-Europe Index (53% of international allocation) | 13% | Vanguard International Equity Index Fund, European Portfolio |

Note:  The Morgan Stanley Capital Perspective (MSCI) Pacific and Europe Indexes together comprise the MSCI Europe Australia Far East (EAFE) Index.

index, representing virtually the entire domestic market. This fund, introduced in 1992, marks the first time that it has been possible to buy a representative sample of the U.S. stock market in a single portfolio.

For the international portion of the core holding you may again use just one fund, the Vanguard International Equity Index Fund, which has two separate portfolios - one covering Japan, Australia, New Zealand, Hong Kong and Singapore - the other covering 13 western European countries.

In both cases the portfolios are weighted according to market size. Table 45 shows that 47% of the international capitalization is in the Pacific area, mainly Japan, and 53% is in Europe. This translates to 12% and 13%, respectively, of the total core holding in this example.

This core portfolio, using just two funds (one having two portfolios), will give you a stake in most of the world's market value, and it will provide it both simply and extraordinarily inexpensively. You can customize it to produce whatever proportions you prefer. It is, of course, not necessary to use Vanguard funds if you can find others with the same diversification at the same or lower cost.

The use of index funds in a core holding is simply one alternative. In addition, or instead, you may select other funds which approach the elusive ideal of being "all weather funds." The most suitable general types of fund for this purpose are the most consistently high performing growth and income and equity income funds. These will still need managing according to your chosen methods, but they tend to be less volatile than most equity funds and also, in general, somewhat more consistent in performance than the more aggressive funds.

If you choose to adopt the concept of a core holding that will either represent the world market and be passively managed, or else use funds requiring rather limited management and that are rather conservative, then with the rest of your equity portfolio you may try quite actively to beat the market. While your core portfolio almost looks after itself, you are free to devote most of your efforts to whatever level of more aggressive management you may choose with the remainder of your portfolio. For example, if you choose to follow a fairly aggressive upgrading of your funds, switching periodically into the top performing funds in the pursuit of maximum gain, you may do so in the knowledge that a substantial part of your equity portfolio is quietly working away for you in a solid core holding. The more aggressive your fund selection and management, the greater is the merit of the concept of a core holding.

The use of a core holding is, in a sense, another dimension of diversification, only in this case it is diversification of your own management styles rather than that of a fund manager.

The actively managed part of the portfolio should first be characterized by risk level. You have earlier decided on a suitable risk level for your entire investment portfolio and the correct permanent allocation of assets between equity and fixed income portfolios. You now know the risk level of whatever core holding you chose, so the risk level of your more actively managed funds should bring the total into balance. This does not mean that all the actively managed funds should have the same risk level, but that their average should be appropriate. For example, if you have determined that because of your high proportion of low risk fixed income holdings your overall equity portfolio can have an average beta of about 1.0, and if your core holding is half of your equity portfolio and is conservatively invested in low volatility growth and income funds, then your more actively managed funds can have an average beta greater than 1.0. This would permit the inclusion of some quite aggressive funds. This is only an example, and you may, for example, have a smaller proportion of fixed income funds or a lower risk tolerance.

Having determined the average risk level, it is now necessary to ensure that the selected funds have appropriate and diversified objectives and management styles, and that they cover a selection of market segments. (Here refer again to the Investment Style Matrix shown in Table 26.) Table 46 provides some examples of alternative fund objectives, management styles and market segments, together with representative funds reflecting these characteristics. These are by no means the only variables, but reflect some of the more important ones. The funds listed are only a few examples and are not specific recommendations.

A certain skill is required in blending these different variables. If the portfolio proportionately reflects them all it will result in something close to an index fund, but at much higher cost. On the other hand, concentrated focus on just one or two variables will increase risk and also potential reward, if the judgement is correct. To beat the market it is essential to be somewhat selective, otherwise you will own the market. The stage of the market cycle and the relative strength of the different fund types can guide you. If, for example, you wish to own some high volatility aggressive growth funds, do so at the beginning of the market rise, not towards the end of the rising leg of the cycle. In an actively managed portfolio you may want to own some growth funds with above average betas, but in this case make sure that the risk-adjusted return has been satisfactory. Higher risk may be acceptable, but only if rewarded with high returns. In an actively managed, more aggressive portfolio, to buy a sector fund on a hunch is, at best, speculative, but to buy it based on recent relative strength and current momentum may cause you to be well rewarded for a while.

The concept of a fairly conservative core holding, used together with an actively managed and perhaps more aggressive group of funds, appeals to many experienced investors.

TABLE 46

**EXAMPLES OF DIFFERENT FUND CHARACTERISTICS**

Some of The Choices Available For an Equity Portfolio Utilizing Different Fund Characteristics

| Fund Characteristic | Example | Representative Funds |
|---|---|---|
| Objective | Capital Appreciation | T. R. Price Capital Appreciation, Fidelity Capital Appreciation, Counsellors Capital Appreciation |
| | Income | Lindner Dividend, Financial Industrial Income, Vanguard Equity Income |
| Management Style | Aggressive Investing | Kaufmann, Strong Discovery, Founders Special |
| | Growth Investing | Gabelli Growth, Janus, IAI Regional, Brandywine |
| | Value Investing | Vanguard Windsor, Gabelli Asset, Mutual Shares |
| | Fully Invested | Twentieth Century Funds, all Index Funds |
| | Enhanced with Options | Value Line Leveraged Growth, Analytical Optioned Equ. |
| Market Segment | Large Companies | Vanguard World – U.S. Growth, Twentieth Century Select |
| | Small Companies | Janus Venture, Founders Frontier, SIT Growth, Babson Enterprise, Pennsylvania Mutual, Montgomery Small Cap |
| | International | T. R. Price International Stock, Harbor International |
| | International, Emerging Markets | Fidelity International Opportunities, T. R. Price New Asia, Montgomery Emerging Markets |
| | Global | Scudder Global, Dreyfus Strategic World Investing |
| | Sector | Vanguard Specialized Energy, T. R. Price Science and Technology, Financial Strategic Portfolios – Health Scien Fidelity Utility |

They have money on both the hare and the tortoise. It is just one example of how a portfolio may be managed. The important point is to adopt a system of portfolio management which provides an adequate comfort level to you, personally, and then to stick with it in a disciplined manner for the long term.

## DEFERRING TAXES - IRA's AND VARIABLE ANNUITIES

Deferring taxes may not reduce your tax liability, it simply provides a longer period for your assets to grow and compound before the inevitable occurs. Short-term tax-deferral produces only modest benefit, but over a period of several decades the benefits can be substantial. For example, if $1,000 is invested at 15% annual return and subject to 33.3% tax, the after-tax yield of 10% will compound over five years to become $1,610. If tax is deferred, then it becomes $2,011 less 33.3% tax on the gain, which gives an after-tax value of $1,674. This is less than 4% more than paying the tax annually. However, if deferral continues on the same basis for 25 years, the two after-tax figures become $10,835 and $22,258 respectively, more than doubling the return by tax-deferral. As always with successful investing, time is on your side.

There are several effective ways to defer taxes on equity funds, and the simplest and least expensive should always be used first. The available opportunities include the following:

1.  Use every type of tax-deferred retirement account and savings account that is available to you. You should fully utilize your Individual Retirement Account, or IRA. You are also probably eligible to contribute to a tax-deferred self-employment retirement account, or your employer's salary-deferral plan or savings plan. In some cases, the employer matches part of your contribution. Such

plans become a very powerful means of building wealth. Do not be deterred if the initial contribution is not tax deductible, it is still an excellent proposition. Company 401(k) plans differ widely but are nearly always bargains. Company matching contributions vary widely from around 10% of the employee's contribution to well over 100%. However constituted, use all the available tax-deferred savings and defined contribution retirement accounts to the full.

2. Manage your funds to minimize current taxes:
   A. Do not purchase a fund just before a taxable distribution is due. Part of your purchase price will, in effect, be returned to you - after taxes!
   B. Recognize the tax advantage of a fund having a low turnover ratio. It permits capital gains to accumulate within the fund until appreciated stocks are sold. This is a particular advantage of most index funds, which need to change portfolio composition rather rarely. Typically, about half the total return from stocks has arisen from capital appreciation, which is only taxed when realized.
   C. The longer you hold an appreciating fund, the longer you will benefit from the compounding of its unrealized capital gains. Selling an appreciated fund is a taxable event and will reduce your money available for subsequent reinvestment.
   D. All other things being equal, purchase a fund having a tax loss to carry forward. This will reduce future tax liability to shareholders. Check with the fund.

From these comments it is obvious that, over an extended period, a core holding of index funds, which are not traded and which have a very low turnover ratio, permits a great deal more tax-deferral than frequent trading of funds having a high turnover ratio.

3. Purchase a mutual fund or similar vehicle within a tax-deferred variable annuity insurance contract. This is becoming a popular form of tax-deferred investment and is available to anyone who needs more tax-deferral than can be achieved with approved tax-deferred pension plans and saving schemes. It should not be confused with a variable life insurance policy, which may also use equity and fixed income investments but which contains a greater element of insurance.

If you are concerned about the financial soundness of the insurance company, call one or more of the insurance rating companies. The principal ones are A. M. Best and Company, Moody's Investors Service and Standard and Poor's Corporation. For telephone numbers, see Appendix A. For A. M. Best, first call (908) 439-2200 to get your insurance company's Best I.D. number. If you need further information on an insurance company, call your State Insurance Commissioner's office.

Basically, the investor may purchase a variable annuity insurance contract, which provides some very limited form of insurance, such as the value of the original investment at the end of the period. The assets invested may be assigned to one or more different portfolios or "sub-accounts," which typically cover equity growth, growth and income, asset allocation, international securities, taxable bonds and a money market. These sub-accounts are often managed by mutual fund companies. The insurance company may also offer a general account with a specified interest rate for a number of years.  At the end of the contract period the accumulated assets, whatever their value, may be withdrawn as a lump sum and subject to ordinary income tax on the gain, or they may be paid out as a regular taxable annuity for life or for a fixed period.  The main variable is the performance of the underlying investments, which varies with the management company. This cannot be changed without terminating the contract and possibly paying a significant penalty.  It may be possible to arrange a tax-free exchange from one company to another by making a "1035 exchange" which refers to that section of the tax code.

The performance of the various portfolios within the many different insurance company policies is tracked by Morningstar in a dedicated monthly publication entitled Variable Annuity Performance Report.  This publication tracks more than 600 portfolios or sub-accounts and is essential for a comprehensive comparison of performance.

Before buying an insurance contract, be cautious.  You are entering the world of insurance salesmen and vendors of load funds.  Typically, you will pay for insurance, whether you want it or not.  You will most likely pay a load, an annual maintenance fee, a daily administrative charge and a surrender charge if you terminate the contract within a specified period of up to ten years.  You may be providing the person who sold it to you a steady income for as long as you hold the contract.  This form of tax-deferral does not usually come inexpensively.  A report by Forbes magazine in 1991 concluded that with such insurance contracts "the additional fees typically consume the tax savings for the first 20 years." There is also a 10% penalty tax on withdrawals before age 59 1/2.

There is always a break-even point, where the additional operating costs (or the possible reduced performance due to lack of free choice of fund management) will offset the advantage of tax deferral. To take an example, let us assume that the total federal and state marginal tax level of the investor is 35%. If it is much lower than that, just forget about most tax-deferred annuities. Then let us assume that the average return is 9% per year. If the returns are lower than this, once again forget about most tax-deferred annuities. We will assume a single premium payment. We then need to estimate the additional cost, and the possibly reduced benefit factor (i.e. the inability to freely switch to another fund family), which together we will call the penalty. The additional cost can be determined by adding the various types of charges described in the prospectus. You will need to read the contract carefully. The average expenses for the equity funds, including insurance expenses and fund operating expenses, total just over 2%. Add to this an annual contract charge of about $30 and a possible surrender charge averaging 5.7%. In some states a premium tax is payable on the proceeds of an annuity, varying from zero to 3.0%. This is deducted by the insurance company before regular tax is paid. The sum of all these charges, less the cost of a no-load fund of your choice, represents the cost side of the equation. It might total perhaps 1% to 2%, but you would need to calculate this for yourself.

If we assume that the total penalty is only 1%, which seems like an underestimate, it would take nine years to break-even before there was any benefit from the tax deferral. If, more likely, the penalty is 2%, it would take more than 20 years, and if it were 3%, it would take about 37 years. If the average investment return was above 9%, it would shorten the break-even period. If it should fall to 6%, then a 2% penalty would prevent the contract from ever breaking even.

While the insurance companies started this investment product, the mutual fund industry has now seen the potential profit to be made. Fidelity purchased its own insurance company in 1986 to package copies of its taxable mutual funds. Several other mutual fund companies now offer these contracts in collaboration with an insurance company.

The major disadvantage of most variable annuity contracts is clearly the unreasonable cost to the investor. If it were possible to find a variable annuity contract which had no sales load, no surrender charge, low insurance premiums and minimal mutual fund or sub-account operating expenses; all combined with a proven fund performance record, then this would come close to the ideal investment. Until 1991, this would have been impossible, but now it can be done! For this reason, variable annuity insurance contracts have entered a new and promising era.

Several of the better mutual fund companies provide their funds, or similar portfolios, within insurance contracts, but until recently they all had either a sales load or a surrender charge or frequently both. For example,

Nationwide Life Insurance Company offers a series of sub-accounts managed by companies such as Neuberger and Berman, Twentieth Century and Oppenheimer. The Phoenix Mutual Life Insurance Company offers four exclusively global no-load sub-accounts managed by the Templeton Funds. Fidelity also offers a no-load annuity through their own insurance company, but they still have a surrender charge during the first five years.

Finally, both Scudder and Vanguard saw the real opportunity to offer their mutual funds using a variable annuity contract which minimized investor expenses.

Scudder, in conjunction with Charter National Life Insurance Company, offers their Horizon Plan variable annuity contract having no annual maintenance fee, no sales load and no surrender charge after the first year. The annual insurance and fund operating expenses total about 1.45% of assets annually (their international sub-account has somewhat higher total expenses). This is no greater than the expenses of very many regular mutual funds having no element of insurance or tax-deferral. The annuity started in 1988, but only more recently reduced its fees to this level, perhaps due to the introduction by Vanguard of their ultra low cost variable annuity in 1991. The horizon plan still maintains the contractual right to re-introduce an annual mainte-nance fee and to increase the insurance cost.

The Vanguard variable annuity plan is a true innova-tion. It is marketed primarily by Vanguard rather than the insurance underwriter, National Home Life Insur-ance Company. It is a plain no-frills plan with limited options but excellent economy. It has no sales load, no surrender charge and total annual insurance and fund operating expenses totaling about 1.0% of assets, plus an annual contract charge of $25. This achieves the remarkable performance of providing all the insurance and mutual fund services at well below the cost of a typical mutual fund alone. This is achieved partly by using index funds.

The investment options are limited to a money market sub-account based on the Vanguard Prime Portfolio, a high grade bond account based on Vanguard Bond Market Fund (an index fund), a balanced account based on Vanguard's Wellington Fund, and an equity index fund based on Vanguard Index Trust 500 portfolio. The use of this annuity contract permits long-term compounding of both bond and stock index funds in an inexpensive tax-deferred vehicle.

In summary, if you are in a high tax bracket, have a long time horizon, and have exhausted all other forms of tax deferral, it may be worth placing a part of your equity investments in a variable annuity insurance contract. Select only those with a proven track record, no loads, no extended surrender charges and low total expenses. Both Scudder and Vanguard offer such contracts. Vanguard achieves the lowest cost by offering index funds.

## FIXED INCOME PORTFOLIO

### BUYING AND SELLING

The fixed income portfolio will require less active management than the equity portfolio, once the portfolio objectives have been clearly established and the best individual funds selected.

Bonds of all types are subject to the effects of interest rate cycles, declining in value as rates rise and vice versa. Most bond fund managers actively manage the maturity of their bond holdings, within the limits of the fund objectives, in an attempt to minimize losses due to rising interest rates and to benefit from declining rates. The shorter the maturity, the less influence changes in interest rates have on current bond prices.

In managing the portfolio, it is necessary to establish a clear investment time horizon for different portions of the portfolio. Money which may be needed at very short notice should be placed in money market funds. Money needed in a year or two may be placed (with a little more risk) in short-term bond funds, and as the time horizon extends, investment may be made in long-term bond funds and international bond funds. International bond funds, although usually not holding long-term bonds, should be considered as longer term investments because of the additional exchange rate risk. For most of the time, at a given credit risk level, the longer the maturity the greater the return.

This varies at different times and can easily be checked by referring to the Wall Street Journal which shows, under the broad heading of "Credit Markets," a yield curve showing yields for comparable bonds of differing maturities. Many bond funds have an average bond maturity of around ten years, but short-term bond funds may be only one to two years and long-term funds may be over 20 years.

When should you buy and sell bond funds? Most of the comments on managing equity funds also apply to bond funds, except that the price volatility of bonds is likely to be much less. Whereas typical standard deviations of equity funds will be between 4% and 5% a month, that of a bond fund will normally be between 1% and 2%. The exception is likely to be high yield corporate bonds, irreverently known as junk bonds, which have a higher risk and a historical standard deviation of between 2% and 3%. They also have a significantly higher default rate than other types of bonds.

Shorter term timing of bonds has generally proved even less successful than with stocks, and few newsletters offering bond timing services have consistently beaten a buy-and-hold approach over recent years. Nevertheless, it is unwise to make major purchases of long-term bond funds when bond prices are at a cyclical low. It is a very simple matter to plot the moving average of a relevant bond index and make major investments only when the price is, for example, below its 12-month moving average. A simple alternative, of course, is to dollar cost average.

A relevant bond index can be found, together with much other useful information on the front page of Section C of the Wall Street Journal. Lehman Brothers long-term Treasury bond index, Salomon mortgage bond index, Merrill Lynch corporate bond index and the Bond Buyer municipal bond index are all reported here and represent most types of bond. The commonly used bond market indexes are described in Appendix D. The recent average maturity of different bond funds and the proportion of different bond types and credit ratings in a fund can be found in Morningstar Mutual Funds. The same source also provides a detailed profile and rating of all funds that are included.

The reasons to sell a bond fund are similar to those discussed for equity funds, and include consistently poor relative risk-adjusted performance and adverse changes in fund management or policies. They also include changing objectives of the investor.

In the case of bond funds, however, the expense levels are even more critical than in equity funds, for two reasons. First, the historical total returns are lower and, therefore, expenses take up a higher proportion of the return than they do in a normal equity fund. Second, bond managers have been shown to have less impact on bond fund returns and, therefore, find it harder to justify their fees. A study by Morningstar published in the Wall Street Journal showed that, with the possible exception of junk bond funds, expenses were the most important determinant of total return in bond funds. The best performing funds in a given comparable group were nearly always those having the lowest expenses. In fact, when dividing fund expenses into high, medium, and low groups, virtually the only difference in total returns between the low and medium expense levels over a five-year period was attributable to the difference in their expense levels. In the case of the high expense level group, their performance was even less than could be attributed to their higher expenses. Fund expense levels tend to remain relatively constant from year-to-year, but expenses can escalate if the fund size shrinks substantially or if it alters its expense policy. Economies of size permit larger funds to have the lowest expense levels. Expenses should periodically be checked against those of similar funds. International bonds fund usually have somewhat higher than average expenses, for unavoidable reasons.

## TAX REDUCTION

The high-tax-bracket fixed income investor wishing to reduce the tax burden does not need to adopt tax deferral strategies. He or she can quite simply invest in tax-free municipal bond funds and totally avoid federal tax liability on interest income. State tax liability on interest can usually also be avoided if a municipal bond fund exists which holds bonds solely issued in the state of residence of the investor. We have previously discussed the merits of tax-free municipals, and how to calculate the taxable equivalent yield in order to check which is better for your portfolio, based on your marginal tax rate.

This is one of the few remaining simple tax shelters for higher income individuals and, although the yields are lower than on taxable bonds, on an after-tax basis they usually produce a higher return. In managing a fixed income portfolio, every purchase of a taxable bond fund should first be compared with the alternative of tax-free municipal bond funds of comparable risk, on an after-tax basis. All fixed income investments must be compared on the basis of total return, on a risk-adjusted basis, after tax. Without this comparison no rational selection can be made. The same criteria apply when periodically reviewing your existing fixed income portfolio. Remember though, that capital gains by municipal bond funds are fully taxable.

## USING MONEY MARKET FUNDS

Money market funds have an important role in a fixed income portfolio, both as a cash haven between longer term investments, and in their own right as an element of fixed principal and very low risk in a portfolio which is otherwise fluctuating in value. They obviously serve to reduce the standard deviation of the entire portfolio. As with bond funds, the returns depend upon tax status, expense levels, risk level and maturity. Tax-free money market funds should again be the comparison against which all taxable money market funds are judged. Yields of money market mutual funds are quoted regularly in the Wall Street Journal and Barron's. Expense levels have a major impact on returns, but are reflected in the yield which is the main factor by which money market funds should be selected. Risk is not of serious concern, since the SEC dictates both the credit worthiness and duration of the fund's holdings. Nevertheless, some people prefer to use money market funds which only hold debt issued by the federal government. These have the advantage of producing income which is not normally subject to state income tax.

A specialized newsletter entitled "Income and Safety," published by the Institute For Econometric Research, covers a large number of taxable and tax-free money market funds, reporting monthly both the 30-day yields and comparative risk ratings. It also covers taxable and tax-free bond funds, reporting yields, expenses and services offered. Most, but not all, money market funds permit writing checks against the account, with minimum check levels varying usually from no minimum to a $500 minimum. This is a convenient way of promptly reinvesting the assets of a money market fund, when required.

When managing your fixed income portfolio, don't forget that if you do not need the money for a while, you may be better advised to place it in a very short-term bond fund, rather than a money market fund. There will be minor fluctuations in the NAV of the fund, but in return, you will get a higher yield. Good taxable and tax-free short-term bond funds exist, having average maturities of one to three years. Scudder, T. Rowe Price and Vanguard offer such funds.

CHAPTER 14

# WHERE TO FIND THE BEST INFORMATION

Successful investing requires knowledge. What you don't know can't help you, but what you do know may. The required knowledge is of two different types. First is the principles and practice of mutual fund investing, which is covered by this book. Second is an ongoing supply of useful, up-to-date, factual information. This is required for the selection of specific funds, and the ongoing management of the portfolio. We do not mean speculation about what the Federal Reserve Board or the government may or may not do in the future, or what the economists are saying about the future of the economy. This type of information abounds but is generally worthless. Rather, we are concerned with a timely supply of reliable quantitative information on what is actually happening and what has actually happened, thus indicating existing trends which may be evaluated.

Such facts exist, but have to be sifted and separated from a mass of irrelevant information. Many oysters have to be opened to find the few pearls of information. Finding these can take many months of research and considerable expense.

In this chapter we shall save you from that task and bring to your notice some of the most useful information sources. It is not intended to be an exhaustive list, but merely to skim the cream of the best. Prices of publications are generally not provided, as they change with time and most can be purchased at discounts well below the listed price.

The telephone numbers of the sources for all publications cited are provided in Appendix A. Most are just a free telephone call away and many newsletters will supply a free sample copy.

In selecting a few sources of information it is important to choose those that have a style you feel comfortable with. Don't use too many; remember that a man with many watches rarely knows the time! Also don't be surprised if market performance numbers vary from source to source. This is not an error but is usually due to slightly different methods of calculation.

Unless you are able to only use library data, it will cost you something to stay properly informed. However, if that lets you select good performing no-load funds, the cost will prove to be one of your best investments.


## NEWSPAPERS


Most of the necessary information on fund prices, market indexes and interest rates can be found in the Wall Street Journal or Investor's Business Daily, and if not there, it will be in Barron's each week.

Section C of the Journal provides a number of domestic market indexes in the "Market Diary," while international indexes appear on the page headed "World Markets." Interest rates are shown on the page covering "Credit Markets." The dividend yield of the Dow Jones Industrial Average, and the S&P 500 index appear each Monday, set in a block within the charts of the Dow Jones averages in Section C. The NAV of funds appear daily, but the yield on money market funds usually appears only on Thursdays. The Lipper Mutual Fund indexes appear usually on Mondays. The Journal also provides articles on mutual funds, personal finance and a year-end investment outlook.

Barron's contains much of its useful statistical information in a section entitled "Market Laboratory" at the back of each issue. It also presents articles on mutual funds and a basic quarterly review of fund performance. Both Barron's and the Wall Street Journal are owned by Dow Jones and Company Inc., and tend to emphasize the market averages reported by that company.

Investor's Business Daily presents its own mutual fund index which is shown graphically, together with its 200-day and 50-day moving averages and a relative strength line. It contains useful mutual fund tables including three-year performance rankings. It also provides regular mutual fund profiles.

International investors may refer to The Asian Wall Street Journal and The Wall Street Journal Europe, both published by Dow Jones and Company, Inc. and to the Financial Times of London, known simply as the Financial Times. This covers mainly United Kingdom and European financial news. The Financial Times also publishes the Investor's Chronicle, covering primarily the domestic United Kingdom market and somewhat similar in scope to Barron's. For current price quotations on hundreds of overseas-based funds refer to the International Herald Tribune, published in Paris and printed simultaneously in 11 cities around the world, including New York.

## MAGAZINES AND JOURNALS

Following the steady increase in ownership of mutual

funds, an increasing number of magazines run periodic surveys of mutual fund characteristics and performance. This is not their original data, but information purchased from specialized organizations such as CDA, Lipper Analytical Services and Morningstar. Those that report performance separately in up and down markets are to be preferred but those very few that may report it on a risk-adjusted basis are the only ones of significant value, as far as performance is concerned.

Forbes magazine is a valuable independent-minded source of information on corporate America. It also provides the Forbes Index of Economic Activity, periodic articles on mutual funds including a column by Mark Hulbert, and an annual fund survey published each year in the first issue of September. This survey has been published every year since 1956, and is still one of the better. We saw in Chapter 8 that the predictive value of their "Honor Roll" is, at best, limited, but the survey of funds and the fund directory are comprehensive. Other magazines reporting surveys of fund characteristics and performance include Financial World, Business Week, Kiplinger's Personal Finance Magazine and Money. Consumer Reports also runs periodic surveys of mutual funds.

For international investors wanting in-depth reporting on economic, political and social events around the world, the best source is the Economist magazine. This is not primarily an investment publication, although it does provide interesting economic and financial data. It specializes in informative features on world affairs, including those of the United States. It is a London based magazine, published in the United States. A similar in-depth focus, but limited to the Far East, is well provided by the Far Eastern Economic Review, published in Hong Kong.

For strictly international statistical stock market data, consult Morgan Stanley Capital International Perspective at your library. The monthly and quarterly editions contain different information.

For general investment information on the United Kingdom and details of hundreds of United Kingdom based domestic and international unit trusts (mutual funds) consult the monthly magazine "What Investment?" published in England.

The most useful general investment periodical is the Journal of the American Association of Individual Investors (AAII), a non-profit organization dedicated to "Assisting individuals in becoming effective managers of their own assets." Membership provides ten monthly issues of the Journal, an annual handbook of mutual funds and a tax planning guide. Members are also offered discounts to magazines, attendance at seminars and membership of local chapters, many of which have mutual fund groups. Each issue of this journal contains short, informative articles on a range of investment topics, including mutual funds. The editorial style reflects practical realism. AAII introduced a new publication in 1992, entitled Quarterly Mutual Fund Update. This covers over 500 no-load and low load funds and provides total return values for each of the previous four quarters and the prior three years. It also provides performance comparisons with fund groups having similar objectives and a simple risk index.

For those wishing to study the more academic aspects of investing, the scholarly journals such as the Financial Analyst's Journal and the Journal of Portfolio Management should be consulted.

## HANDBOOKS

Several organizations produce an annual handbook listing and characterizing hundreds, or even thousands of funds. Some cover the broad field of mutual funds, some exclude money market funds and some cover just no-load and low load funds.

The Individual Investor's Guide to No-Load Mutual Funds is supplied free of charge to all members of the American Association of Individual Investors, as mentioned earlier. It is distributed in June of each year and covers over 500 no-load and low load funds.

The Handbook for No-Load Mutual Funds, by Sheldon Jacobs, is published by The No-Load Fund Investor. It lists over 1,200 funds, including money market funds and contains articles on mutual fund investing.

Donoghue's Mutual Fund Almanac, published by the Donoghue organization, covers over 2,200 funds, including load funds and money market funds.

Mutual Fund Encyclopedia, by Gerald Perritt, published by Dearborn Publishing covers over 1,100 load and no-load funds with articles on mutual funds.

Investor's Guide to Fidelity Funds, by Martin and McCann, is published by John Wiley and Sons. It is an independent publication covering more than 100 Fidelity funds.

The Independent Guide to Vanguard Funds, published by Fund Family Shareholders Association, covers more than 50 Vanguard funds.

The quarterly Mutual Fund Performance Guide, by Charles Schwab and Company, lists more than 500 funds which may be purchased through the Company. It is free of charge.

Most of these handbooks provide basic performance data for several prior periods and information on minimum investment requirements, expenses and shareholder services. They rarely provide important information on risk, fund management or fund investment characteristics. For this type of information it is necessary to refer to the best fund reporting services.

The tax implications of owning mutual funds may change as frequently as the tax laws, but a useful source of current information is the IRS publication #564, which describes the tax implications of mutual fund ownership. This is not, of course, strictly a handbook, but a useful free leaflet.

## TRADE ASSOCIATIONS

The Investment Company Institute is the national association of the American investment company industry and represents the sponsors of about 3,000 mutual funds, with more than 36 million shareholders.

The Institute acts as a source of information on the industry and offers leaflets, brochures, books, films and videos, usually at modest prices. Their annual Mutual Fund Directory is published by Probus Publishing and includes their entire membership.

The Mutual Fund Education Alliance provides The Investor's Guide to Low Cost Mutual Funds, listing over 260 funds available by direct purchase from the fund companies, rather than via distributors. It also provides a good 60 minute audio cassette and booklet covering some of the basics of mutual fund investing. The membership is listed in Appendix C.

The 100% No-Load Mutual Fund Council provides a directory of over 120 funds having no loads or 12b-1 charges. This is a most useful list from which to select funds. The membership is listed in Appendix B.

## FUND REPORTING SERVICES -
## WHERE THE PROS GO FOR INFORMATION

The closer you can get to the original source of information, the more reliable and comprehensive it usually is. The task of compiling, checking and presenting detailed information on thousands of mutual funds is a demanding task performed by only a few specialized companies. These are mainly the fund reporting services that provide input to professional money managers and to many other publications and news media. This is where you go to get really comprehensive information on funds.

Here you can find a lot of useful information which is not in a fund's prospectus, but which is almost essential to know before making an informed decision about a fund. The reports of these services are not inexpensive and may cost several hundred dollars a year, but they are likely to be available at your library. If not, you might want to try a short-term trial subscription and perhaps share it with another investor.

The "Bible" on mutual funds is Morningstar Mutual Funds (formerly Mutual Fund Values), published by Morningstar Inc. of Chicago. With this, you need consult no magazines or handbooks - this does far more for you. Broadly, Morningstar Mutual Funds (MMF) does for mutual funds what the Value Line Survey does for individual stocks. It is published every two weeks in two parts and tracks over 1,000 stock and bond funds but not money market funds. Every two weeks the summary information on every fund is updated, and every 20 weeks, on a rolling basis, the detailed profile of each fund is revised.

Perhaps the greatest challenge with MMF is to ensure that you get from it all that it offers. The service comes with a 40-page guide on how best to use it and a definition of the various measures reported.

Each fund is profiled on one page, which contains a performance update, performance ranking, performance/risk analysis, price performance and relative strength graph, list of major portfolio holdings and an overall rating. It incidentally also contains risk adjusted performance, alpha, beta, standard deviation, $R^2$ value, expenses, credit analysis of bond funds, tenure of fund manager, standard portfolio statistics, and a great deal more, including an analysts's commentary on the state of the fund. The ranking system is based on stars; from one to five depending on the historical risk-adjusted performance.

Morningstar also produces a more modest and less expensive monthly publication entitled Mutual Fund Performance Report, which contains summary statistics of fund characteristics and includes extensive historical performance rankings. For investors interested in mutual funds within variable annuity insurance contracts, Morningstar provides a monthly Variable Annuity Performance Report covering more than 600 sub-accounts of variable annuities and life policies and also an annual Variable Annuity Sourcebook. The Company also publishes, each March, a two-volume Mutual Fund Sourcebook, containing vital statistics on over 1,800 funds, including many profiles of the careers of fund managers. Other services include Morningstar Closed-End Funds, an information source similar to Morningstar Mutual Funds, and a series of two Annual Conferences, one of which covers funds sold directly to the public. Morningstar also provides Business Week magazine with its Mutual Fund Scoreboard. Although a relatively new company, Morningstar has become perhaps the premier mutual fund reporting service.

Another good fund reporting service is CDA Investment Technologies Inc. Its monthly CDA Mutual Fund Report analyzes about 1,300 funds and includes a rating scale based on performance and risk, in addition to comprehensive information on each fund.

CDA Mutual Fund Charts is a quarterly service that covers over 1,500 funds and shows total return over a ten-year period. It includes comparable performance of several indexes for comparison.

Lipper Analytical Services reports extensively on mutual funds, but unfortunately they decline to do business with the public. However, in conjunction with Standard and Poor's

Corporation, they publish Mutual Fund Profiles Quarterly. This provides rather brief information on a wide range of funds.

Perhaps the oldest fund reporting service is Wiesenberger and Company. Established in 1940 by Arthur Wiesenberg, it has earned a place in the tradition and history of mutual funds. Wiesenberger Investment Companies is a huge, 1,000 page annual book, covering thousands of investment companies and containing about 19 chapters on the conventional and traditional selection and management of funds.

## NEWSLETTERS

A good investment advisory newsletter can essentially provide four things:
1. A market timing service.
2. A fund selection service.
3. A disciplined approach to investing which the subscriber may follow.
4. Timely, factual information permitting subscribers to make their own decisions.

There are hundreds of newsletters covering every aspect of investing. Select Information Exchange (SIE) of New York City offers, free of charge, a 64-page catalog describing over 800 investment newsletters. They also offer a sample of 25 newsletters covering mutual funds, at a cost of less than $1 per newsletter. However, if you are in a hurry, call up the newsletter directly. Some of the timing services having the best track records do not specifically focus on mutual funds, but most of the mutual fund newsletters offer some type of timing service.

The selection of a good newsletter is very important and justifies considerable time spent in examining many. Be skeptical, they mainly look good at a distance. The one you select should meet at least three requirements: it should have a good independently verified long-term performance record, have objectives similar to your own, and should provide you with a comfort level and confidence sufficient to make you act on its recommendations. You may, of course, decide to follow perhaps only its fund selection or its timing recommendations.

Before acting on timing advice, remember that in spite of the claimed achievements and unquestioning self confidence of many newsletters, they are as a group a contrary timing indicator. That means that most of them are usually wrong — they cannot foretell the future any better than you can, believe it or not. In recent years only a small minority has actually beaten the market. However, as a source of current facts, newsletters can be invaluable, and the best ones have a track record at least as good as the better institutional investors and professional money managers.

Whatever your interest in mutual fund investing, there are newsletters to meet your needs. Table 47 gives some small indication of the diversity of the areas covered and some of the newsletters available. Many other newsletters cover most of the areas listed and those cited are examples, not endorsements. For comprehensive listings of newsletters, consult the Oxbridge Directory of newsletters or Hudson's Newsletter Directory, which are likely to be at your library.

The task of selecting newsletters has been greatly aided by an independent evaluation service provided by Mark Hulbert, editor of the Hulbert Financial Digest newsletter and author of The Hulbert Guide to Financial Newsletters, which describes and rates more than 100 selected investment newsletters.

The database accumulated by Hulbert over more than ten years provides a wealth of practical market experience unavailable elsewhere. For example, he is able to establish that the presence of a telephone hotline has not contributed to newsletter performance over a five-year period. He is again able to

TABLE 47

**THE DIVERSITY OF INVESTMENT NEWSLETTERS**

Examples of Some of the Many Areas Covered By Investment Newsletter

| Area Covered | Example of Newsletter |
|---|---|
| Advising Institutions | The Bank Credit Analyst |
| Asset Allocation | Asset Allocation Review |
| Bond Funds | Income and Safety, Bond Fund Advisor |
| Conservative All Weather Funds | All-Weather Fund Investor, The Mutual Fund Letter |
| Fidelity Funds | Fidelity Monitor, Fidelity Insight, Fidelity Mutual Fund Guide |
| Fund Charts and Rankings | Mutual Fund Trends, Growth Fund Guide |
| Fund Management | L/G No-Load Fund Analyst |
| Fund Timing | Mutual Fund Strategist, Chartist Mutual Fund Timer |
| Fund Upgrading | No-Load Fund X, Weber's Fund Advisory |
| Global Timing | Global Fund Timer |
| International Funds | International Fund Monitor |
| Market Value Timing | Growth Fund Guide |
| Model Portfolios | L/G No-Load Fund Analyst |
| Money Market Funds | Income and Safety |
| Moving Averages | Telephone Switch Newsletter |
| Municipal Bond Fund Timing | Bond Fund Advisor |
| Newsletter Evaluation | Hulbert Financial Digest |
| Performance Projections | Mutual Fund Forecaster, Growth Fund Guide |
| Retirement Investing | The Mature Investor |
| Sector Funds | Sector Funds Newsletter |
| Technical Analysis of World Markets | Pring Market Review |
| Vanguard Funds | Vantage Point, The Vanguard Adviser |

support the importance of consistency of performance. The newsletters which performed well during the first five years of his observations, on average, performed about twice as well as the others during the second five years of his observations. Some claim that newsletter performance is entirely due to chance: Hulbert has shown that over a ten-year period, about 15% of the newsletters had a performance so superior that it became statistically significant and was most unlikely to be due to chance. Calculating the standard deviations of many of the recommended portfolios, he found that about 40% were more risky than the total market and about 60% less so. A few had ten times the risk of the total market and a few had only one tenth. Select a newsletter with a level of risk you are willing to accept.

Few of the mutual fund newsletters tracked in the Hulbert Guide To Financial Newsletters, 4th Ed. 1991, succeeded in consistently beating the market. Over a ten-year period and a seven-year period, only one model portfolio within a newsletter did so, and that was the "class 3" portfolio of higher quality growth funds reported by the No-Load Fund X. This newsletter follows a very simple system, using the sum of performance rankings over multiple periods and periodically upgrading to the highest ranking funds, as we discussed in Chapter 8. It does not include a timing system. Over a five-year period this portfolio again beat the market and so did two other newsletters: The Mutual Fund Strategist and The Telephone Switch Newsletter. The Mutual Fund Strategist includes both a timing system and a fund selection system. Funds are selected on a simple intermediate term relative strength basis, not too different from the intermediate term rankings of The No-Load Fund X newsletter. The Telephone Switch Newsletter uses a timing system based solely on a 39-week moving average.

During a shorter three-year period, The Mutual Fund Strategist also beat the market and so did several other funds, which may or may not have the consistency to remain in this list of leaders. Most of the newsletters that beat the market over extended periods did so with less risk than the total market, thus considerably enhancing the significance of their achievements.

The consistent performers have a few things in common. They use very simple common sense systems, they minimize risk, and they focus on the intermediate to longer term, rather than either the very short-term of a few weeks or the very long-term of many years. They also are generally not the most noisy and highly promoted newsletters — they don't need to be. Those that arrive in your junk mail are unlikely to be the best.

When considering newsletters, it is important to realize not only that most do not beat the market, but also the longer the time period of measurement the fewer that do. Of all the newsletters and separate portfolios tracked by Hulbert (not just the mutual fund letters), only eight beat the market over a ten-year period and only four beat it significantly by more than 10%.

However, many of the newsletters which have not beaten the market have significantly reduced risk for their subscribers. They have also succeeded in presenting timely and useful data, which is the main purpose of some newsletters. For example, Mutual Fund Trends, published by Growth Fund Research Inc., presents each month performance rankings of about 170 funds and market indexes. It covers the prior 13, 26 and 39 weeks and provides performance rankings during market moves from recent highs to lows and lows to highs. It also provides charts of each fund listed, showing weekly price range, 13 and 39-week moving averages and a relative strength line. It presents excellent tabular and graphic information but makes no specific recommendations. It is for investors who wish to make up their own minds, once given the facts.

Another comprehensive newsletter for the more sophisticated investor is the L/G No-Load Fund Analyst, written by Litman and Gregory and published by L/G Research Inc. This provides model portfolios and notes monthly; comprehensive statistical tables quarterly; and detailed reports on about 50 good funds annually. It supplies qualitative as well as quantitative fund analyses and although providing model portfolios, it is also quite suitable for those investors wishing to make their own decisions.

A fairly recent addition to the newsletter scene is the 5-Star Reporter introduced by Morningstar in September, 1992. It claims to be "teacher, reporter and database rolled into one" and achieves these objectives with the usual Morningstar quality and finesse. It presents no recommended portfolios but rather helps the discerning investor to construct and manage his or her own winning portfolio. It is reasonably priced and may become the yardstick against which other quality newsletters are judged.

In summary, first decide which of the four types of newsletter service are important to you. Select a newsletter after careful examination of many. Do you feel comfortable with it and has its performance been independently verified? Remember that the majority of letters do not consistently outperform the market, but are more likely to reduce market risk. Only the very best newsletters are worthwhile, and these can be invaluable. If you prefer to make your own decisions once given the facts, there are good newsletters which facilitate this. Subscribe to only one, or at most two, newsletters, and then stick with them — that's what you bought them for.

In general, the newsletters that employ the investment management techniques described in this book produce the best and most consistent results.

## COMPUTER SOFTWARE

For those investors who prefer to access information from a computer, there is an increasing supply of software programs.

FundVest, Inc. provides the Fund Master TC program from Time Trends software. This is used with a modem and database, such as the Dow Jones News/Retrieval. It can produce a wide range of charts and performance rankings.

Rugg and Steele, Inc. offers the Mutual Fund Selector and the Portfolio Manager software programs. These are designed to help investors select mutual funds and to track, monitor and evaluate their portfolios. A special edition of the Mutual Fund Selector is available, covering the annual fund survey appearing in Kiplinger's Personal Finance Magazine.

The American Association of Individual Investors supplies an inexpensive disc for IBM or Macintosh computers containing six years of data on the funds included in their annual handbook, The Individual Investor's Guide To No-Load Mutual Funds. They also provide on disc their Quarterly No-Load Mutual Fund Update, introduced in 1992.

The Business Week Mutual Fund Scoreboard is available on disc either quarterly or monthly and provides current information on more than 1,600 mutual funds. You may subscribe to an equity and/or a fixed income diskette for use on an IBM or compatible machine. It is a menu driven program which supports multiple search and sort criteria on over 25 information fields. The data source is Morningstar, Inc.

CDA Technologies, Inc., produces a quarterly diskette based on its CDA Mutual Fund Report covering about 1,300 funds.

One of the most interesting recent developments is the introduction of Morningstar Mutual Funds on Disc, using CD-ROM technology. This provides an enormous amount of current information on more than 2,000 funds. It is a menu driven system with over 90 fields of information on each fund and over 50 fields of information with which to screen, rank and compare mutual funds over a 15-year prior period. It is available with monthly, quarterly or annual updates and requires an IBM or compatible PC having at least 640k of memory, a hard disc drive and CD-ROM drive. It represents the most sophisticated tool available for the study of mutual fund performance.

# PART FOUR

# SUMMARY

CHAPTER 15

# THE DO'S AND DON'TS OF SUCCESSFUL INVESTING

## THE DO'S

1. Do start saving and investing early in life — building wealth safely takes time.
2. Do have a clear-cut investment objective and a realistic plan to get there. If you don't know where you are going, you are unlikely to get there. Be ambitious, have a plan and then just do it!
3. Do understand the sinister long-term impact of taxes and inflation in all your investment decisions. Real returns after taxes and inflation are all that matter.
4. Do establish your own particular break-even point. This is the return you need to create wealth, after considering both taxes and inflation.
5. Do keep your investing simple, and be guided by common sense. There is no magic. You now know as much as most experts.

6. Do be skeptical. If an investment looks too good to be true, it probably is. Very high risk is usually not adequately rewarded.

7. Do have patience and discipline in your investing. This is how most great fortunes have been built over time.

8. Do establish separate equity and fixed income portfolios. Don't attempt to switch between them. It's too risky if you are wrong.

9. Do achieve carefully balanced and widely diversified equity and fixed income portfolios.

10. Do match your investments to your risk tolerance. Understand both your financial and your temperamental ability to tolerate risk.

11. Do let your investment time horizon dictate your investment choices. Invest for the long term whenever possible.

12. Do exploit the incredible power of compounding and tax-deferral. Used together over time they are the best way of creating wealth.

13. Do very carefully select the best investments in a given category. It only requires a little study, and we have shown you how to do it.

14. Do manager your portfolio objectively. Avoid being swayed by the emotions of fear and greed. Ignore predictions and follow existing trends — they are reality.

15. Do exploit investor psychology. The majority is usually wrong. Avoid being influenced by popular fads.

16. Do always evaluate an investment on a risk-adjusted basis. No other way makes sense.

17. Do recognize where you are in a market cycle and make cool decisions based on market value, moving averages of market price and interest rate changes. Ignore the emotions of the moment.

18. Do recognize the classic signs of major turning points in the market. We have spelled them out, so refer to them.

19. Do remember that there is no single asset class for all seasons and no single fund for all seasons. They have times when they are hot and times when they are not.
20. Do consider the concept of holding a core portfolio with part of your equity assets. Use fairly conservative funds which are likely to track the market; index funds may be ideal. Try to beat the market only with the remainder, if you wish.
21. Do invest internationally with your most patient money. Use open-ended, geographically diversified funds with proven management having global experience.
22. Do look for funds with past consistency of high performance, combined with current high relative strength.
23. Do always favor a fund having a positive alpha value.
24. Do use intermediate term performance ranking and relative strength lines as important guides in fund selection and upgrading.
25. Do become fully invested in growth-type funds whenever the price/dividend ratio of the S&P 500 index is in the teens and rising. This is bargain time, be aggressive.
26. Do sell most domestic equity funds if the price/dividend ratio of the S&P 500 index exceeds $34. The market represented by this index is now seriously overvalued.
27. Do follow the long-term stock market trends shown by multiple moving averages of market price and also interest rate signals, (if you wish to time the market to reduce the losses from major bear markets).
28. Do refer to a good fund reporting service to help you evaluate a fund before buying it, in addition to reading the prospectus. This will provide vital information which is not in the prospectus.
29. Do remember that newsletters are generally a contrary indicator and are most frequently wrong. The best are excellent. Select one that has an independently verified record of consistent performance, or one that provides

you with the factual data needed for you to make your own decisions.

30. Do remember that you are the general manager of your investments. Use expert fund managers and advisors. Free advice from those trying to sell you an investment is worth, at best, what you paid for it.

31. Do use patience, discipline, common sense and knowledge. With this and a cool head, you will build a fortune over time. As your wealth grows, manage it with care — it is easy to lose.

32. Do maintain an overall perspective. Playing the money game and building wealth should not be an end in itself. Wealth is simply an economic lubricant to facilitate a more secure and enjoyable life-style. Enjoy it!

## THE DON'TS

1. Don't try to make a fortune in a hurry — you are more likely to lose what you have.

2. Don't try to tell the future - you can't.

3. Don't attempt short-term market timing - it doesn't work.

4. Don't speculate — unless you are prepared to lose your money with equanimity.

5. Don't look for the single perfect investment - it doesn't exist.

6. Don't invest in anything too complicated or in anything you don't fully understand. Investing should be simple.

7. Don't be gullible and don't buy on emotions. Get the facts, think about it, take time. Don't buy anything on the same day that you first think about it.

8. Don't try to jump from one asset class to another in search of greater gain — the risks are too great.

9. Don't believe that a top performing fund of a previous

period will necessarily be a future consistent winner - it most likely won't be.

10. Don't put more than 10% of your total investment assets into one mutual fund, with the exception of a money market fund or a broad-based index fund. You need to diversify globally across fund categories and management styles.

11. Don't make major new long-term general domestic equity investments when the price/dividend ratio of the S&P 500 is much over $30 (i.e. a dividend yield below 3.3%). The market represented by this index is no longer a good value.

12. Don't buy a fund with a significant negative alpha value.

13. Don't buy a fund where the management has recently changed, unless you know the new manager's track record. Be cautious if the fund won't tell you who's managing it.

14. Don't buy a fund just before a distribution is made. You will be taxed on the partial return of your money.

15. Don't buy international funds as short term investments. You have the additional exchange rate risk.

16. Don't buy single country funds, unless you are prepared to accept high risk.

17. Don't buy full-load funds. Avoid low load funds wherever possible. Don't buy a fund with a 12b-1 charge unless you wish to contribute to the distribution costs of the fund distributor.

18. Don't buy a variable annuity insurance contract having a load or an extended surrender charge. Avoid annuities having annual total insurance and sub-account charges above 1.5%.

19. Don't pay average total annual expenses of more than about 1.0% for domestic equity funds, 0.7% for taxable bond funds and 0.5% for tax-free bond funds and all money market funds.

20. Don't stay with an intermediate-term loser with poor relative strength; there are always winners so upgrade.
21. Don't be influenced by day-to-day random market fluctuations or by the endless futile speculations aimed at feeding investor fear or greed. Ignore them and stick to your established plan.
22. Don't panic when the market seems to fall apart. When everyone is selling and nobody is buying is the ideal time to buy.
23. Don't be discouraged by setbacks. The very best managers have them, and they are the best because they have learned from them. So can you. You can't turn back the clock, but you can wind it up again!

# APPENDIXES

# APPENDIX A

## Telephone Numbers For Sources Of Information And Publications Cited

All-Weather Fund Investor ........................................ (800) 621-8322
American Association of Individual Investors .............. (312) 280-0170
Asset Allocation Review ......................................... (800) 221-7514
Bank Credit Analyst .............................................. (514) 398-0653
Barrons ............................................................... (800) 628-9320
Best, A.M. ........................................................... (900) 420-0400
Bond Fund Advisor ............................................... (617) 721-4511
Business Week ...................................................... (800) 635-1200
Business Week's Mutual Fund Scoreboard Disc .......... (800) 553-3575
CDA Investment Technologies Inc. .......................... (800) 232-2285
CDA Mutual Fund Report ...................................... (800) 232-2285
Charles Schwab & Company .................................. (800) 526-8600
Chartcraft Weekly Mutual Funds Breakout ................ (914) 632-0422
Chartist Mutual Fund Letter ................................... (310) 596-2385
Chartist Mutual Fund Timer ................................... (310) 596-2385
Consumer Reports ................................................ (914) 378-2000
DAL Investment Co. .............................................. (415) 986-7979
Dearborn Financial Publishing ............................... (800) 621-9621
Donoghue Organization ......................................... (800) 343-5413
Economist, The ..................................................... (800) 456-6086
Far Eastern Economic Review (Hong Kong) ...... FAX: (852) 572-2436
Fidelity Insight ..................................................... (617) 235-4432
Fidelity Monitor .................................................... (916) 624-0191
Fidelity Mutual Fund Guide .................................... (800) 544-6666
Financial Analysts Journal ...................................... (212) 957-2860
Financial Times, The (of London) ............................ (800) 628-8088
Financial World .................................................... (800) 666-6639
Forbes ................................................................ (800) 356-3704
Fund Exchange .................................................... (800) 423-4893
Fundline ............................................................. (818) 346-5637
FundVest ............................................................. (508) 663-3330
Growth Fund Guide .............................................. (800) 621-8322
Growth Fund Reserach .......................................... (800) 621-8322

Global Fund Timer ................................................(800) 256-3136
Hudson's Newsletter Director ...............................(914) 876-2081
Hulbert Financial Digest .......................................(703) 683-5905
Income and Safety ..............................................(800) 327-6720
International Herald Tribune ..................................(800) 882-2884
Investment Company Institute ...............................(202) 293-7700
Investor's Chronicle (London) ...............................44-81-680-3786
Investor's Business Daily .......................................(800) 443-3113
Investor's Intelligence ...........................................(914) 632-0422
Kiplinger's Personal Finance Magazine .....................(800) 544-0155
L/G No-Load Fund Analyst....................................(415) 989-8513
L/G Research Inc. .................................................(415) 989-8513
Lipper Analytical Services .......................................(212) 393-1300
Marketarian Letter ...............................................(800) 658-4325
Money Magazine...................................................(800) 633-9970
Moody's Investor Services ......................................(212) 553-0300
Morgan Stanley International Cap. Perspective ..........(212) 703-2965
Morningstar Inc. ...................................................(800) 876-5005
Morningstar Mutual Funds......................................(800) 876-5005
Morningstar Mutual Funds on Disc ..........................(800) 876-5005
Mutual Fund Education Alliance, The .......................(816) 471-1454
Mutual Fund Forecaster .........................................(800) 327-6720
Mutual Fund Letter ...............................................(312) 649-6940
Mutual Fund Performance Report ............................(800) 876-5005
Mutual Fund Sourcebook .......................................(800) 876-5005
Mutual Fund Strategist ...........................................(802) 658-3513
Mutual Fund Trends ..............................................(800) 621-8322
National Bureau of Economic Research....................(617) 868-3900
No-Load Fund Investor ..........................................(914) 693-7420
No-Load Fund X ...................................................(800) 323-1510
100% No-Load Mutual Fund Council .......................(212) 768-2477
Oxbridge Director of Newsletters ............................(212) 741-0231
Pring Market Review .............................................(800) 221-7514
Probus Publishing .................................................(800) 426-1520
Rugg and Steele ...................................................(800) 237-8400
Schabacher Investment ..........................................(301) 840-0301
Sector Fund Newsletter...........................................(619) 748-0805
Select Information Exchange ...................................(212) 247-7123
Social Investment Forum........................................(612) 333-8338
S&P Insurance Rating Services ...............................(212) 208-8000
Standard & Poor's/Lipper Mutual Fund Profile ..........(800) 221-5277

# APPENDIX B

## Mutual Fund Companies That Are Members Of The 100% No-Load Mutual Fund Council

Formed in 1989, the 100% No-Load Fund Council is a group of mutual fund companies offering funds which are totally free of any initial sales charge, 12b-1 fees, contingent deferred sales charge, long-term redemption charge or dividend reinvestment charge.

However, this does not guarantee that they have low operating expenses — some do not. This should be checked in the prospectus in all cases. Most members offer cost efficient funds, and some have excellent long-term track records. The members of the Council and their telephone numbers are as follows:

Acorn Fund ...............................................................(800) 922-6769
Analytic Optioned Equity Fund ...............................(714) 833-0294
Avondale Total Return Fund ...................................(800) 845-8303
Armstrong Associates ..............................................(214) 720-9101
Beacon Hill Mutual Fund.........................................(617) 482-0795
Benham Management ..............................................(800) 472-3389
Caldwell Fund ..........................................................(800) 338-9477
Century Shares Trust...............................................(800) 321-1928
Eclipse Financial Asset Trust ..................................(800) 872-2710
Evergreen Group .....................................................(800) 235-0064
Fairmont Fund .........................................................(800) 262-9936
Fasciano Fund .........................................................(800) 338-1579
Greenspring Fund ....................................................(301) 435-9000
Jones and Babson Group.........................................(800) 422-2766
Lindner Funds..........................................................(314) 727-5305
Meridian Fund .........................................................(800) 446-6662
Monetta Fund ..........................................................(800) 666-3882
Montgomery Small Cap Fund..................................(415) 627-2400
Nicholas Family of Funds ........................................(414) 272-6133

Oakmark Fund ........................................................(800) 476-9625
Olympic Trust Fund ..............................................(213) 623-7833
The Primary Funds ...............................................(800) 443-6544
Safeco Funds .........................................................(800) 426-6730
Sit "New Beginning" Funds ....................................(800) 332-5580
Stratton Funds ......................................................(800) 634-5726
Twentieth Century Investors ...................................(800) 345-2021
United Services Advisors .........................................(800) 873-8637
Value Line Funds ..................................................(800) 223-0818

# APPENDIX C

## Mutual Fund Companies That Are Members Of The Mutual Fund Education Alliance, The Association Of No-Load Funds

This group of mutual fund companies represents funds whose shares are available directly to the public, without the use of brokers and with little or no sales charge or commission. It does not quite live up to its name of "no-load," as some members, such as Fidelity and Fundtrust, offer low load funds. It also does not guarantee that the funds are free of 12b-1 charges, so check the prospectus carefully. However, it does provide a useful starting point in that all of these funds are sold directly to the consumer and many pass on this cost benefit. Members include some of the finest fund families and are as follows:

Benham Group*......................................................(800) 472-3389
Bull and Bear Group ..............................................(800) 847-4200
Dreyfus Corporation...............................................(800) 782-6620
Fidelity Investments ...............................................(800) 544-8888
Financial Funds/Invesco Funds ..............................(800) 525-8085
Founders Mutual Funds ..........................................(800) 525-2440
Fundtrust Funds ....................................................(800) 638-1896
Gabelli Funds ........................................................(800) 422-3554
GIT Investment Funds.............................................(800) 336-3063
Janus Capital Corporation .....................................(800) 525-8983
Jones and Babson*................................................(800) 422-2766
The Kaufman Fund ................................................(800) 237-0132
Lexington Group....................................................(800) 526-0056
Safeco Mutual Funds* ...........................................(800) 426-6730
Scudder, Stevens and Clark....................................(800) 225-2470
Stein Roe Mutual Funds .........................................(800) 338-2550

Charles Schwab & Co. ..........................................(800) 435-4000
Strong Funds .......................................................(800) 368-1030
T. Rowe Price Associates .......................................(800) 638-5660
Twentieth Century Mutual Funds* ............................(800) 345-2021
United Services Advisors* .......................................(800) 873-8637
Vanguard Group of Investment Companies ...............(800) 662-7447

*Also members of the 100% No-Load Mutual Fund Council.

# APPENDIX D

## COMMONLY USED MARKET INDEXES

Indexes representing a given section of an investment market may be derived in several different ways, and care must be taken to select not only an appropriate index to represent a given market sector but also an index which is calculated in a manner appropriate to its intended use.

An index may be a simple arithmetic average of the price of a group of similar investments. An example is the Dow Jones Industrial Average. It may also be calculated using a geometric average, in which case the price changes of higher priced stocks have no greater effect on the average than similar percentage changes in the price of lower priced stocks. A geometric average is also sometimes known as an equally weighted index. An example is the Value Line geometric index. It is calculated by multiplying together the number (n) of individual values, taking the $n^{th}$ root and dividing this by n.

Alternatively, an index may be capitalization weighted, also known as market value weighted. In this case, the price of each stock is weighted by the market capitalization of the company; which in turn is the price of a share of stock, multiplied by the number of shares outstanding. An example is the S&P 500 index. This is by far the most common type of index.

Most stock indexes are capital value indexes and do not reflect the reinvestment of distributions. These are only reflected in total return indexes.

Many of the market indexes described below have sub-indexes covering narrower areas of specialized investments. Most of the popular market indexes are reported weekly in Barron's and may also appear in the Wall Street Journal and in Investor's Business Daily.  The most commonly used are those that follow.


## DOMESTIC STOCK MARKET

*Dow Jones Industrial Average*
A price weighted simple average of 30 large common stocks listed on the New York Stock Exchange.  It represents only a small proportion of the total market but is widely quoted in the popular press.

*Dow Jones Transportation Average*
A price weighted average of 20 transportation stocks listed on the New York Stock Exchange.

*Dow Jones Utilities Average*
A price weighted average of 15 public utility stocks listed on the New York Stock Exchange.  It tends to be an indicator of interest rate expectations.

*Dow Jones Composite Average*
A price weighted average of the 65 stocks in the Industrial, Transportation and Utilities Averages.

*Dow Jones Equity Index*
A broadly based index of 700 stocks, representing the majority of the total market capitalization, including New York Stock Exchange, American Stock Exchange and over-the-counter issues.

*Standard and Poor's 500 Index*
A capitalization weighted index of 500 stocks, comprising 400 industrial, 40 financial, 40 utility and 20 transportation stocks.

It mainly represents stocks traded on the New York Stock Exchange, with a small representation of American Stock Exchange and over-the-counter issues. The largest 20 stocks represent over a quarter of the index. The total index represents less than 10% of the total number of companies traded but about three quarters of the total market value. It is the stock market performance benchmark most often used by money managers. The median market capitalization is about $12 billion.

*Standard and Poor's MidCap 400 Index*
A capitalization weighted index based on 400 stocks of medium-sized companies having a market capitalization from $200 million to $5 billion. About 1/3 of the index represents the largest 50 companies. Approximately two-thirds of the index represents industrial stocks, the remainder being mainly utility and financial stocks. About 62% of the stocks are traded on the NYSE, 3% on AMEX and 35% are NASDAQ stocks. The index was created in 1991.

*Standard and Poor's 100 Index*
Represents 100 stocks from the S&P 500 index for which derivative products, such as index option contracts and futures are traded. It is a capitalization weighted index, with the largest three or four stocks comprising 20% to 25% of the value of the index. It does not necessarily represent the 100 largest stocks in the S&P 500, as sometimes assumed.

*New York Stock Exchange (NYSE) Composite*
A capitalization weighted index of all the more than 1,600 stocks traded on the New York Stock Exchange.

*American Stock Exchange (AMEX) Market Value Index*
A capitalization weighted total return index of the more than 800 stocks traded on the American Stock Exchange.

*National Association of Securities Dealer Automatic*
*Quotation System (NASDAQ) Composite Index*
A capitalization weighted index of more than 4,000 smaller
stocks sold over-the-counter (OTC) and not traded on a stock
exchange. More than one-third of these companies are very
small, having a market capitalization of less than $10 million.
The median capitalization is about $20 million.

*Russell 1000 Index*
A capitalization weighed index with adjustment made for cross
ownership. It comprises 1,000 stocks having market capitalization over $300 million, and typically represents 90% of the
value of the total market.

*Russell 2000 Index*
A capitalization weighed index with adjustment made for cross
ownership. It represents smaller companies having a market
capitalization of from $20 million to $300 million, which
accounts for 8% to 9% of the total value of the market. The
median capitalization is about $65 million.

*Value Line Composite Index*
An index containing about 1,700 stocks traded on the New
York Stock Exchange, the American Stock Exchange and
over-the-counter. It represents about 95% of the total stock
market value. This index is expressed separately both as a
geometric average and as an arithmetic average.

*Wilshire 5000 Equity Index*
A capitalization weighted index of more than 6,000 stocks,
about 86% of the value of which are traded on the New York
Stock Exchange, 3% on the American Stock Exchange and
11% over-the-counter. This is one of the broadest and most
useful market indexes. It is also reported as an equal weighted

or geometric average.

## Wilshire 4500 Equity Index
An index comprising the Wilshire 5000 stocks, less those contained in the S&P 500 index. As such, it is a useful measure of the market, excluding many of the very large capitalization stocks. The median capitalization is about $30 million.

## INTERNATIONAL STOCKS

### Morgan Stanley Capital International (MSCI) Indexes
MSCI produces many international stock market indexes published monthly and quarterly in Morgan Stanley Capital International Perspective. These include national, regional, global and industry indexes. All are capitalization weighted.

### MSCI World Index
An index comprising more than 1,400 stocks from 19 countries, and representing 60% of the market capitalization of each country.

### MSCI Europe, Australia, Far East, Index (MSCI EAFE)
The EAFE Index is widely used as a benchmark for the performance of broadly diversified international mutual funds. It includes more than 1,000 stocks in 16 countries, but is dominated by the Japanese market. It notably excludes the United States, Canada and South Africa, which are included in the World Index. It has a median market capitalization of approximately $14 billion.

### Other MSCI Indexes
Separate indexes are prepared for Europe, the Far East, the Pacific, the Nordic Countries, North America and 20 individual countries.

AMEX International Market Index
A narrowly based capitalization weighted index of 50 large companies in European countries, Australia and Japan. It is used for trading derivative products such as index option contracts and futures, on the American Stock Exchange.

## BONDS

*The Bond Buyer 40-Municipal Bond Index*
The average yield of 40 actively traded tax exempt revenue and general obligation municipal bonds.

*The Bond Buyer 20-Bond Index*
The average yield of 20 general obligation municipal bonds.

*Merrill Lynch 500 Municipal Bond Index*
The average yield on 500 mainly investment grade municipal bonds. Sixteen sub-indexes exist on various types of 25-year revenue bonds and 20-year general obligation bonds.

*Dow Jones Bond Averages*
Simple averages of the prices of 20 bonds; ten industrial and ten utility bonds.

*Ryan Labs Treasury Index*
A total return index of United States Treasury notes and bonds.

*Lehman Brothers Treasury Bond Index*
A market value weighted index of virtually all outstanding United States Treasury notes and bonds. This index is frequently used as a benchmark for comparing the performance of mutual funds holding United States Treasury obligations.

*Lehman Brothers Government/Corporate Bond Index*
A market value weighted index of United States government and investment grade corporate bonds used as a broad benchmark to measure the performance of many bond mutual funds.

*Salomon Brothers Broad Investment Grade Bond Index*
A total return index covering all major Treasury, United States government agency, mortgage and corporate bonds. The index contains more than 3,700 bonds.

*J. P. Morgan Overseas Government Bond Index*
Reports the price (in local currency and U.S. dollars) and the yield of 11 national government bond indexes, together with a non-U.S. and a global index.

*Salomon Brothers World Government Bond Index*
A market capialization weighted dollar based index of approximately 1,000 government bonds from major countries including the U.S.

## MUTUAL FUNDS

*Lipper Analytical Services Mutual Fund Indexes*
Lipper produces a total return index of mutual funds in each of the following categories:
  Growth Fund Index
  Growth and Income Fund Index
  Equity Income Fund Index
  Balanced Fund Index
  Gold Fund Index
  Science and Technology Fund Index
  International Fund Index
These are narrow based indexes of 10 to 30 funds in each

category. Lipper also reports the average performance of a wide range of equity and fixed income fund categories, in addition to these fund indexes.

### Investor's Business Daily Fund Index

A narrow based index of 20 mutual funds, whose investment objectives include capital appreciation and growth, with a minor component representing natural resources and international funds.

### Donoghue's Money Market Averages

These are simple averages of the maturity, seven-day yield and 30-day yield of taxable money market funds.

Performance averages for a wide range of mutual fund categories can also be found in the reports of fund monitoring services, such as Morningstar Mutual Funds and Wiesenberger Investment Companies.

# APPENDIX E

## The Future Value Of A Fixed Sum At Various Rates Of Compounding

The table shows what a dollar invested today will be worth in the future at annual rates of return varying from 2% to 20%. For example, if $1.00 is invested at 10% annual return, after ten years it will become $2.59. This can be found by looking across the ten-year line to where it meets the column headed 10%. Similarly, $1 invested at 18% for 30 years becomes $143.37. These are nominal dollars compounded annually, before taxes and inflation. Compounding quarterly or monthly will significantly increase the final amount.

Annual Return

| No. of Years | 2% | 3% | 4% | 5% | 6% | 7% | 8% | 9% | 10% | 12% | 14% | 16% | 18% | 20% |
|---|---|---|---|---|---|---|---|---|---|---|---|---|---|---|
| 1 | 1.02 | 1.03 | 1.04 | 1.05 | 1.06 | 1.07 | 1.08 | 1.09 | 1.10 | 1.12 | 1.14 | 1.16 | 1.18 | 1.20 |
| 2 | 1.04 | 1.06 | 1.08 | 1.10 | 1.12 | 1.14 | 1.16 | 1.18 | 1.21 | 1.25 | 1.29 | 1.34 | 1.39 | 1.44 |
| 3 | 1.06 | 1.09 | 1.12 | 1.15 | 1.19 | 1.22 | 1.25 | 1.29 | 1.33 | 1.40 | 1.48 | 1.56 | 1.64 | 1.72 |
| 4 | 1.08 | 1.12 | 1.16 | 1.21 | 1.26 | 1.31 | 1.36 | 1.41 | 1.46 | 1.57 | 1.68 | 1.81 | 1.93 | 2.07 |
| 5 | 1.10 | 1.15 | 1.21 | 1.27 | 1.33 | 1.40 | 1.46 | 1.53 | 1.61 | 1.78 | 1.92 | 2.10 | 2.28 | 2.48 |
| 6 | 1.12 | 1.19 | 1.26 | 1.34 | 1.41 | 1.50 | 1.58 | 1.67 | 1.77 | 1.97 | 2.19 | 2.43 | 2.69 | 2.98 |
| 7 | 1.14 | 1.22 | 1.31 | 1.40 | 1.50 | 1.60 | 1.71 | 1.82 | 1.94 | 2.21 | 2.50 | 2.82 | 3.18 | 3.58 |
| 8 | 1.17 | 1.26 | 1.36 | 1.47 | 1.59 | 1.71 | 1.85 | 1.99 | 2.14 | 2.47 | 2.85 | 3.27 | 3.75 | 4.29 |
| 9 | 1.19 | 1.30 | 1.42 | 1.55 | 1.68 | 1.83 | 1.99 | 2.17 | 2.35 | 2.77 | 3.25 | 3.80 | 4.43 | 5.15 |
| 10 | 1.21 | 1.34 | 1.48 | 1.62 | 1.79 | 1.96 | 2.15 | 2.36 | 2.59 | 3.10 | 3.70 | 4.41 | 5.23 | 6.19 |
| 11 | 1.24 | 1.38 | 1.53 | 1.71 | 1.89 | 2.10 | 2.33 | 2.58 | 2.85 | 3.47 | 4.22 | 5.11 | 6.17 | 7.43 |
| 12 | 1.26 | 1.42 | 1.60 | 1.79 | 2.01 | 2.25 | 2.51 | 2.81 | 3.13 | 3.89 | 4.81 | 5.93 | 7.28 | 8.91 |
| 13 | 1.29 | 1.46 | 1.66 | 1.88 | 2.13 | 2.40 | 2.71 | 3.06 | 3.45 | 4.36 | 5.49 | 6.88 | 8.59 | 10.69 |
| 14 | 1.31 | 1.51 | 1.73 | 1.97 | 2.26 | 2.57 | 2.93 | 3.34 | 3.79 | 4.88 | 6.26 | 7.98 | 10.14 | 12.83 |
| 15 | 1.34 | 1.55 | 1.80 | 2.07 | 2.39 | 2.75 | 3.17 | 3.64 | 4.17 | 5.47 | 7.13 | 9.26 | 11.97 | 15.40 |
| 16 | 1.37 | 1.60 | 1.87 | 2.18 | 2.54 | 2.95 | 3.42 | 3.97 | 4.59 | 6.13 | 8.13 | 10.74 | 14.12 | 18.48 |
| 17 | 1.40 | 1.65 | 1.94 | 2.29 | 2.69 | 3.15 | 3.70 | 4.32 | 5.05 | 6.86 | 9.27 | 12.46 | 16.67 | 22.18 |
| 18 | 1.42 | 1.70 | 2.02 | 2.40 | 2.85 | 3.37 | 3.99 | 4.71 | 5.55 | 7.68 | 10.57 | 14.46 | 19.67 | 26.62 |
| 19 | 1.45 | 1.75 | 2.10 | 2.52 | 3.02 | 3.61 | 4.31 | 5.14 | 6.11 | 8.61 | 12.05 | 16.77 | 23.21 | 31.94 |
| 20 | 1.48 | 1.80 | 2.19 | 2.65 | 3.20 | 3.86 | 4.66 | 5.60 | 6.72 | 9.64 | 13.74 | 19.46 | 27.39 | 38.33 |
| 21 | 1.51 | 1.86 | 2.27 | 2.78 | 3.39 | 4.14 | 5.03 | 6.10 | 7.40 | 10.80 | 15.66 | 22.57 | 32.32 | 46.00 |
| 22 | 1.54 | 1.91 | 2.36 | 2.92 | 3.60 | 4.43 | 5.43 | 6.65 | 8.14 | 12.10 | 17.86 | 26.18 | 38.14 | 55.20 |
| 23 | 1.57 | 1.97 | 2.46 | 3.07 | 3.81 | 4.74 | 5.87 | 7.25 | 8.95 | 13.55 | 20.36 | 30.37 | 45.00 | 66.24 |
| 24 | 1.60 | 2.03 | 2.56 | 3.22 | 4.04 | 5.07 | 6.34 | 7.91 | 9.84 | 15.17 | 23.21 | 35.23 | 53.10 | 79.49 |
| 25 | 1.64 | 2.09 | 2.66 | 3.38 | 4.29 | 5.42 | 6.84 | 8.62 | 10.83 | 17.00 | 26.46 | 40.87 | 62.66 | 95.39 |
| 26 | 1.67 | 2.15 | 2.77 | 3.55 | 4.54 | 5.80 | 7.39 | 9.39 | 11.91 | 19.04 | 30.16 | 47.41 | 73.94 | 114.47 |
| 27 | 1.70 | 2.22 | 2.88 | 3.73 | 4.82 | 6.21 | 7.98 | 10.24 | 13.10 | 21.32 | 34.38 | 55.00 | 87.25 | 137.37 |
| 28 | 1.74 | 2.28 | 2.99 | 3.92 | 5.11 | 6.64 | 8.62 | 11.16 | 14.42 | 23.88 | 39.20 | 63.80 | 102.96 | 164.84 |
| 29 | 1.77 | 2.35 | 3.11 | 4.11 | 5.41 | 7.11 | 9.31 | 12.17 | 15.86 | 26.74 | 44.69 | 74.00 | 121.50 | 197.81 |

# APPENDIX F

## The Future Value Of Regular Periodic Investments At Various Rates Of Compounding

The table shows what a dollar regularly every year will become in the future at annual rates of return varying from 2% to 20%. For example, if $1.00 is invested each year at 10% annual return, after ten years the $10 invested will become $15.93. Similarly, $1.00 invested each year at 18% for 30 years becomes $790.94. Compounding quarterly or monthly will significantly increase the final amount. For example, $1.00 per year equally divided into four quarterly investments, and the whole sum compounded quarterly at a 10% annual return for ten years, will become $16.85. At 18% for 30 years, it will become $1,087.60.

| No. of Years | Annual Return | | | | | | | | | | | | | |
|---|---|---|---|---|---|---|---|---|---|---|---|---|---|---|
| | 2% | 3% | 4% | 5% | 6% | 7% | 8% | 9% | 10% | 12% | 14% | 16% | 18% | 20% |
| 1 | 1.00 | 1.00 | 1.00 | 1.00 | 1.00 | 1.00 | 1.00 | 1.00 | 1.00 | 1.00 | 1.00 | 1.00 | 1.00 | 1.00 |
| 2 | 2.02 | 2.03 | 2.04 | 2.05 | 2.06 | 2.07 | 2.08 | 2.09 | 2.10 | 2.12 | 2.14 | 2.16 | 2.18 | 2.20 |
| 3 | 3.06 | 3.09 | 3.12 | 3.15 | 3.18 | 3.21 | 3.24 | 3.27 | 3.31 | 3.37 | 3.43 | 3.50 | 3.57 | 3.64 |
| 4 | 4.12 | 4.18 | 4.24 | 4.31 | 4.37 | 4.43 | 4.50 | 4.57 | 4.64 | 4.77 | 4.92 | 5.06 | 5.21 | 5.36 |
| 5 | 5.20 | 5.30 | 5.41 | 5.52 | 5.63 | 5.75 | 5.86 | 5.98 | 6.10 | 6.35 | 6.61 | 6.87 | 7.15 | 7.44 |
| 6 | 6.30 | 6.46 | 6.63 | 6.80 | 6.97 | 7.15 | 7.33 | 7.52 | 7.71 | 8.11 | 8.53 | 8.97 | 9.44 | 9.92 |
| 7 | 7.43 | 7.66 | 7.89 | 8.14 | 8.39 | 8.65 | 8.92 | 9.20 | 9.48 | 10.08 | 10.73 | 11.41 | 12.14 | 12.91 |
| 8 | 8.58 | 8.89 | 9.21 | 9.54 | 9.89 | 10.25 | 10.63 | 11.02 | 11.43 | 12.29 | 13.23 | 14.24 | 15.32 | 16.49 |
| 9 | 9.75 | 10.15 | 10.58 | 11.02 | 11.49 | 11.97 | 12.48 | 13.02 | 13.57 | 14.77 | 16.08 | 17.51 | 19.08 | 20.79 |
| 10 | 10.94 | 11.46 | 12.00 | 12.57 | 13.18 | 13.81 | 14.48 | 15.19 | 15.93 | 17.54 | 19.33 | 21.32 | 23.52 | 25.95 |
| 11 | 12.16 | 12.80 | 13.48 | 14.20 | 14.97 | 15.78 | 16.64 | 17.56 | 18.53 | 20.65 | 23.04 | 25.73 | 28.75 | 32.15 |
| 12 | 13.41 | 14.19 | 15.02 | 15.91 | 16.86 | 17.88 | 18.97 | 20.14 | 21.38 | 24.13 | 27.27 | 30.85 | 34.93 | 39.58 |
| 13 | 14.68 | 15.61 | 16.62 | 17.71 | 18.88 | 20.14 | 21.49 | 22.95 | 24.52 | 28.02 | 32.08 | 36.78 | 42.21 | 48.49 |
| 14 | 15.97 | 17.08 | 18.29 | 19.59 | 21.01 | 22.55 | 24.21 | 26.01 | 27.97 | 32.39 | 37.58 | 43.67 | 50.81 | 59.19 |
| 15 | 17.29 | 18.59 | 20.02 | 21.57 | 23.27 | 25.13 | 27.15 | 29.36 | 31.77 | 37.27 | 43.84 | 51.65 | 60.96 | 72.03 |
| 16 | 18.63 | 20.15 | 21.82 | 23.65 | 25.67 | 27.88 | 30.32 | 33.00 | 35.94 | 42.75 | 50.98 | 60.92 | 72.93 | 87.44 |
| 17 | 20.01 | 21.76 | 23.69 | 25.84 | 28.21 | 30.84 | 33.75 | 36.97 | 40.54 | 48.88 | 59.11 | 71.67 | 87.06 | 105.93 |
| 18 | 21.41 | 23.41 | 25.64 | 28.13 | 30.90 | 33.99 | 37.45 | 41.30 | 45.59 | 55.74 | 68.39 | 84.14 | 103.74 | 128.11 |
| 19 | 22.84 | 25.11 | 27.67 | 30.53 | 33.75 | 37.37 | 41.44 | 46.01 | 51.15 | 63.43 | 78.96 | 98.60 | 123.41 | 154.73 |
| 20 | 24.29 | 26.87 | 29.77 | 33.06 | 36.78 | 40.99 | 45.76 | 51.16 | 57.27 | 72.05 | 91.02 | 115.37 | 146.62 | 186.68 |
| 21 | 25.78 | 28.67 | 31.96 | 35.71 | 39.99 | 44.86 | 50.42 | 56.76 | 64.00 | 81.69 | 104.76 | 134.84 | 174.02 | 225.02 |
| 22 | 27.29 | 30.53 | 34.24 | 38.50 | 43.39 | 49.00 | 55.45 | 62.87 | 71.40 | 92.50 | 120.43 | 157.41 | 206.34 | 271.03 |
| 23 | 28.84 | 32.45 | 36.61 | 41.43 | 46.99 | 53.43 | 60.89 | 69.53 | 79.54 | 104.60 | 138.29 | 183.60 | 244.48 | 326.23 |
| 24 | 30.42 | 34.42 | 39.08 | 44.50 | 50.81 | 58.17 | 66.76 | 76.78 | 88.49 | 118.15 | 158.65 | 213.97 | 289.49 | 392.48 |
| 25 | 32.03 | 36.45 | 41.64 | 47.72 | 54.86 | 63.24 | 73.10 | 84.70 | 98.34 | 133.33 | 181.87 | 249.21 | 342.60 | 471.98 |
| 26 | 33.67 | 38.55 | 44.31 | 51.11 | 59.15 | 68.67 | 79.95 | 93.32 | 109.18 | 150.33 | 208.33 | 290.08 | 405.27 | 567.37 |
| 27 | 35.34 | 40.70 | 47.08 | 54.66 | 63.70 | 74.48 | 87.35 | 102.72 | 121.09 | 169.37 | 238.49 | 337.50 | 479.22 | 681.85 |
| 28 | 37.05 | 42.93 | 49.96 | 58.40 | 68.52 | 80.69 | 95.33 | 112.96 | 134.20 | 190.69 | 272.88 | 392.50 | 566.48 | 819.22 |
| 29 | 38.79 | 45.21 | 52.96 | 62.32 | 73.63 | 87.34 | 103.96 | 124.13 | 148.63 | 214.58 | 312.09 | 456.30 | 669.44 | 984.06 |